6/09

(RE)VISUALIZING NATIONAL HISTORY:
MUSEUMS AND NATIONAL IDENTITIES IN EUROPE
IN THE NEW MILLENNIUM

GERMAN AND EUROPEAN STUDIES

General Editor: Jennifer Jenkins

(RE)VISUALIZING NATIONAL HISTORY

MUSEUMS AND NATIONAL IDENTITIES IN EUROPE IN THE NEW MILLENNIUM

Edited by Robin Ostow

UNIVERSITY OF TORONTO PRESS
Toronto   Buffalo   London

© University of Toronto Press Incorporated 2008
Toronto Buffalo London
www.utppublishing.com
Printed in Canada

ISBN 978-0-8020-9221-2

Printed on acid-free paper

Library and Archives Canada Cataloguing in Publication

(Re)visualizing national history : museums and national identities in Europe in
the new millennium / edited by Robin Ostow.

(German and European studies)
Includes bibliographical references and index.
ISBN 978-0-8020-9221-2 (bound)

1. Museums – Political aspects – Europe. 2. Europe – Politics and government.
3. Nationalism – Europe – History. 4. Museums – Social aspects – Europe.
I. Ostow, Robin, 1945– II. Series.

AM40.R49 2008   069'.094   C2006-906601-9

University of Toronto Press acknowledges the financial assistance to its publishing
program of the Canada Council for the Arts and the Ontario Arts Council.

University of Toronto Press acknowledges the financial support for its publishing
activities of the Government of Canada through the Book Publishing Industry
Development Program (BPIDP).

To the memory of Miriam Furst Ostow, who recently left this world, and to Miriam Lubrich, who makes us all so happy

Contents

Acknowledgments   ix

Introduction: Museums and National Identities in Europe in
the Twenty-First Century   3
ROBIN OSTOW

**Part One. The Twenty-First Century: New Exhibits and
New Partnerships**

1 Exhibition as Film   15
   MIEKE BAL

**Part Two. Reconfiguring National History: Centralized and
Local Strategies**

2 The Terror of the House   47
   ISTVÁN RÉV

3 Putting Contested History on Display: The Uses of the Past
   in Northern Ireland   90
   ELIZABETH CROOKE

Part Three. Restoring National History with International Participation

4 Museums, Multiculturalism, and the Remaking of
   Postwar Sarajevo   109
   EDIN HAJDARPAŠIĆ

5 Building a Jewish Museum in Germany in the
   Twenty-First Century   139
   BERNHARD PURIN

6 Remusealizing Jewish History in Warsaw: The Privatization and
   Externalization of Nation Building   157
   ROBIN OSTOW

**Part Four. Displaying War, Genocide, and the Nation:
From Ottawa to Berlin, 2005**

7 Constructing the Canadian War Museum/Constructing
   the Landscape of a Canadian Identity   183
   REESA GREENBERG

8 Peter Eisenman's Design for Berlin's Memorial for the Murdered
   Jews of Europe: A Juror's Report in Three Parts   200
   JAMES E. YOUNG

Contributors   215

Index   219

Acknowledgments

This volume has been made possible by the very generous contributions of many individuals and institutions. Its central questions and ideas grew out of a research grant awarded me by the Social Science and Humanities Research Council of Canada for a project on Jewish museums in Europe. My work on Europe's Jewish museums led me to broader questions regarding the relations between major museum exhibitions and national histories and identities – and, more specifically, to the metamorphoses and new articulations of these histories and identities that have been emerging since the Cold War ended in 1989. Further questions centred on the role of the new modes of exhibitions, especially their political potential.

In 2004, Susan Solomon and I organized a conference: (Re)Visusalizing National History: Museology and National Identities in Europe in the New Millennium. With our co-organizer, David-Thierry Ruddel, we invited colleagues – museum scholars and practitioners – from different parts of Europe and from North America to share their findings and to think with us. This conference was sponsored by the University of Toronto's Chancellor Jackman Program for the Arts, the Faculty of Arts and Sciences, the Joint Initiative for German and European Studies, and the School of Graduate Studies, under Michael Marrus. Special thanks to Janet Hyer and Edith Klein, who were responsible for the administration, and to all the conference participants, including those who were unable to contribute chapters to this book.

Support for the publication of this book came from the University of Toronto's Joint Initiative for German and European Studies. In the later phases of development, small grants were made available by the Centre for European, Russian, and Eurasian Studies at the University of Toronto and the Faculty of Arts at Wilfrid Laurier University. David Peirson, Dean of the Faculty of Graduate Studies at Laurier, personally edited the photographs. At the University of Toronto Press, Len Husband and Frances Mundy greatly enhanced the quality of the manuscript, in the most gracious possible way.

Many individuals in Warsaw, Toronto, and New York provided information, ideas, and insights for my own chapter on the new museum in Warsaw. In addition to all those mentioned and quoted in the text, Eleonora Bergman, Renata Piatkowska, Agnieska Rudzinska, Michael Shudrich, and Magdalena Sieramska gave generously of their time and expertise. In Toronto, Piotr Wrobel contributed ideas and encouragement. Krystyna Piskorz provided sensitive translations of key documents, as well as explications and contextualizing materials.

Colleagues, friends, and family supported me intellectually, technically, and personally as the project was taking shape. They include Franziska Becker, Marie-Helène and Gernot Behr, John Borneman, Annegret Ehmann, Nanette Funk, Barbara Kowalenko, Ute Lischke, Gero Lenhardt, Oliver Lubrich, Michael Lucas, Andrea Margles, Sigrid Meuschel, Ken Morrison, Alice Musiol, Rachel Newman, Jana Oldfield, Doina Popescu, Menachem Rosensaft, Elaine Stavro-Pearce, and Dorothy Zolf McDonald. Natascha, Naomi, Nuri, and the larger Ostow clan are the best inspiration and support system anyone could be graced with.

Susan Solomon has been a major partner in this endeavour, which owes its existence in great part to her efforts.

To all, thanks so much. Needless to say, I take full responsibility for the contents.

(RE)VISUALIZING NATIONAL HISTORY:
MUSEUMS AND NATIONAL IDENTITIES IN EUROPE
IN THE NEW MILLENNIUM

Introduction:
Museums and National Identities in Europe in the Twenty-First Century

ROBIN OSTOW

The splitting of some European countries in the late twentieth century, the reunification of others, and the reshaping of the continent as a polity and as an ideology have made it urgent to reconfigure national discourses, circulate new national values, and develop new histories and images to reflect the changed realities. With individual states now coming under pressure to distance themselves from the destructive nationalism of the late nineteenth and the twentieth centuries, and to exhibit their commitments to democracy, multiculturalism, rule of law, human rights, peacekeeping and a free market economy, the visual representation of these new values and identities has become a central issue. Museums provide one site for such representation. Indeed, Dipesh Chakrabarty (2002, 6) noted that in 'late democracies,' museums have emerged as 'a key site for cultural politics arising over questions of the past.'

The challenges to museums – institutions traditionally charged with displaying national identities – involve more than merely rehanging, reordering, adding, or removing display objects. The surge in identity politics that marked the end of the Cold War has challenged traditional museum structures and operations. In some museums, groups that had long been excluded are now represented on curatorial teams and in the development of new exhibits. At the same time, the global migration of display objects, of capital, of museum professionals, and of signs and images is reshaping museums, whose position in their national political and cultural landscape has been shifting.

Worldwide, the past two decades have seen the strongest wave of museum building since the nineteenth century, and this wave is continuing in Europe, from Bilbao to Warsaw and beyond, complemented by the reorganization of existing museums, especially in Central and Eastern Europe. Simultaneously, a growing interest in museums has resulted in a considerable scholarly literature exploring their history, their display strategies, and their politics. Susan Crane (2000) links museums to the literature on collective memory as it has been defined and analysed by Maurice Halbwachs (1992) and Pierre Nora (1984), among others. Mieke Bal (1996), one of the contributors to this volume, has analysed the techniques of narration as well as the basic frameworks of understanding that inform how an exhibit's display objects relate to one another and to viewers. These relationships infuse exhibits with meanings that usually support the categories and ideologies on which the political order depends. Jean Baudrillard (1996) has interrogated the social role of objects from the past, the eroticism of collecting and displaying, and the process of ordering objects – for example, in a museum. He has related these activities to the need to bring a sense of order and control to the chaos of history. Ultimately, he interprets the display of objects from the past as a visualization of the idea of continuity, of overcoming time and death.

But for this volume, perhaps the most important research has explored the relationship of museums to the nation and the state. Benedict Anderson (1991) has highlighted the role museums play in visualizing nations and empires and in displaying to the public the role assumed by states and monarchies as guardians of the national or imperial heritage. Tony Bennett's definitive book, *The Birth of the Museum* (1995) employed a Foucaultian approach to analyze the establishment of national museums in the nineteenth century as educational spaces – as institutions whose purpose was to turn the state's inhabitants into citizens and to narrate the nation and equate it with the idea of progress.

In addition, a rich literature has developed around how national identities are reshaped, how new national values are circulated, and how this relates to the European identities and values that have emerged since the collapse of communism and the rise of the European Union (EU). This literature, which includes official EU documents, emphasizes democracy, the rule of law, human rights, the protection of minorities, and peacekeeping, all based on a functioning market economy and an economic union. Jürgen Habermas (1992) has pointed to the importance to a united Europe of citizenship and a common political culture. Jacques Derrida (1990) has argued for a multiplicity of European identity that allows it to coexist with national and other identities. Luisa Passerini (2002) has described European identity as a process rather than a finished product.

Other scholars have pointed to Europe's history before the development of the EU and to the lingering ghosts of nationalism, war, and imperialism. Tony Judt (1992) has described how the idea of Europe relates to collective national memories of Nazism. Timothy Garton Ash (2000) has focused on the gaze from the countries of Eastern Europe, where being 'Central European' means playing back to the West its own fantasies of the region. Ariane Chebel D'Appollonia (2002, 190) has foregrounded the need to create powerful European myths and symbols 'as strong as those that sustain the individual nations of which it is composed' to enable the EU to compete with aggressive nationalism. And more recently, Will Kymlicka (2005, D4) has argued that the EU 'provides a safe shelter for nationalism ... nationalist projects can be pursued safely within the EU because ... the overarching structure ... contains national rivalries.'

The essays in this volume bring these two literatures together. They view the wave of museum and monument building in Europe as part of an effort to forge consensus in politically unified but deeply divided nations. Each contributor explores the how museums are exhibiting new (and some old) national values, and – equally important – how new museums (and new exhibits in older museums) are reflecting and refracting the relations among old and new social groups in Europe and North America. This collection is interdisciplinary; it represents the perspectives of history, art history, sociology, literature, and political science. The contributors come from Canada, Northern Ireland, Hungary, Germany, the Netherlands, the United States, and Bosnia; they include scholars of international standing as well as younger scholars and museum practitioners. The views presented are those of museum insiders *and* outsiders.

The contributors explore the effects of post-1989 social and political changes on the structures of museums and their exhibits. In the nineteenth and twentieth centuries, national governments built large museums to demonstrate their wealth and power; but the recent weakening and impoverishment of many governments (most dramatically those in Eastern Europe) has led to the neglect of national museums – for example, in Sarajevo. In Northern Ireland, lingering divisions are reflected in the failure of the established national museums to address the 'Troubles' of the past decades.

Economic and cultural developments in the museum world have also contributed to the reshaping of exhibits. The recent wave of museum building has tightened the market for conventional display objects. At the same time, authentic objects from Eastern Europe – for example, Poland – have been 'loaned' to larger museums in the West. And as Bernhard Purin's contribution points out, this process has been aggravated by a new sensitivity to 'looted art.' The shrinking supply of authentic objects, combined with the emergence of a public – especially in the West – that is accustomed to film and television and to retrieving information from data banks, has led to a proliferation and a new aesthetic of high-tech museum installations. In the case of the Jewish museum project in Warsaw, though, plans for a completely image-based exhibit have generated sufficient backtalk to persuade the professional staff to commit themselves to some 'hard' items.

The museums, exhibits, and the memorials that are the focus of this book are the result of profound political and cultural changes, but they are also informed by local histories that are more varied and more nuanced. The House of Terror in Budapest, established under the aegis of Hungary's right-wing government of the early 1990s, is a univocal, top-down display of one version of Hungarian history. By contrast, the small museums and exhibits discussed by Elizabeth Crooke are community-based and represent the views of mobilized local groups. Other museums have brought in, and give voice to, new constituencies that are often external to the state. At the Bosnian National Museum in Sarajevo, non-governmental organizations (NGOs) such as UNESCO have become involved, and their commitment to multiculturalism is reflected in the national values and narrative on display. Bernhard Purin describes how postwar Jewish museums in Germany and Austria have evolved; they are no longer administered by and representative of the views of non-Jewish Germans and Austrians; Jews have joined the curatorial staffs, and in some cases descendents of emigrated Jews have formed communities around Jewish museums in their ancestral cities and towns. Their active participation has expanded the displays of local Jewish history geographically, chronologically, and even confessionally, in that some members of this museum community are no longer Jewish. The Jewish museum project in Warsaw was driven largely by groups outside Poland that had their own visions and agendas. The intense pressure they placed on the Polish government to build an expensive museum representing the martyrdom of a minority has led to popular resentment.

Memorials and museums have somewhat different mandates. The former tend to focus public attention on one event – most often an act of bloodshed; the latter usually express visually a broader story based on art, science, or history, sometimes in combination. National museums often display epic narratives and highlight moments of national grandeur. In practice, though, museums often contain memorial displays, and memorials reference the broader history that lends them meaning. The large outlays of capital for these museum and memorial projects tend to be justified as necessary to prevent the return of nationalist bloodbaths. In the cases investigated in this book, however, the national narratives and identities on exhibit represent a broad spectrum. The exhibit in Budapest is interpreted by István Rév as fascist. Images of nationalism with a multicultural face and of postnationalism are embodied in two adjacent museums in Sarajevo. Transnational 'world memory' frames the Partners (The Teddy Bear Project) exhibit in Munich. The new Canadian nationalism is made concrete in the museum of Canada's foreign wars that reopened in a new building in 2005 in Ottawa.

And the variation in the histories presented is echoed in the broad range of uses and statuses of display objects. István Rév argues that, in the House of Terror, objects often serve as tools to confuse and manipulate the public: real documentary photographs of war are not distinguished from pseudo-documentary or fictional ones. The Warsaw museum is an unsuccessful attempt to bypass real objects altogether and to work only with media images. In Sarajevo, the museum is closed for several months every year and only one of its heritage objects, the Sarajevo Haggadah, is carefully preserved; this points to the state's inability to preserve and display the treasures in its custody. The Ars Aevi exhibit, which is housed in tents, suggests a similar inability on the part of the international art community. However, the new Jewish museum in Munich is committed to working with authentic objects and to interrogating their history within the framework of the broader national history.

Several essays in this book highlight the increasing significance of film in museum exhibits, and its multiple uses. Mieke Bal's contribution points out that cinema, as the art of the masses, was often used often for political mobilization during the twentieth century and serves as a link between art and politics. At a more abstract level, Bal approaches film – in particular, its ability to engage viewers emotionally – as a metaphor for analysing exhibits. As the visitor moves through space and views the displays sequentially, the journey through the exhibit takes on a cinematic quality; film techniques inform the positioning of display objects and the organization of the visitors' walk through the exhibit. István Rév notes how film clips of mass gatherings are employed to lend the exhibit at the House of Terror the epic sweep and emotional power of the large fascist demonstrations in 1930s Italy.

The Jewish museum project in Warsaw will be referencing films about the Warsaw Ghetto uprising of 1943 to mediate the visitors' relationship to events that have left few physical traces on the city. In this exhibit, the visitors will nor merely watch film footage; they will walk through what might be a film set and become incorporated into the images projected on the gallery's walls. In this way, they will not just see history on film; they will become part of it. They will experience history's dramatic moments as if they were extras in the film version. The film, made decades after the historical events, will become (as in the House of Terror) the hyperfact that reveals the barely visible historical fact: the visitor/participant will acquire a bottom-up, Rosencranz-and-Guildenstern view of Polish Jewish history. Experiences of this kind change the viewer's relation to the history on display from one of distance and analysis, to one of neurological and emotional responses to intense external stimulation. In her chapter on the Canadian War Museum, Reesa Greenberg links this kind of exhibit experience to William Connolly's model of neuropolitics – that is, the use of formal elements of mass culture to mobilize thought processes unconsciously and to affect how perception is organized.

In the planned museum in Warsaw, not just the distance but the very separation of the visitor from the display will be erased. The visitor will become part of the exhibit and will perform a small part of the historical narration. Dipesh Chakrabarty (2002) explores the shift from the older, classical positioning of the visitor as viewer (also voyeur; R.O.) and decipherer of history to a new status as a subject who performs and experiences history. He links this development to recent changes in the concept of democracy. He argues that particularly in Europe and North America, the process of becoming a citizen has been uncoupled from the educational project of learning abstract reasoning and has been extended to larger groups of people through its (re)rooting in performance and experience. Democratic participation through performance and experience requires less formal education and can encompass individuals from diverse cultural backgrounds.

Above and beyond all this the case studies reveal a continuum with regard to the intellectual activity or passivity of the museum visitor. Mieke Bal argues that Ydessa Hendeles's exhibit Partners (the Teddy Bear Project) is a 'new kind of show' that 'activates the viewer, compelling her to create rather than consume the exhibition as narrative.' The opposite extreme is encountered in the House of Terror, where the visitor is manipulated through frightening and misleading displays and texts.

In 1992, Tony Judt traced the postwar idea of Europe to the suppression in many countries of national memories of collaboration with Nazism. Thirteen years later, he extended this line of thought: 'As Europe prepares to leave World War Two behind ... the recovered memory of Europe's dead Jews has become the very definition and guarantee of the continent's restored humanity' (2005, 804). It surprised me that the Holocaust surfaced as a theme in seven of the eight essays in this collection. Nazism and the Holocaust hover like ghosts over the museums and exhibits discussed in this book. István Rév's essay addresses Hungary's denial of complicity in the deportation of its Jews in the House of Terror, as well as the gripping power of symbols such as Auschwitz – symbols that, he contends, separate good from evil neatly, in a way that other events – for example, Hungary's 1956 revolution – cannot. In Bosnia's national museum, the 'rescued' Sarajevo Haggadah is featured as a display of the moral integrity of the Bosnian nation. Mieke Bal illustrates how, by contrast, Ydessa Hendeles's exhibit Partners (the Teddy Bear Project) owes much of its power and integrity to its ability to display the ambivalences surrounding Nazism and to link that movement to 'world memories' of nationalism and violence.

Finally, the Holocaust in Europe, the Troubles in Northern Ireland, and Canada's participation in overseas conflicts raise a key question for nations in the twenty-first century – the possibility for healing and regeneration following the violence of what Hobsbawm (1994) has called the 'short twentieth century.' This theme echoes Baudrillard's contention that objects from the past are collected and displayed as a way of overcoming death. And it is foregrounded in almost all the case studies in this book. Bernhard Purin's museum project in Munich aims at healing by elucidating the history of the art displayed and in this way bringing the ghost of the Holocaust into the museum. Through the return of looted art, Purin is performing an act of restitution; by using the new media to reach out to communities of Jewish emigrants and their descendents around the world, he plans to reintegrate them into the German community, thereby reconstituting its integrity. Elizabeth Crooke's contribution to this volume offers a more sceptical look at the claims of healing found in some museum projects in Northern Ireland. The project she found most convincing grew out of the visit to Northern Ireland by the deputy chair of the South African Truth and Reconciliation Commission.

Edin Hajdarpašić provides an example of the failure of healing in Bosnia's National Museum. There, in 2002, the fifteenth-century

Sarajevo Haggadah was exhibited to display Bosnia as a nation that respects and protects its minorities. But the narrative of preservation and protection has reconstituted religion as a major fault line compartmentalizing Bosnia's population – one that reduces multiculturalism to 'multiconfessionalism.' The aftermath of the exhibit has also highlighted the neglect of the museum around the Haggadah and the state's current inability to exhibit its history.

My own essay centres on a museum project that justifies itself as an act of healing the relations between Poles and Jews by literally filling in what has long been an empty Jewish space in downtown Warsaw. On closer inspection, though, the museum plans point to an exhibit that reflects the political and economic ties of Polish, American Jewish, and Israeli elites, leaving many concerns of local Jews and non Jews in Warsaw unaddressed. Similarly, Reesa Greenberg's piece points to the divisive effects of efforts in the 1990s to build a Holocaust gallery in the Canadian War Museum. Consensus for the reorganization and relocation of this museum was achieved only after the museum adopted an architecture that dehistoricized and universalized war, emptying the narrative of references to conflicts internal to Canada and focusing instead on wars fought abroad, counterbalanced by the regenerative powers of Canada's natural landscape.

The issues of healing and redemption bridge the Atlantic. Ydessa Hendeles's Partners (The Teddy Bear Project) exhibit, which came to Munich from Toronto, is anti-redemptory. It focuses on the ambivalences of the partnership between Germans and their Jewish victims, and it provides no images or promises of healing. By contrast, the Holocaust memorial in Berlin – designed by Peter Eisenman, an American – is an example of healing imported from New York. James Young elaborates on the history of the design from 1998, when it was first selected by a five-member jury, to the completion of the memorial seven years later. The plan to erect a Holocaust memorial covering a field of five acres in the centre of Berlin was debated by politicians and by the German public for many years. In 1998 it was rejected by many Germans, who saw it as reducing German history to the Holocaust and as an overwhelming display of German guilt in the heart of the old/new capital. Young notes that the German Parliament voted to proceed with the controversial memorial in the same year that it began to demonstrate new national values – by participating in NATO's intervention against the genocide in Serbia and by changing its citizenship laws so as to favour residency rather than blood. Inaugurated in the spring of 2005, the memorial – a forest of 2,711 concrete pillars that suggest gravestones, above a subterranean 'place of information' – provides an abstract environment for contemplation (and sometimes, for play) directly over Hitler's bunker. The site combines Chakrabarty's two exhibition models. The place of information provides knowledge for the formation of an educated German citizenry. Among the 2,711 pillars, not quite vertical, on a sloping field, visitors experience feelings of being lost, overwhelmed and thrown off balance by the Holocaust.

This memorial was expected to close what Judt has called 'a sixty-year cycle of denial, education, debate and consensus' (2005, 830) and to allow Germans to live with their Nazi past. Yet several months after its inauguration, observers noted a glaring disconnect between the memorial's positive reception by the media and the more mixed responses of Berliners. This monumental gesture of commemoration at the official level supports the legitimacy of the Federal Republic of Germany in Europe. At the same time, neo-Nazi marches in Germany's eastern states and calls to establish another memorial in Berlin to commemorate the expulsion of Germans from territories that are today parts of Poland and the Czech Republic point to more varied and unsettled memories at the local level.

BIBLIOGRAPHY

Anderson, Benedict. 1991. *Imagined Communities: Reflections on the Origins and Spread of Nationalism*. London: Verso.

Ash, Timothy Garton. 2000. 'Conclusions.' In *Between Past and Future: The Revolutions of 1989 and Their Aftermath*, edited by Sorin Antohi and Vladimir Tismaneanu, 395–402. Budapest: Central European University Press.

Bal, Mieke. 1996. *Double Exposures: The Subject of Cultural Analysis*. New York: Routledge.

Baudrillard, Jean. 1996. *The System of Objects*. Translated by James Benedict. London: Verso.

Bennett, Tony. 1995. *The Birth of the Museum: History, Theory, Politics*. New York: Routledge.

Chakrabarty, Dipesh. 2002. 'Museums in Late Democracies.' *Humanities Research* 10, no. 1: 5–12.

Chebel d'Appollonia, Ariane. 2002. 'European Nationalism and European Union.' In *The Idea of Europe: From Antiquity to the European Union*, edited by Anthony Pagden, 171–90. Cambridge: Cambridge University Press.

Crane, Susan, ed. 2000. *Museums and Memory.* Stanford: Stanford University Press.

Derrida, Jacques. 1990. *The Other Heading: Reflections on Today's Europe.* Bloomington: Indiana University Press.

Habermas, Jürgen. 1992. 'Citizenship and National Identity: Some Reflections on the Future of Europe.' *Praxis Internationale* 12, no. 1: 1–19.

Halbwachs, Maurice. 1992. *On Collective Memory.* Chicago: University of Chicago Press.

Hobsbawm, Eric. 1994. *The Age of Extremes: The Short Twentieth Century 1914–1991.* London: Little, Brown.

Judt, Tony. 1992. 'The Past Is Another Country: Myth and Memory in Postwar Europe.' *Daedalus*, 121, no. 4: 83–112.

– 2005. *Postwar: A History of Europe since 1945.* New York: Penguin.

Kymlicka, Will. 2005. 'Saul Tilts at the Market Windmills.' *Globe and Mail*, 28 May. D3, D4.

Neubauer, Hans-Joachim. 2005. 'Picknick zwischen den Stelen.' *Rheinischer Merkur*, no. 22, 2 June.

Nora, Pierre. 1984. *Les lieux de mémoire.* Paris: Gallimard.

Passerini, Luisa. 2002. 'From the Ironies of Identity to the Identities of Irony.' In *The Idea of Europe: From Antiquity to the European Union*, edited by Anthony Pagden, 191–208. Cambridge: Cambridge University Press.

PART ONE

The Twenty-First Century:
New Exhibits and New Partnerships

1 Exhibition as Film

MIEKE BAL

Photography as Storyboard, Exhibition as Film

If taken at all seriously either as art form or as a predominantly visual discourse, exhibitions are usually interpreted or framed in terms borrowed from other art practices. This transfer between disciplines and practices is quite useful; it helps museologists conceive of their practices artistically and coherently, while providing critics with conceptual tools to illuminate exhibitions as meaningful wholes in relation to their visitors. For example, in my book *Double Exposures* (1996), I conducted a mostly critical examination of a few famous exhibition sites in museums of worldwide reputation. The key metaphor in that analysis was narrative, conceived as a meaning-producing sequentiality emerging from the viewer's walk through an exhibition. Putting one thing next to another, in other words, produces a time-bound relationship between the two, one that moves from the first to the second.

In that study I used this metaphor as a tool for a critical reading of exhibitions. Here, by contrast, I don't want to elaborate on what bothers me in many displays, but, in the opposite spirit, offer some thoughts about this and other metaphors as tools for enhancing the aesthetic and political efficacy of exhibitions. Thus my goal is not criticism but rather theorizing by means of a careful analysis of actual displays. I will do this through a close look at an exhibition I found the best – the most effective, gripping, and powerful – I have ever seen. I am talking about the award-winning exhibition Partners, curated by Canadian art collector and curator Ydessa Hendeles.

This exhibition does important political work in that, without in the least universalizing art, it both addresses a transnational world and refrains from endorsing the neonationalism that is presently rampant in Europe and the United States. It also establishes long-repressed albeit ambivalent links, expressed in the exhibition's title, as history has forged them between the Jewish and the German peoples, as well as between the two sides of the Atlantic. This political efficacy is wrought by means of what is the primary thrust of the show – namely, a profoundly effective, indeed thrilling, aesthetic. I seek to understand how, far from being opposite or even distinct domains, political work and aesthetic work operate together in an inextricable merging that strengthens both.

But I elaborate this general point in a more specific way than that. For this aesthetic is intimately linked with the predominant medium of the exhibition, which is photography, aligned with sculpture and video. In light of my earlier insight that exhibitions, by virtue of the spectator's movement through the space and the temporal sequentiality involved in the visit, are always to some extent narrative, the medium of photography in the exhibition tends to take on cinematic effects. This effect has been enhanced in Partners, so much so that a tension between photography and film is the primary aesthetic at play. In this respect, Partners is exemplary – indeed, a meta-exhibition.

Therefore, for an understanding of the artistic *work* that Partners does, I find it most productive to deploy the metaphor of *film*. Specifically, since many of the works exhibited here are, or are derived from, photography, I submit understanding Partners as a proposal to consider photography – the medium, the art – as a *storyboard* or visual scenario for a cinematic vision of art presentation. As we shall see later, photography's allegedly privileged connection to reality is part of that function. Hence, so is its connection to, or engagement with, the transworld conceptions of nation and display that we are studying in this book. It is this inextricable bond between aesthetics and politics that makes this exhibition not only astonishingly effective but also, specifically, emblematic for the topic at issue in the conference from which this volume emanated.

I contend that this relationship between art and the politics of nationhood is brought in according to a particular aesthetic vision that binds the contemplation of art with a repositioning of the subject in relation to the world. This works as follows. The thrust of the cinematic vision I see in this exhibition is to establish, or at least encourage, an *affective* relationship not only between the art and the viewer but also among the artworks themselves. These relationships among the artworks constitute the exhibition's *syntax*, which is *affective* in nature. Between a *perception* that troubles us and an *action* we hesitate over, *affect* emerges. Photography, the key element in Partners, projects this relationship of affect as the possibility of *translating* heterogeneous *emotions* into one another. The common foundation on which such translation can work is the notion that through art, it is possible to identify with other people's pasts as they lived them; in other words, to 'have' other people's memories. And in such cases, where memories travel as much across the Atlantic as through time, I propose to discuss the affective syntax in terms of *world memories*. This term, then, suggests how I would like to attempt to move, with Ydessa Hendeles's Partners as my partner, from neonationalism to postnational thinking.

Exhibition as ... Competing Models

Partners occupied fourteen exhibition rooms in the Haus der Kunst (House of Art) in Munich. Thirteen of these rooms were medium or small and surrounded the fourteenth, a large central space (see fig. 1.1). The different rooms were devoted to objects ranging from early photographs to contemporary sculpture. Neither strictly sequential nor circular, the exhibition had a single entrance, leading into an exhibit of three very different objects, none of which belonged to canonical art: an early self-portrait of Diane Arbus, made before she became an artist and for a private purpose; an antique toy of a Minnie Mouse figure carrying Felix the Cat in a suitcase; and a studio photograph of a group of bandits. After this small entrance room, the exhibition offered several possible itineraries.

In light of this organization, my favourite conceptual metaphor of narrative, while never irrelevant for exhibitions where visitors move through time, is perhaps not the most obviously operative one. Thus, already at this very basic level of the floor plan, the exhibition raises the question of the metaphors that can be brought to bear on it. Most frequently, one speaks of exhibitions in terms of either theatre or narrative. Theatre recalls the mise-en-scène that all exhibitions imply, narrative invokes the walking tour the visitor makes through it. In museums devoted to national collections, it is the nation itself that either gets staged or is narrated in nationalism's favourite genre, the epic. The relevance of the conceptual metaphor of *theatre* as a frame of reference is easy to grasp. In exhibiting a number of artworks under the best possible viewing

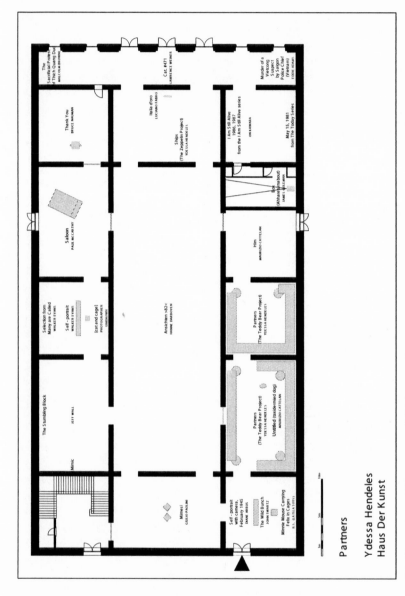

Partners

Ydessa Hendeles
Haus Der Kunst

1.1 Floor plan of Partners, exhibition catalogue.

conditions, curators need to develop a *scenography*. They arrange objects in a space that, by virtue of those objects' status as art, becomes more or less fictional. The gallery suspends everyday concerns and isolates the viewer *with* the art.

But the gallery space also isolates the viewer *from* the art. The objects can be approached, but only to a limited degree and most often without being touched. This turns the gallery space into a stage separated from the spectator sitting in the dark. To make a convincing exhibition, the curator arranges the objects like still personages, as a tableau vivant. The distancing this entails constitutes the limit of the usefulness of the metaphor of theatre. Partners deploys this metaphor but does not restrict itself to it.[1]

To be sure, an exhibition is necessarily the result of a mise-en-scène, and Partners is no exception. But what does this mean? In theatre, mise-en-scène is the materialization of text (word and score) in a form accessible for public, collective reception; a mediation between a play and the multiple public, that is, each individual in it; an artistic organization of the space in which the play is set; and an arranging of a limited and delimited section of real time and space. As a result of all this arranging, a differently delimited section of fictional time and space accommodates the fictional activities of the actors, who perform their roles in order to build a plot. In the case of exhibitions, it is important to realize that the role of actor is not limited to the objects on display; both the visitors and the objects are the actors, and it is the interaction between them that constitutes the play.

The subject of this activity – the (stage) director – makes a work of art. Her tools are time, space, actors, props, and light. Her activities are the projection of dramatic and musical writing into a particular time-space, or *chronotopos*; specifically spatial co-ordination; the highlighting of some meanings over others; and the keying of text and score in between performers and public. This is sometimes 'totalizing,' and always – to use a term I prefer – *mise-en-pièce(s)*.[2]

To speak with Hans-Thiess Lehmann, mise-en-scène is a mediation from logos to landscape.[3] The activity of mise-en-scène makes for an intervention that turns words – in the case of exhibitions, the conceptual understanding by the curator of the artworks – leading to the formation of abstract meanings, into a spectacle receptive to the turmoil of liberated meanings variously attached to concrete, visible, and audible phenomena and signs. Borrowed from theatre, mise-en-scène indicates the overall artistic activity whose results will shelter and foster the performance of the concrete realization of the art. In its mobility, and in the change over time that it entails, mise-en-scène fits nicely as a metaphor for the experience of an exhibition, because theatrical mise-en-scène creates an affective relationship with the spectators on the basis of, among other things, spatial arrangements. It is also a metaphor that theatre shares with film.

The *narrative* conception of exhibitions has been discussed in the catalogue for Partners – explicitly by Ernst van Alphen in his essay 'Exhibition as Narrative Work of Art' (2003), and implicitly by Ydessa Hendeles in her 'Notes on the Exhibition' (2003). This idea is based on the visitor's journey through the exhibition as constitutive of a series of events constituting a 'plot.' Narrative and theatre share the element of plot, but there is also a major difference between them. Instead of standing still *in front of* an imaginary stage, as in theatre, the viewer now walks *through* a forest of objects. And instead of being a spectator of the play, she is now a co-narrator, fulfilling in her own way the script that predetermines the parameters within which the story can be told. This temporal dimension of exhibitions is the guiding principle of narratological analysis. As in reading a novel, where the reader accumulates an understanding and affective relationship with the events and characters, walking through an exhibition creates, in the experience of the visitor, an accumulative relationship with the art on display.

In the catalogue, Van Alphen offers a narrative model for exhibitions as an alternative to the three traditional principles of coherence, derived from (1) the centrality of the individual artist, (2) a chronological unfolding of an artist's or a group of artists' 'development,' and (3) thematic unification. These principles are unsurprising, and hence unchallenging. By contrast, a narrative exhibition asks of the viewer that she establish connections as she moves through the exhibition, building up a 'story,' which has, as its outcome, or dénouement, an *effect*. This effect is an impression that binds together the different experiences evolving from the confrontation with the artworks.

Such shows need not have the typical coherence of traditional exhibitions. On the contrary, since they activate the viewer, compelling her to create rather than consume the exhibition-as-narrative, such shows can harbour heterogeneous objects that only cohere because of the narrative constantly 'under construction.' As Van Alphen argues, Hendeles's series of ground-breaking exhibitions at her Art Foundation in Toronto bear the hallmark of narrativity in this sense. Partners brings this art of storytelling, by means of a particular installation of objects, to a hitherto unsurpassed level of intensity.

In Van Alphen's analysis of this exhibition, the narrativity is concep-
tualized primarily through Peter Brooks's theory of plot and repetition.
Harking back to a structuralist model, according to which a plot is constructed from building blocks arranged in a tension between similarity
and difference or in an ongoing transformation, Brooks sees narrative
as a constant postponement that frustrates but also maintains a desire
for the ending. This desire is the basis of the activity of the reader, who
performs what Brooks (1984) calls 'reading for the plot,' to cite the title
of his major book on this topic.

But as with novels, exhibition narrative also achieves this effect by
means of a specifically narrative *rhetoric*. In her straightforward, osten-
sibly descriptive 'Notes' in the catalogue, Hendeles hints at some
particular *poetical* figures that articulate this narrative. It is in these figures that the unique effectivity of this exhibition can be perceived. One
such figure is *contrast*. This figure is at work, for example, between the
quietness of the gallery in which On Kawara's work from the *Today*
series (1966–present) and elements from his *I Am Still Alive* series
(1969–present) is installed, and the loud, pounding sounds of the adjacent gallery where James Coleman's *Box (Ahhareturnabout)* from 1977 is
staged (Hendeles 2003, 223). The contrast is effective because the
soundproof door between the two rooms turns the loudness of *Box* into an
unexpected shock. The equally noisy ragtime music of Paul McCarthy's
Saloon (1995–6) works differently, because this noise reaches the visitor
earlier on, creeping up on her, from soft and unclear to loud and
bizarrely out of date.

Hendeles also hints at subtle *counterpoints*, such as between the
themes of murder and suicide that are found in Darboven's *Ansichten
>82<* and that are reiterated in the photojournalist narratives of
Malcolm Browne and Eddie Adams (Hendeles 2003, 220), on display at
opposite ends of the long, narrow gallery. But after Darboven's work,
these two embedded themes are no longer clear opposites. Rather, they
are complex entanglements with the real world, in which perpetrator
and victim positions are not always in crystal-clear opposition, partly
because the individual does not act alone. But whereas the contrast
between Kawara and Coleman proceeds in a forward movement of
linear time, the resonance between Darboven's work and the two pho-
tojournalistic series emerges retrospectively. This difference – between
prospective and retrospective resonance – is of a narratological nature.[4]

A third figure Hendeles mentions is *reiteration*. This figure is at work,
for example, in the continuation – in Partners (The Teddy Bear Project)

from 2002–2003 – of a duality proposed in a preceding gallery. The duality between comfort and danger, affection and hostility, established as early as the entrance gallery by the toy called Minnie Mouse Carrying Felix in Cages, continues in the later, overwhelming installation of thousands of pictures of teddy bears. Whereas Hendeles focuses on the repetition of these dualities, Van Alphen places the narrativity effect in the subtle transformations in the differences within the similarities. Perhaps Hendeles's focus is as distinct from Van Alphen's as poetry is from prose narrative. Hendeles establishes a version of what Dutch curator Rudi Fuchs has called *couplets* – often unexpected analogies and resonances produced by means of juxtapositions.[5]

Theatre, narrative, poetry: these genres, I contend, help us understand how exhibitions, not the particular artworks in them, *work*. How they produce effects that imprint themselves on us and make us leave the galleries different from when we entered them. By means of this transformative work, these genres elude the facile discourse of admiration. In this sense they are much more productive than nationalist display or epic narrative and in combination can contribute to overcoming an outdated and dangerous nationalism. These three models are operative in Partners. But what makes them exceptionally effective is the overarching model of *cinema*.

Exhibition as Film, after Photography

Cinema, as the new art of the twentieth century – the century of this exhibition – is specifically relevant here for three reasons. First, it encompasses the three models I have just mentioned and binds them together: film requires mise-en-scène, unfolds narratives, and deploys poetic strategies to enforce its affective impact, slowing down the forward thrust of the plot. Second, cinema is the art of the masses. Thus it was highly invested in becoming an effective tool for political activism both in the Soviet politics of an Eisenstein – who used a montage of dialectical contrast as his primary tool – and in the early Hollywood tradition of Griffith, whose organicist montage of oppositions produced its own mass politics. Third, and most importantly for my analysis, cinema is not simply a continuation of photography. Rather, this new medium of the early twentieth century *responds* to photography, critically and ambivalently. This response concerns not only movement and time but also, more subtly, the insistence on the limits of visibility *inherent* in time, which cinema inscribes in the black intervals in and between frames.[6]

Cinema, then, takes off where photography reaches its literal limits: the frame. Thus photography serves as cinema's scenario or storyboard, and cinema is photography's commentary: a metaphotography. This is emphatically – but as we shall see, not exclusively – the case in Partners. With photography as its storyboard, this exhibition animates that visual scenario by means of cinematic strategies. These strategies include the obvious ones, such as the construction of a space that is proper to the exhibition and that offers connections to the outside world without coinciding with it; the tension between movement and time, each possessed by its own rhythm; and the deployment of stylistic figures such as those of montage (e.g., dissolves) and framing (e.g., close-ups) that thicken the narrative and change its pace. The cinematic that, I contend, is the soul of this exhibition – its beating heart that makes our hearts beat – comes to operate most powerfully at a few key junctures.

One such moment or juncture is the transition towards an artwork that the curator-collector has herself contributed as an artist, called Partners (The Teddy Bear Project). This immense photo archive of thousands of snapshots, studio pictures, and other inconspicuous forms of photography – all uniformly matted and framed – is the heart of the exhibition, next to the entrance gallery if one elects to move forward ahead instead of turning left (see fig. 1.2). Here, the collector has ordered the wall-covering photographs according to taxonomies that repeat, and thus mock, nineteenth-century models of exhibiting; in the process, she slows down the narrative to the extreme. All of the photographs have one element in common, whose importance the artist – as I must now call her – has not found but rather created through her acts of collecting: in each a toy teddy bear is visible.

The categories established centre on these toys. One child, two children, twins with teddy bears; soldiers, sailors, hunters with teddy bears; women, dressed or naked, with teddy bears; children aiming sometimes adult-size rifles at small teddy bears. Bears in strollers or baby carriages, group portraits with a teddy bear, babies competing with teddy bears in size and cuteness. Two galleries, with winding staircases in them, so that two floors of walls covered from ceiling to floor confine and hold the visitor in a necessarily time-consuming act of voyeurism, intimacy with unknown people, most but not all of whom must be dead by now. After these two crowded galleries, a near-empty third one beckons.

In this next gallery, a sculpture of a young adolescent boy kneeling in a pose of prayer is all there is. It turns its back to those who exit the photo galleries. Slowed down by the time-consuming, indeed time-stopping photo

1.2 Overview of Ydessa Hendeles's Partners (The Teddy Bear Project), photo installation 2002–3.

galleries, one is not too rushed to see the boy's face. Eventually, though, this moment becomes inevitable. A moment of total shock occurs when one walks through that third gallery to see the boy's face. The face is Hitler's. The sculpture, *Him*, is by Maurizio Cattelan, from 2001 (fig. 1.3).

Indeed, it is when Cattelan's sculpture *Him* enters the picture that, for me, the narrative model suddenly yields to the altogether different cinematic one. We encounter this sculpture when exiting the two crowded rooms of Partners (The Teddy Bear Project). The contrast between the intimate installation of the photo archive, which invites us to dwell, explore, and remain in this installation-within-the-installation, and the lone figure seen from the back in an otherwise empty gallery, produces the estranging sense of a sharp cut between one episode and the next, set in a completely different space. The visual contrast is comparable to the auditory contrast between the quiet Kawara and the loud Coleman installations. The contrast between quiet and loud is here one between multitude and singularity, between overwhelming

1.3 Maurizio Cattelan, *Him*, 2001.

and meditative, between welcoming warmth and cold loneliness. The lone figure kneeling on the cold stone floor is cut out – literally.[7]

This contrast sets up an expectation of contrast at the level of content as well. Indeed, a sometimes convincing, sometimes deceptive sense of comfort and safety is created by means of an old-fashioned, homey living room, illuminated by domestic lamps and overwritten by the even more old-fashioned nineteenth-century museum of natural history, with its odd classificatory drive and crowded showcases. This cozy ambience contrasts with the danger to which this child-size kneeling doll seems to be exposed. But the doll turns its back to us. This has the effect of pulling us closer, compelling us to approach, to walk to the other side, to see its face, bend over in the typical physical condescendence with which we approach children, people in wheelchairs, small people. Perhaps we seek to keep it company.

The movement performed by the viewer is the kinetic equivalent of a zoom-in, from a long shot to a close-up. And after we turn around and zoom in, the face we finally come to see – against the backdrop of the Teddy Bear galleries that continue to beckon us – destroys any sense of safety, warmth, or comfort that may linger.

A Canadian Jewish curator showing us Hitler in one of Germany's most history-laden buildings – how does this gesture address the dangers of nationalism by means of a specifically cinematic aesthetic? The tension between expecting a face we do not know and seeing one we do – but that half a century of taboo building has taught us we must not look into – generates a suspenseful sense of fear, if only for a split second. This face, so low that we have to mentally or even physically crouch down to look it in the eyes, is cinematic, symbolically and physically at the same time, in that it is the close-up isolated, abstracted from Hendeles's photo installation Partners (The Teddy Bear Project) where it was visually absent but constantly if implicitly evoked. It thus stands for cinema as a commentary on photography. Close-ups *exaggerate* photography; they push realism to its limits, and sometimes beyond, when the view comes so close that the image ceases to be legible, that the grain of the photograph and the grain of the skin become one, whereby the object recedes behind its representation. The close-up in cinema re-becomes photography, but 'beyond' cinema: it stops time, undermining the linearity of temporality that the cinematic has just instored. This is the primary function of the close-up in film: it imposes a qualitative leap that is indifferent to linear time. And since time and space are intricated in the same move, close-ups undermine spatial continuity as well.

They are not aggrandizements of a segment of the image. Rather, they are *abstractions* that isolate the object from the time-space coordinates in which we were moving as if 'naturally.' Close-ups immediately cancel the whole that precedes them, leaving us alone, thrown out of linear time, alone with a relationship to the image that is pure *affect*.[8]

Exhibition as Film 'before' Photography

In its function as cinematic close-up, Cattelan's sculpture *Him*, technically not a photograph, does three things to the relationship between photography and cinema and to the complementary relationship between the exhibition space and the outside world. And it does so in exemplary fashion. First, it instils the sense in us that incredibly, this excessively realistic sculpture is more photographic than all of the thousands of photographs in the gallery just exited: it is more precise, more readable, because larger in scale. At the same time, and second, the *object* of the photorealistic representation is shocking enough to stop us in our tracks. Here, physical and psychic stopping coincide, aggrandizing each other's effect. Finally, as with Diane Arbus's tiny self-portrait, which opens the show and programs our mode of being in it, the eyes can be looked into but don't look back. If Arbus's miniature is a model for the kind of photographic look that this show mobilizes, then Hitler's glassy eyes are mercifully out of reach. Rather, his large eyes which are looking, but not at us, must be looking into a mirror – the mirror of history that we have just left. It can be said that this sculpture is 'mirroring evil.'[9]

Close-ups are cinematic images that counter the linearity of time; thus the deployment of this form here to (re?)present a figure who orchestrated the greatest catastrophe in history is a way of protesting against a certain conception of nation, history, and time. The conception against which this sculpture as exhibited after Partners (The Teddy Bear Project) militates in a way it might not in a different exhibition context, is the historical conception that construes time as inevitably linear and unstoppable and that simultaneously relegates the past to a distance. Producing a close-up of Hitler is a way of bringing him, and everything he stands for, *into the present tense*.

Here, the relation between photography and cinema as its successor and commentator changes gears, to become a relationship of preposterous reversal, in which photography comments on cinema as *its* (surviving) successor. It is from the retrospective vantage point of the present tense that the temporality of the thousands of photographs in

Partners receives its multilayered density – a density that is, I contend, the aesthetic point of this 'affective syntax.' We look back, and the coziness becomes impenetrable. I, personally, had to go back, physically, thus becoming aware of the way this exhibition *counters* narrative linearity while at the same time remaining a multilayered narrative. Compared to Hitler's overreadable face, the snapshots, already caught in the long shot of multitude, were even harder to read yet in greater need of reading. Thus I spent more time with them on this second visit, even though reading them all was both impossible and pointless.

The pace of the film I am now watching is slowing down. Strikingly, Agnès Varda's 2004 film about Partners interprets the installation cinematically in precisely this way. In her film, the face of Hitler is superimposed retrospectively on the photographs, colouring them a sickly green. The mannequin's eyes sometimes seem to be a lens through which one looks at the snapshots. Seeing, after the fact, a literally cinematic representation of my personal sense of unease, which I experienced as cinematically produced, was a rather unnerving experience indeed.

At an earlier moment, the sheer number of photographs had the same uncanny effect that mass graves can have. Their tense is the past, rigorously, so that we don't know whether the people in them are still alive. But now, 'after' Hitler, I want to know whether and when they died, and how many of them survived the dead man in the next room. Now I see them through the face that overlayers them. Cinema has a technique for this. Hitler's face, then, is edited in, like a *dissolve*. The superposition of two images, one singular, one massively multiple, is a dissolve that creates memory space. In form, it is no different from Leni Riefenstahl's dissolve in *Triumph of the Will* (1935), in which an image of a crowd of soldiers melts into an image of Hitler speaking, thus 'creating a third image where Hitler is made up of all the small men that represent Germany,' a composite image that quotes 'the depiction of power and the 'body of society' in the cover illustration of *Leviathan* by Thomas Hobbes from 1651' (Iversen 2003, 3).

I tend to see in this backward movement – in the flashback constructed by the contrast between *Him* and Partners (The Teddy Bear Project), which all but imposes a return to the latter *through Him* – a quotation as critical commentary on political visions such as those both Hobbes and Riefensthal 'imaged.' This quotation compels us to do two things that cinema has taught us are possible, albeit difficult. First, it makes us reflect *from within* – from within the formerly cosy galleries and from within the composite image produced by the dissolve and now inevitably surrounding us – on the tension inherent in Partners (The Teddy Bear Project) between safety, comfort, and childhood innocence, on the one hand, and the dangers of conformism, its bond with commerce, and the serious, formative potential of play, fantasy, and fiction, on the other hand. The phantom of 'the nation' is inherent in those dangers.

Second, this tension is compounded by the tension on which this work thrives – between the value of each singular person, a value embodied in the sometimes elaborate stories that accompany the pictures in the display cases, and the absorption of each person in multitudes, the multitude of Hitler's soldiers, of those who went along with his soothing discourse for so long, for too long, until it was too late and the Hobbesian social body was formed, so that the multitude of victims could arise. And through the transitional object of the teddy bear, the question of emotional complicity peeps in from around the corner.

But since this dissolve specifically involves a close-up and a long shot, it produces a memory space that binds both the past to the present, and this exhibition-visit to tragedy. For each of us visitors, that past tense has different connotations, inflections, but its affect cannot be held at bay. And for each of us, the memories which that affect yields are composite – not our own, but translated through innumerable stories and images. They are, as film theorist Kaja Silverman (1996) has argued, *heteropathic* memories – that is, the memories of others felt in a strong affect-image as a gift to those who perished.[10]

It is in this respect that the *worldwide* provenance of the snapshots becomes an important element of this Teddy Bear work. In her 'Notes' (2003), Hendeles mentions the many countries all over the world from which the photographs came. The act of clutching a teddy bear is presented here as a worldwide act of conforming to that awkward partnership between the two nations that share this history in this act of exhibiting today, Germany and North America. Symbolically, the history of the teddy bear itself, with its dual, staggered 'invention' and implementation as a globally popular toy, testifies to that ambiguity. Like the American Indian according to Karl May, the toy was invented, copyrighted, mass-produced and sold, named and cherished, in an episodic history in which now Germany, then the United States, took the leading role.

Thus wherever we rest our gaze when we return to Partners (The Teddy Bear Project) after, with, and through Cattelan's *Him*, the innumerable memories – each of which is individual, irretrievable, but for this single snapshot – imprint themselves in our present tense, in our visit to that current exhibition space, in the former Haus der Deutsche Kunst (House of German Art), which Hitler had ordered built to house purely German art in isolation from the 'degenerate art.' This enables a *translation* of all those emotions into *world memories*.

At this point, in order to give more substance to the conceptual metaphor of cinema as a way of understanding the power of this exhibition, I would like to discuss a number of cinematic devices that respond to photography.

A first device is the recomposition of movement out of instants. In this, cinema is rigorously *metaphotography*. Obviously, the fact that the teddy bear pictures are more often than not *posed* photographs makes them stand in *opposition* to cinema's movement-images. From the vantage point of today, such a contrast turns photography inevitably into a meta-cinema. But even so, at the same time their installation itself is still cinematic. Cinema, according to Gilles Deleuze, is essentially dependent not on photography in general but rather on the snapshot that freezes the instant. As a 'post-photographic' form of photography, cinema decom-poses and recomposes movement in relation to equidistant instants. [11]

In this respect, as a commentary on photography, Partners (The Teddy Bear Project) makes two interventions that inflect our experi-ence of cinema. First, the posed production quality of many of the photographs recedes in favour of their informal, amateurish quality, which delimits the pose in time and inscribes its brief duration so that they become snapshots in Deleuze's sense of *instantanées*. The ambigu-ous category here is the *posed* snapshot. Second, the uniform matting and framing along with the equidistant hanging (metaphorically?) reintroduce the equidistant instants of cinema's recomposition of movement. Closely in line with Deleuze's view of cinema, the installa-tion offers a precarious and provisional stability that is, as this philoso-pher's great predecessor Henri Bergson would have it, 'a slice of becoming.' Thus, Hendeles's installation harks back to photography, its 'storyboard' from the vantage point of cinema.

A second cinematic device that 'handles' photography is pro-spective. After starting our visit with Diane Arbus's self-portrait – so small and thus so large – and immersing ourselves twice in Partners (The Teddy Bear Project), after the close-up and dissolve of *Him* and its imposed flashback, the encounter with many of the non-photographic sculptures is *photographically 'incurved.'* With this verb, I am pointing not only to the tight bond between affect and action, but also, specifically, to a baroque conception of point of view derived from another of Deleuze's works, according to which point of view *enfolds* the viewer rather than allowing him to take in a spectacle at a distance, without involvement. The point of view of 'the fold' compels the viewer to enter the fabulation of the art-work, to travel inside and out again and emerge transformed by the experience. This principle, one might say, is literalized and aggrandized in the intimate rooms of Partners, where immersion, not linear perspective, reigns supreme. With the affect of that experience still with us, the voyeuristic engagement with Paul McCarthy's *Saloon* that *that* work imposes is turned on its head: unlike a voyeur, we cannot remain aloof; our subjectivity has been transformed by the earlier moment.

A third cinematic device is a play on the 'mechanical reproducibility' of the photograph. An example is the effect of the photo installation on Paolini's sculpture *Mimesi* from 1975–6 (fig. 1.4), exhibited in the gallery one enters after the confrontation with *Him*. This sculpture of a dual copy of a classical sculpture similarly appeals to the enfolded look I just mentioned. Standing for classical beauty – celebrated as the ultimate confusion between art and sex, between aesthetic and erotic attraction – the Medici Venus so flagrantly copied here as one of innumerable copies is photographic not only in its resemblance to the alleged original, but also in its doubling, in its multiplication in situ, which entices us to look at this sculpture differently from the way its prestigious original would require. The two figures do not offer their bodies to us, nor do they confront our gaze. Instead, self-absorbed, narcissistically gazing into the mirror, they flaunt their indifference, denying us access to both the close-up of their faces and their supposedly attractive bodies. And in the umpteenth reiteration of the fake modesty of the *pudica* gesture, this gesture suddenly comes back to life as 'real': their modestly covered genitals are now 'really' out of visible reach.

How, then, is *Mimesi* cinematic? Decomposed, doubled, and recomposed as one image of two equidistant instants, this sculpture brings the Venus to a life – of movement and becoming – that it never had. But in the sequence of the film, after the beginning and as an alternative to *Him*, the snow-white, larger-than-life double form confronts us with the issue of beauty in history, the perverted aesthetic of *ethical indifference*. The latter is this exhibition's antagonist, evoked every time the tight bond between aesthetics and politics is foregrounded, in an ever-subtle manner. It reminds us of the bond between art and politics in the creation of this great exhibition space itself, of the specific moment when the Haus der Kunst was created as much as of the current post-Holocaust need to

1.4 Giulio Paolini, *Mimesi*, 1975–6.

reconnect art and the world. The self-sufficiency of the dual figure is not a given; it is actualized in contrast, resonance, and narrative sequentiality with those images that posit the impossibility of such autarchy.

This brings me to a fourth 'cinephotographic' device: precisely because of the *Mimesi* artwork's isolated, venerated position both in the history of art and in this gallery, where it stands alone, the self-duplicating simulacrum of art flaunts its own *framed* position. Like montage, framing is a fundamental element in cinema, one that it shares with its predecessor and partner, photography. The frame determines the whole of what can be seen at any given moment. By delimiting what is present, the frame also stipulates what is absent. White recalls the disappearance of colour from classical sculpture, thereby turning the elimination of colour and of the present into the collapsed, defining feature of the classical in art; in the same way, the frame that isolates this work physically eliminates what it forcefully excludes and thus recalls.

The frame can be *saturated* – as it is in the long shots pulled up close in Partners (The Teddy Bear Project) – or it can be *rarefied*, and the two galleries where this is the case are the framing rooms of *Him* and *Mimesi*. With the former, we saw how the depth of the frame reintroduced the saturated background of the photo-installation, which was thus able to reclaim its status as principal scene. In the case of *Mimesi*, the cinematic device is different, for here the saturated images of the teddy bear rooms are not quite so acutely present, either because we retraced our steps or because, after the first gallery, we chose to go to *Mimesi* first. Here, the compelling desire to see makes us walk around the sculpture, surrounding it, as in an inversion of the panoptical gaze of surveillance foregrounded in our cultural awareness by the work of Michel Foucault. Thus we *enact* cinema, we play the starring role, caught up in a scopophilic system of double exposure.

A fifth device is a continuous colour-montage. The example, here, is Hanne Darboven's installation *Ansichten >82<* from 1982, installed in the large central gallery of the museum. While the harsh white still saturates our retinas, the romantic soft focus, the starry-eyed black-and-white sailor, the orange ship, and the rhythmic repetition of Darboven's installation at the centre of the exhibition quite suddenly reverse our physical position. After walking around the sculpture, we are now inside it. Indeed, after *Mimesi*, and possibly also after Partners (The Teddy Bear Project), Darboven's *Ansichten >82<* presents itself like the inside of a gigantic sculpture. Unlike The Teddy Bear Project, this work, in its imposing hall, with (again) equidistant tableaux, is at first so cold that the ship's orange colour beckons with its warmth. Temperature alone suffices to establish a connection between Darboven's ballad of suicide and murder and two tableaux by Jeff Wall, which also use orange.[12] By extension, the themes of suicide and murder, much toned down in these works set in the mood of comedy, remain present as threats, and taint the falling woman in *The Stumbling Block* and the bullying street guy in *Mimic* with the same duality of potential violence. Our 'film' takes on a decidedly postmodern incongruity here. It is for all these reasons that I contend that this exhibition too exemplifies an aspect of exhibition practice that may well be inherent to it: its fundamentally preposterous temporality. In Partners, this aspect is more strongly present because it is overdetermined by the reversal of roles between cinema and photography.

But the continuity remains cinematic – enough, at any rate, to allow readings of Walker Evans's self-portrait, in the next room on the right, as potentially murderous, and of his confined subway riders displayed on the opposite wall as locked up in the tragedy of history. And so we arrive at the back gallery, where suicide and murder are literally, photographically, represented before our eyes, as action-images, in two facing series of journalistic photography. Malcolm Browne's *The Sacrificial Protest of Thich Quang Duc* (11 June 1963) and Eddie Adams's *Murder of a Vietcong Suspect* (1 February 1968) are the twin emblems of that other war.

This exhibition translates emotions into instances of *world memory*. By this term I mean more than the mere provenance of the collection from all over the world. I mean acts of memory that do not encompass the whole world (which is impossible and would be pointless), but that go out into the world, address it, and link up with it on its own terms.[13] The decisive move in Hendeles's curatorial practice that makes this point that she has is *translated* – literally, carried over – her conceptual work with art from Toronto to Germany, to Munich, to the Haus der Kunst – a building and institution that in itself is a dissolve of past and present images, a visual state foregrounded by the felicitous decision to restore as much as possible of the Troost architecture from 1937. This is, literally, *a transnational move* that raises transhistorical questions – for example, of the meaning of partnership.

Through this displacement, the Partners exhibition is no longer the mise-en-scène of a fictional, fabulous space, but the arrangement of a segment of the world that is itself syntactically linked to other places it has affected and touched in the past, and that it continues to touch in the present. This linkage is Partners's alternative to nationalism. Cinema facilitates the absorptive fabulations that fill this real space with the glue of affect.

The Affect-Image of World Memory

This is an appropriate moment to spell out what the concept of *affect* is doing here – why it is so central both to the very possibility of world memory and to the deployment of the cinematic in exhibition practices. I am using the word 'affect' in an effort to make the tripartite connection that leads up to my main thesis, which is, that this exhibition is a paradigm of exhibitions considered in terms of the cinematic. Through the etymological sense of *aesthetics* as binding through the senses, *affect* connects the aesthetic quality of this exhibition and the art it includes, to what I like to see as a new and totally contemporary *politics of looking* – for which cinema offers the tools and photography the conceptual reflection. To understand affect without resorting to psychology, our best resource is Deleuze's first book on cinema. There, he exposes Bergson's vision of *perception*, a vision that Deleuze puts to work in his theory of cinema. Perception, in the Bergsonian/Deleuzian sense, is a *selection* of what, from the universe of visuality, is 'usable' in our lives.[14]

Perception makes visible the usable 'face' of things. This is why perception is bound up with framing: both cinema and exhibitions make such a selection for us, proposing a particular perception. This selective perception prepares the possibility for action. 'Action-images,' as Deleuze calls them, show us how to act on what we perceive. Deleuze uses the verb *incurver*: to 'incurve' the visible universe is to measure a virtual relationship of action between us and the things we see. *Mutuality* is key here: images can act on us as much as we can act on them. As I wrote earlier, between a perception that troubles us and an action we hesitate about, *affect* emerges. Affect-images present a temporarily congealed relationship between perception and the action that coincides with subjectivity. In other words, the viewer sees (what is within the frame), and hesitates about what to do; she is thus *trapped in affect*. Affect, writes Charles Altieri (2003, 49), in a remarkably negative definition, comprises the range of mental states in which an agent's activity cannot be adequately handled in terms of either sensations or beliefs but requires attending to how he or she offers expressions of those states.

Affect-images are important because, like the close-ups whose form they often take, they arrest linear time. The specific receptivity that such images entail connects them to aesthetic effect. This is why it matters that Hendeles's filmic exhibition is made mainly out of *art* – a choice that is not indifferent, of course, to the effect of the exhibition-as-film. And those objects – like the Minnie Mouse toy at the beginning, which was used both on the cover of the catalogue and on the advertising posters and banners for the exhibition; and like the teddy bears of Partners (the Teddy Bear Project), the snapshots of which were not originally made to be art – become art in this exhibition. They are treated, displayed and hence turned into artworks. 'Art preserves,' wrote Deleuze and Guattari in *What Is Philosophy?* (1994). This exhibition demonstrates what it is that art preserves and how it does this.

As pointed out by Silverman, Deleuze and Guattari describe the objects of preservation as 'bloc[s] of sensations, that is to say, a compound of percepts and affects.' These blocs exist independent of the subjects experiencing them. After closing time, the gripping documentary photographs of suicide and murder, the romantic face of Darboven's sailor, and Wall's freeze-framed cinematic image of an act of bullying continue to exist in the dark as blocs of sensations, percepts, and affects, and as syntax: a syntax that 'ascends irresistibly into his [the writer's] work and passes into sensation.' But even if they endure, they do not in themselves have a memory. [15]

For us to understand the contribution made to this cinematic exhibition of photographs as artworks and of objects that in the wake of photography take on its primary characteristics, the relationship of complementary contrast between photography and memory is key. Kaja Silverman (1996, 157) formulated this relationship as follows: 'Whereas photography performs its memorial function by lifting an object out of time and immortalizing it forever in a particular form, memory is all about temporality and change.'

The cinematic cut from Partners (The Teddy Bear Project) to *Him*, the zoom-in to a close-up, the flashback that ensues once the close-up has stalled linear time, and the resulting dissolve all constitute a particular instance of a montage that stitches together photography and memory. As a result – and this is, here, what 'art preserves' – the visitor is able to let the installation 'introduce the "not me" into [her] memory reserve' (1996, 185).

This world memory this exhibition produces through its many cinematic devices is not inherent in the art objects themselves. The syntax is there thanks to the installation, which juxtaposes works to form a sequence that is readable by means of the rhetorical figures mentioned earlier, so as to create narratives. But the heteropathic memories that contribute to creating an affective discourse in the present tense – those memories are virtual, not actual, so long as visitors do not 'perform' the film. Once they do, however, induced by this montage, world memory becomes activated and can become actual – in the present tense, which is not inherent in the image but is one of its potential modes. This makes this exhibition, with all its historical objects, utterly contemporary.

This is the contribution made by the silent, meditative gallery that houses Kawara's date painting and box, his press clipping and its appeal to a media consciousness. In her 'Notes' in the catalogue (2003), Hendeles correctly rejects the notion that the date paintings might be history paintings. The latter genre, like photography, seeks to *commemorate* historical events. Memory, instead, responds to the *images* of events that circulate, and thus constructs these as memorable events. Hendeles writes that instead of commemorating events, Kawara in his work attempts to locate himself in history. In light of Deleuze's concept of the affect-image, one might say that he produces just that: a temporarily congealed hesitation in the face of the images that frame the event for him. He hesitates about whether and how to act, but he is already stretching out, as it were, beyond selective perception alone. In this sense, Kawara's work as installed here is a particularly revealing instance of how photography can be, so to speak, curated beyond itself, to encompass heteropathic – or world – memory. Without *being* photography – it includes only a weak instance of it, in the faded and vulgar press clipping – Kawara's installation becomes a cinematic image that *comments on* photography. The auditive contrast between this gallery and the enclosed dark room staging Coleman's *Box* thus turns out to be more complementary (a partnership of sorts) than contrastive. For there, too, the brief flashes selected from the old footage, made readable rather than visible by the hyperbolic black spaces between them, derive their power from their potential to hold, to not allow time to dominate, to harbour images in the subjectivity 'incurved' by the voice that hesitates between calling and repelling the violence of the punches.

Exhibiting Photography as Meta-Cinema

In view of my interpretation of exhibitions as meta-cinema, I must now speculate on why photography is so prominent in Hendeles's exhibition, the way it is also in her collection. Specifically, why is the combination of historical and contemporary photography so effective? At first glance, the common denominator of the works in this exhibition is that they are cinematic because they are *also* photographic. McCarthy's *Saloon* is perhaps the most programmatic work in this respect: it uses hyperbolically large close-ups; it also deploys a photorealistic mode – aggrandized to grotesque proportions – of representing not only the 'real' face of the cowboy but also the 'real' toys of the pussycat, the pig, and the doll. These figures are toys, not animals or people; the realistic mode thus becomes itself grotesque. This is the critical potential of the simulacrum, the copy without original, copy of copy, photo of toy. The artist deploys this inherently contradictory mode to create a literally *moving* image; and he lets period music accompany these images. If this work, which is emphatically placed at the end and which provides a sound edit that functions as an audio dissolve placed over the works on the path leading up to it, is any indication, the relationship between photography and cinema is not only one of historical development but also – in terms that McCarthy's work justifies – 'preposterous.' With that term, already used above but not explained, I wish to usher in my conclusion, which turns the relationship upside down and seeks to understand photography, in Hendeles's hands, as a critical commentary on cinema.

Preposteriority is the temporal reversal that inhabits all exhibitions. Situated in the present, they rewrite the past and revise our relation to it as well as its meanings as such (Bal 1999). As we stand in front of the two most clearly cinematic sets of photographs – the press photos of the suicide captured by Browne and the murder displayed for Adams's camera – we almost fall back into the most standard Hollywood action movie. Almost, but not quite. For, stopping short of being action-images, these two mutually rhyming sequences are reined in from their potential Hollywood status by Lawrence Weiner's words. It is in this gallery that Weiner's word-picture *Vis intertiae* (cat. #471) from 1980 – on the materiality of slowing down in temporal close-up – spells out how physical, transformative, and perhaps decisive the affect of affect-images is. The picture says:

A change in inherent quality
(vis inertiae)

La réaction d'un objet au
Contact suffisant a entraîner
Un changement de qualité
Inhérente (vis inertiae)

The two series of photojournalism, Browne's and Adam's – recalling, through their generic background, America's nationalistic *hubris* in Vietnam, the presence of words in newspapers, and the way words connect individuals to the world – inaugurate a reading of this exhibition that turns it into commentary on cinema from the vantage point of photography.

Press photographs, like action movies, come and go. They pass quickly, and their visual overload hampers rather than promotes our connection with the world. Occasionally, this crazy pace of media saturation is stopped in its tracks. These two series, like the novel *Uncle Tom's Cabin* in its time, seem to turn action-images into affect-images. Integrating them with other images of violence, in this space, here and now, not only recalls the events and the changes in the course of the Vietnam War resulting from them, but also – beyond that specific historical world-memory – places into an affect-image the very power of images. That is, if we allow them to exercise that power – harboured in an exhibition that does not lock out the world, in a space that *is* world history – to make us hesitate just long enough to be transformed by them.

In our present, which has embarked on and is entangled in a new episode of that ongoing war of which the Vietnam War was an earlier episode – one from which no nation seems to be able to disentangle itself – an exhibition that thinks through cinema with the aid of a photography that is able to critique its successor from 'before' can be seen as deeply political, precisely *because* it is so profoundly and transformatively aesthetic. I find this aesthetic a major contribution to a cultural philosophy that attempts to bridge the gulf between art and the melancholy powerlessness before, or the insidious complicity with, the politics that threatens both art and all our lives. This politics is powerful and complex – too complex, multiple, and subtle to discuss in this context. If, for example, I have refrained from even mentioning the gender politics that clearly run through this show, from the *Wild Bunch* photo of bandits in the first room to *Saloon* and back to that group portrait of bandits looking like nice guys, it was so that I could invite my readers – now, at the end – to return to the beginning and start all over again. But that will have to be another paper.[16]

Meanwhile, this volume will offer fresh insights into how endeavours such as Hendeles's Partnership with history can help museums serve their primary function in a postnational world. Far from confining themselves to reconfirming nationalism, as current exhibitions all too frequently tend to do, thanks to the paradigm of Partners, exhibition makers can deploy different options. I contend that the primary task of exhibitions should be to encourage visitors to stop, suspend action, let affect invade us, and then, *quietly,* in temporary respite, *think.*

NOTES

1 Hendeles herself does consider the metaphor of mise-en-scène crucial for her work (oral communication, 2003). The metaphor of exhibits as still personages was foregrounded – literally so – in the exhibition Louise Bourgeois: Geometria pozadania / Geometry of Desire (Warsaw: Zachêta Pañstwowa Galeria, 2003, curator Adam Budak). There, Bourgeois's totemic sculptures, referred to as Personages, occupied the centre of the main gallery, casually dispersed as if to represent the visitors.

2 Mostly from Pavis (1998, 361-8). This paragraph and the following one come from my book *Travelling Concepts* (2002).

3 Lehmann (1997). I prefer to leave undecided – indeed, insist on the undecidability of – the distinction between phenomenology and semiotics implied in this formulation, which is mine, not Lehmann's.

4 For these and other terms of narratology, see Bal (1997), which is partly based on Genette, *Discours du récit* (1972).

5 The rhetorical figures mentioned in these paragraphs are analysed in Ydessa Hendeles (2003). For a narrative theory based on rhetorical figures rather than plot, see Genette (1972). Rudi Fuchs has used the poetical rhetoric of couplets consistently throughout his career as curator.

6 The fundamental heterogeneity among frames, owing to the black intervals separating each image from the next, turns serial photography into readable rather than visible, images. See Doane (2002).

7 This contrast between multitude and singularity resonates with Michael Hardt and Antonio Negri's reflections on the multitude as site of resistance. See their book *Empire* (2000).

8 See Susan Buck-Morss (1994). She points to the fear of early cinema spectators when confronted with close-ups. Sometimes they clamoured to see evidence that the figure whose head only was visible, had not been beheaded.

9 I am referring to the exhibition Mirroring Evil held at the New York Jewish Museum, curated by Norman Kleeblatt. It is no coincidence that Cattelan's sculpture diminishes the figure of Hitler to the size of a pre-adolescent boy, thus bringing it close to the toys that were so prominent in Kleeblatt's exhibition. See van Alphen, 'Playing the Holocaust' (2002). This is a critical study of the use of toys in relation to historical trauma.

10 Varda's film shows some visitors responses that, in all their variety, confirm the affective investment in (other people's) past that the photo exhibit impels.

11 Deleuze (1983, 14). The following is greatly indebted to Paola Marrati, *Gilles Deleuze* (2003). An excellent in-depth study of Deleuze's cinema books is David Rodowick, *Gilles Deleuze's Time Machine* (1997). Patricia Pisters's, *The Matrix of Visual Culture* (2003) is a wonderfully stimulating 'work-book.' The view of snapshots as frozen moments is challenged in Ulrich Baer, *Spectral Evidence* (2002), who opposes to it the catastrophic reading of the snapshot he borrows from Vilém Flusser, *Towards a Philosophy of Photography* (2000).

12 Jeff Wall, *The Stumbling Block*, 1991; *Mimic* 1982. Available at http://by113fd.boy113.hotmail.msn.com/cgi-bin/getmsg?curmbox =00000000%2d0000%2.

13 The term 'acts of memory' is meant to emphasize the active nature of memory. See Bal, Crewe, and Spitzer (1999).

14 Bergson (1997, 29). See also Bergson (1998).

15 Silverman (1996, 163; 164, emphasis in text; 167).

16 In his catalogue essay, Van Alphen reflects in more depth on the gender issue than I can possibly do here.

BIBLIOGRAPHY

Alphen, Ernst Van. 2002. 'Playing the Holocaust.' In *Mirroring Evil: Nazi Imagery / Recent Art*, edited by Norman Kleeblatt, 66–83. New York: Jewish Museum.

– 2003. 'Die Ausstellung als narratives Kunstwerk / Exhibition as a Narrative Work of Art.' In Ydessa Hendeles, *Partners*, edited by Chris Dercon and Thomas Weski, 143–85. Munich: Haus der Kunst; Cologne: Buchhandlung Walther König.

Altieri, Charles. 2003. *The Particulars of Rapture: An Aestheties of the Effects*. Ithaca, NY: Cornell University Press.

Baer, Ulrich. 2002. *Spectral Evidence: The Photography of Trauma*. Cambridge, MA: MIT Press.

Bal, Mieke. 1996. *Double Exposures: The Subject of Cultural Analysis*. New York: Routledge.

– 1997. *Narratology: Introduction to the Theory of Narrative*. Toronto: University of Toronto Press.

– 1999. *Quoting Caravaggio: Contemporary Art, Preposterous History*. Chicago: University of Chicago Press.

– 2002. *Travelling Concepts in the Humanities*. Toronto: University of Toronto Press.

Bal, Mieke, Jonathan Crewe, and Leo Spitzer, eds. 1999. *Acts of Memory: Cultural Recall in the Present*. Hanover, NH: University Press of New England.

Bergson, Henri. 1997 (1896). *Matière et mémoire*. Paris: PUF.

– 1998 (1907). *L'évolution créatrice*. Paris: PUF.

Brooks, Peter. 1984. *Reading for the Plot: Design and Intention in Narrative*. New York: Alfred A. Knopf.

Buck-Morss, Susan. 1994. 'The Cinema Screen as Prosthesis of Perception: A Historical Account.' In *The Senses Still: Perception and Memory as Material Culture in Modernity*, edited by C. Nadia Seremetakis, 45–62. Chicago: University of Chicago Press.

Deleuze, Gilles. 1983. *Cinéma I: L'image-mouvement*. Paris: Editions de Minuit. Translated as: *Cinema I: The Movement-Image*. H. Tomlinson and B. Habberjam. London: Athlone Press, 1986.

– 1993. *The Fold: Leibniz and the Baroque*. Trans. and with a foreword by Tom Conley. Minneapolis: University of Minnesota Press.

Deleuze, Gilles, and Félix Guattari. 1994. *What Is Philosophy?* Trans. by Hugh Tomlinson and Graham Burchill. London: Verso.

Doane, Mary Ann. 2002. *The Emergence of Cinematic Time: Modernity, Contingency, the Archive*. Cambridge, MA: Harvard University Press.

Flusser, Vilém. 2000. *Towards a Philosophy of Photography*. Trans. by Anthony Mathews. London: Reaktion Books.

Foucault, Michel. 1975. *The Birth of the Clinic*. Trans. A.M. Sheridan Smith. New York: Vintage.

Genette, Gérard. 1972. *Discours du récit*. Vol. 3 of *Figures*. Paris: Editions du Seuil. Eng. *Narrative Discourse: An Essay in Method*. Trans. by Jane E. Lewin, with a foreword by Jonathan Culler. Ithaca: Cornell University Press, 1980.

Hardt, Michael, and Antonio Negri. 2000. *Empire*. Cambridge, MA: Harvard University Press.

Hendeles, Ydessa. 2003. 'Anmerkungen zur Ausstellung / Notes on the Exhibition.' In *Partners*, edited by Chris Dercon and Thomas Weski, 187–229. Munich: Haus der Kunst; Cologne: Verlag der Buchhandlung Walther König.

Iversen, Gunnar. 2003. 'Dissolving Views: Style, Memory and Space.' Paper delivered at the Modes of Seeing conference, University of Trondheim, 6–8 November.

Lehmann, Hans-Thiess. 1997. 'From Logos to Landscape: Text in Contemporary Dramaturgy.' *Performance Research* 2, no. 1: 55–60.

Marrati, Paola. 2003. *Gilles Deleuze: Cinéma et philosophie*. Paris: PUF.

Pavis, Patrice. 1998. *Dictionary of the Theatre: Terms, Concepts and Analysis.* Toronto: University of Toronto Press.

Pisters, Patricia. 2003. *The Matrix of Visual Culture: Working with Deleuze in Film Theory.* Stanford, CA: Stanford University Press.

Rodowick, David. 1997. *Gilles Deleuze's Time Machine.* Durham, NC: Duke University Press.

Silverman, Kaja. 1996. *The Threshold of the Visible World.* New York: Routledge.

Varda, Agnès. 2004. *Ydessa, les ours, et etc.* French documentary, 45 min. Ciné-Tamaris, co-produced by the Musée de Paume, Paris.

PART TWO

Reconfiguring National History:
Centralized and Local Strategies

2 The Terror of the House

ISTVÁN RÉV

The most famous photographs of the 1956 Hungarian Revolution capture the moment when the soldiers and policemen who had been defending the headquarters of the Budapest Party Committee left the building. Faced with a superior force of revolutionaries, the defenders realized that further defence was hopeless and surrendered their besieged headquarters. On their way out, at the very gates of the building, the defeated were received by deadly machine gun fire. *Life* magazine ran a series of close-up pictures of the killing.

Life photographer George Sadovy's photo report of the bloodbath became one of the most famous sequences of war photographs ever made, comparable only to such legendary pictures as the Hungarian-born Robert Capa's war reportage during the Spanish Civil War.[1] When *Life* decided to publish a special issue devoted exclusively to images of the revolution, Sadovy composed a narrative account to accompany his pictures:

> The fighting really began to flare up. People were dropping like flies ... Now the AVH [Hungarian secret police] men began to come out. The first to emerge from the building was an officer alone. It was the fastest killing I saw. He came out laughing and the next thing I knew he was flat on the ground. It didn't dawn on me that this guy was shot. He just fell down, I thought ... Six young policemen came out, one very good-looking. Their shoulder boards were torn off. Quick argument. We're not as bad as you think we are, give us a chance, they said. I was three feet from that group. Suddenly one began to fold. They must have been close to his ribs when they fired. They all went down like corn that had been cut. Very gracefully. Another came out running. He saw his friends dead, turned and

headed into the crowd. The rebels dragged him out. I had time to take one picture of him and he was down. Then my nerves went. Tears started to come down on my cheeks. I had spent three years in war, but nothing I saw then compared with the horror of this. I could see the impact of bullets on clothes. There was not much noise. They were shooting so close that the man's body acted as a silencer.[2]

Sadovy shot several rolls of film on Köztársaság (Republic) Square while covering the siege of the Budapest Party Headquarters (which, incidentally, during the Second World War had served as the headquarters of the Volksbund, the Nazi sympathizer association of Hungarian Germans). *Life* published dozens of his photographs, among them the four-picture series of the massacre of the AVH soldiers, most of them enlisted men without rank.

Sadovy's photos were included in the authorized Communist version of the events on Republic Square, in *Köztársaság Tér 1956* (Republic Square 1956), first published in 1974. Ervin Hollós, who co-authored the book with his wife, was in the building during the siege. Immediately after the uprising was crushed, he became deputy head of the Investigation Department of the Ministry of the Interior, the agency in charge of investigating the 'counter-revolutionary atrocities' during the 1956 events, among them the massacre on Republic Square. Later on, he changed careers, and became the official historian of 1956; in that position he made good use of the confessions he had co-written, as the chief investigator of the 'counter-revolution.'

To situate the narrative and to establish the events of 1956 as a counter-revolution in an memorializable localization system, *Köztársaság Tér 1956* provided extensive photographic coverage of the events in addition to textual account. These pictures came mostly from the pages of *Time*, *Life*, and *Paris Match*. Aided by the photographs, the historians condensed the most important events connected to specific locations – primarily Republic Square – in order to guarantee that future memories would be tied to known and concrete locations.

The pictures were included in the official account in order to 'solidify' the massacre as an immovable event. Photography – so it seems – does not require mediation; it promises non-interventionist objectivity. Because a photographic image is not made directly by human hand – it is simply a mechanical reproduction of 'reality,' it is an action at a distance –, it promises the immediacy of evidence, almost as if it were revelation.[3] It is not made, but seemingly brought forth and revealed, like an object found in the depths of an archive. It does not refer to or resemble reality; rather, it stands for reality and takes the place of the original.[4] Photography is thus an appropriate medium for transforming a particular event into a frozen document, into a sign.

After the revolution the courts made use of this evidence, these photos, when identifying and charging those who had taken part in the massacre on Republic Square.[5] The images were used as *hyperfacts*, capable of referring to and revealing another, more fundamental and until then barely visible fact: the striking similarity of the bloodbath to other images of right-wing, anti-Communist incidents of the past. When seen from a certain perspective, the images suggested their own frame: here, the counter-revolutionary nature of the event. Within that frame, suddenly everything fell into place; the hidden came to light.[6] The non-interventionist 'objectivity' of a photograph and its power to reveal the hitherto unknown are not contradictory: X-rays are capable of showing what has been invisible to the human eye in what is presumed to be an empirically reliable, non-subjective way.[7]

On 2 November 1956, two days after the fall of the Budapest Party Headquarters, *Magyar Függetlenség* (Hungarian Independence), one of the revolutionary newspapers, revealed that after they stormed the building, the revolutionaries had found 'large quantities of half-ready pancakes in the kitchen, enough for considerably more people than those actually found after the siege, but the AVH-men mysteriously disappeared.' When the dead lying in the square were added to the prisoners taken by the revolutionaries, the total, including civilians, came to less than a hundred. The number surprised the victors, who had assumed that hundreds of soldiers and policemen were living in the party headquarters, together with hundreds or even thousands of prisoners, women and children among them.

In the indictment brought at one of the post–Republic Square trials, the Budapest Military Court stated that before the siege, rumours had been circulating among the fighting groups that underground prisons and casemates lay beneath the party headquarters and that hundreds or even thousands of freedom fighters were being held in them.[8] On the morning of the siege, one of the revolutionary military leaders assured his men: 'We are absolutely certain that under the party headquarters there are several floors of underground cellar prisons, full of political prisoners whom it is our duty to free.'[9] The 'White Book,' the official Communist version of the events, would later claim that in the days before the bloody battle, horror stories had been circulating in the city that thousands of prisoners were suffering in the underground labyrinth, some for as many as ten years.[10] One daily wrote about medieval prisons, others about 'the torture chambers of the inquisition,' 'the secret of the tunnels under the party headquarters,' and 'the mysteries of the Communist casemates.'[11]

After the revolutionaries took the building, they immediately tried to contact the prisoners. They investigated the cellars but found no one. They searched for secret entrances that supposedly led to the underground labyrinth, and they listened for noises and hammering from below. Some of the occupants claimed that they had heard cries from below. Later on, *Magyar Nemzet* would report that, on lifting a telephone receiver in an empty office, a member of the occupying forces overheard a conversation between an AVH officer and a guard in the underground prison, who was inquiring anxiously about the outcome of the fighting. 'Let us out! We are prisoners. We want to live!' was purportedly heard from deep below. 'How many of you are there?' came the question from above. 'Hundred and forty,' arrived the barely audible answer from the depths of the bunker.[12]

In the early evening of 30 October, once the fighting had ceased, the revolutionary military units issued warrants for the arrest of those who might have taken part in designing the underground structures, and of officials of the Budapest Sewage Company, who were supposed to know the secret entrance to the underground structures. Hungarian National Radio repeatedly asked anyone who had information about the layout of the casemates to report, without delay, to the headquarters of the rescue operation. The following afternoon, General Béla Király, the commander of the revolutionaries' National Guard, appointed a lieutenant-colonel to oversee the underground search.

Some Western photographers and a few Western film crews stayed on the square after the building was surrendered and took pictures of the search. One photo shows two men – probably from the National Postal Service – listening carefully to a sound detector placed at one of the manholes on the square. At the request of the National Guard, the National Geophysics Institute provided a cathode ray oscilloscope, four Soviet made geophones, and one anode battery with the necessary cables to help with the search.[13] The National Guard ordered the Hungarian-Soviet Oil Exploration Company to send drilling rigs, boring tools, and even drilling vans and a boring rig to the square. Three boring masters were ordered to the city from the Oroszlány coal mines, and experts from the Zala oil fields with sophisticated equipment were brought in to help the searchers.

At first, 20-metre exploratory wells were drilled; on 3 November, the oil drilling equipment began going even deeper. The revolutionaries sent powerful excavators to the site, and one picture, published in *Köztársaság Tér*, clearly shows an enormous ditch excavated by a machine that had been used in the construction of the Budapest Underground. The Budapest Sewage Company sent workers, pick-axes, shovels, ropes, and other supplies. After failing to find the entrance to the labyrinth from the building's cellars, the searchers descended into the sewage system. As described by some of the news-papers, this scene brought to mind Victor Hugo's *Les Misérables*, in which the ex-prisoner Jean Valjean carries the seriously wounded Marius through the labyrinth of sewers under revolutionary Paris.

George Mikes, a London-based Hungarian émigré who worked for the BBC, claimed that the prisons could be reached only through a hidden entrance either from the cellars or from one of the boxes in the City Opera, which stood across from the party headquarters on the opposite side of the square. According to Mikes's account, a captured AVH officer had revealed the secret; however, he had then managed to mislead the explorers. After days of exhausting effort, the rescuers had to give up the search, leaving the 154 prisoners (Mikes's figure), together with their captors, to perish in the depths.[14]

In the early morning of 4 November, four days after the search began, Soviet troops returned to Budapest. With the defeat of the revo-lution, the mystery remained unsolved – the prisoners were never found. The fact that they were not found did not disprove either the existence of the underground prisons or the tragic fate of the prisoners.

The archives of Radio Free Europe (RFE) include an odd collection known as the 'Items.' An 'Item' is an interview that was conducted with a newly arrived emigrant from behind the Iron Curtain to the West, or with a tourist. Most of these people mistakenly believed that they were talking to an interested former compatriot, or a casual acquaintance, or a Western journalist. It did not occur to most of them that they were talking to an employee or a contractee of an intelligence agency, who would be writing a formal official report in their native language, com-plete with an English summary and evaluation comments. The texts, arranged by subject heading, were used later on by the programmers at the national desks of RFE. Before the collapse of the Communist regimes, most of the items were destroyed, partly in order to protect the interviewees, who might be recognized despite the anonymous format of the documents (the initials or pseudo-initials of the interviewers were always noted on the front page). However, thousands of items from the national desks survived the shredding, and today they provide unique information for scholars of Communist times.

The 'Items' form a weird collection. In some cases it is obvious – and we even have direct proof – that the interview is pure fiction. Some interviewers were paid by the piece, so they would try to produce as many interviews as seemed acceptable. One well-known Hungarian writer and social critic who immigrated to London and worked for RFE, composed some of the interviews facing just his typewriter in the solitude of his study. In most cases the tourist or (especially) the recent immigrant wanted to please the interviewer and thus said what he or she assumed the interviewer wanted to hear. (The vast majority of interviewees were young or middle-aged men.) The collection suggests the vague notions that interviewees had about the image of Communism in the West. It is also apparent that typically, this circular impression was formed by listening to RFE broadcasts. In turn, the programmers made use of the interviews when broadcasting anti-Communist propaganda to the East. The stories that were told in reply to the leading questions of the covert agents – who presupposed the obvious anti-Communist leanings of the refugees, who were waiting for their residence permits, and of the tourists, who were stunned by all the commercial wealth of the West – testified to the potency of the self-fulfilling prophecies of the Western propaganda, which were based on the information distilled from the severely biased items.

Among the Hungarian items, under the header 'Resistance,' there are a few interviews that explicitly deal with the storming of the party headquarters and the underground prisons. Item no. 1264/57 came from Vienna (probably from one of the refugee camps). According to the English summary: 'Source comments on the chapter [of the official White Book] "Attack Against the Headquarters of the Party Committee of Budapest." He refuted the statement of the "White Book" that the underground of the headquarters did not exist.'[15]

The source, a forty-nine-year-old former journalist from Budapest, stated that he had kept a diary during the days of the revolution and recorded all the noteworthy events over its course. He was present when, after the siege ended, the victors entered the building and tried unsuccessfully to find the entrance to the underground cells. On 3 November a journalist reported to a captain of the army's technical division that he had found telephone and electricity cables that led beneath the building. On the captain's orders, geophysical equipment was immediately shipped from one of the coal-mining districts. By radio, the rescue teams were able to make contact with the 131 prisoners, who said that they had been forced to descend to the underground prisons from room No. 3 of the party headquarters:

> Forty of us from the investigation team searched the building from roof to cellar but were unable to locate room No. 3, as the rooms of the building, unfortunately, were not numbered … We decided to return the next morning, on November 4, and to carry on, with the help of explosives. In view of the start of the Soviet attack, however, we had no opportunity to revisit the site. According to the catering book we found in the building, the kitchen catered for 250 people, and this clearly proves the existence of the underground prison and the secret passage, through which at least a hundred members of the AVH could leave the building via the tunnel of the underground railway. The political prisoners, however, remained forever under the ground. The circumstances of the construction of the party headquarters substantiate my claim. The construction of the building started parallel with the building of the underground railway [sic]. [Before World War II the building served as the headquarters of the Volksbund.] A delegation of forty Soviet engineers arrived in Budapest to supervise the construction of the tunnels, and not a single Hungarian engineer was allowed the see the full plan, they were shown only small segments of the complete master plan. All of us who worked at the construction were completely convinced that we were not building an underground railway, but nuclear shelters, instead.[16]

Item No. 3169/57 also came from one of the Austrian refugee camps. Its source was a thirty-two-year-old technician from Budapest. The title of this item – 'Underground Railway in Budapest and Party Headquarters at Köztársaság-Ter' – is the first mention of the assumed direct connection between the underground prisons and the underground railway. The English summary remarks: 'Source took part in the attempts to locate the underground rooms with technical equipment for eight days' (the siege took place on 30 October, the Soviet troops occupied Budapest on 4 November).[17] The technician insisted:

> In order to see the story in a clear context, we have to go back to the construction of the Budapest underground railway. At one point of the line, a

detour was built in the direction to Köztársaság tér, but the tunnel did not turn back anywhere to the main underground line ... This work was headed by an AVH officer whose cover name was Kovacs. He was a local party secretary, but, in order to mislead the workers, he had been expelled several times from the Party ... This part of the tunnel was built mostly by prisoners sentenced to death who, without exception, were executed later on. As it proved to be impossible to supply all the necessary workforce from among prisoners sentenced to death, a few of the construction workers survived, and, when the works stopped after 1953, all of them were sent to far away workplaces in remote parts of the country. Some of them returned during the days of the revolution, and they were the ones who were able to provide precise information about the whereabouts of the detour-line ...

After midnight, on October 29 [the siege took place on 30 October], the investigators transported an aerial detector from one of the mines to the Square, which enabled the search team to listen to the vulgar conversation of the AVH officers, the crying of the children and the screaming of the women. We could determine the direction of the tunnel, which led to a spiral staircase beneath the royal box, now reserved for the Secretary General, of the City Opera, on the opposite side of the Square ... In a cellar we accidentally discovered a telephone switch. One of the members of the National Guard happened to know the secret password which enabled him to start a conversation with the AVH officers under the ground. The officers, believing that they were talking to one of their comrades, requested him to turn on the water tap, and asked him about the outcome of the siege. Naturally, we did not tell them that the Headquarters had fallen, and the revolutionaries had occupied the building ... On the square, with the help of taping equipment, the military managed to capture ciphered messages coming from below the ground, but they were not able to decipher the secret code ... We decided that next day, November 4, we would break through the wall at one end of the tunnel of the underground railway, but at daybreak the Soviet troops arrived, and the search had to be stopped ... On that day the Soviet military occupied the building, and during the coming days, the rattle of firearms could be heard from the direction of the Party Headquarters ... The Soviets imposed a curfew until seven in the morning, but when I ventured into the street, immediately after the end of the curfew, I saw corpses every morning, children and women among them, lying flat on their faces in the Square. In my estimate, during the next two weeks, about a hundred bodies were collected from the Square after the end of the nightly curfew. Obviously, these were the people who had been kept under the ground.[18]

The text suggests how the bright – albeit artificially lit – utopia of the Stalinist underground was turned into an image of hell. The mirror image of the cellars under the party headquarters is also featured among the items.' An interview originating from the Vienna News Bureau on 2 September 1957 describes, as the title puts it, 'How the "White Book" Was Put Together.'

According to the source:

> The fighting was still going on in Budapest, when, in the former Head-quarters of the AVH, in 16 Jászai Mari Square [this building – commonly referred to as the 'White House' – after 1956 became the Ministry of Interior, and later on, until 1989, was occupied by the Central Committee of the Party], or precisely in the cellars of the said building, the idea of the 'White Book,' that would uncover the counter-revolution, was born. Please do not fool yourselves: this was not a cold, unfriendly, and dirty coal-cellar, but a basement equipped with all imaginable comforts, an ample quantity of foodstuffs, hoarded in the 'operation officers' shelter,' three levels below the ground. Only their uniform distinguished those who stayed in this luxurious cellar from the rats. These rats with a human figure were the employees of the Political Department of the National Police Headquarters and their relatives ... The only resistance these 'heroes' were able to think of was heroically resisting the temptation to leave the secure cellar and face up to the revolution.[19]

Following the depiction of the scene, the interviewee then gives a detailed description of the 'curly dark hair,' 'the thin stature,' and 'the characteristic nose' of the rats in whose minds the idea of the 'White Book' was born. These people understood that, without the help of genuine documents, it would be impossible to prove to the world and to the UN that the 'Hungarian Revolution was neither the Revolution of the People, nor the Revolution of the Hungarian Youth but the instead, it was the "Horthyst-fascist mob, financed by counts, barons, bank directors and the United States that wanted to overthrow the most glorious achievement of the 20th century: the people's democracy."'[20]

The source insists that the photographs included in the 'White Book' – among them the pictures of the massacre on Republic Square – had been doctored in the safe and secluded cellar three floors underground, in the 'Headquarters of the AVH.'[21] The AVH 'rats' retouched the pictures in the depths of their well-appointed cellar so as to turn the barbarity of the Communist secret police into sinister accusations against the Hungarian revolutionary youth.[22]

In 1992 the first post-Communist conservative government commissioned a two-part film report on the underground prisons from Hungarian National Television (HNT; the country's only television channel at the time). The investigative report was aired in early March of 1994, shortly before the parliamentary elections, as part of HNT's *Unlawful Socialism* series.[23] By that time the popularity of the first post-Communist conservative government – which had been in office since May 1990 – was fading dangerously. All the polling agencies were predicting a Socialist victory – perhaps even an absolute majority – in the upcoming elections.

In 1989, as part of the transition from one-party rule, the Hungarian Socialist Worker's Party reinvented itself as the Hungarian Socialist Party and divested itself of many of its buildings, among them the party headquarters and the Central Committee building. The renamed party moved its offices to the huge former headquarters of the Budapest Party Committee on Republic Square.

After the first democratic elections in 1990, the Socialist Party had ended up with a tiny block of seats in Parliament. The election had been won by a right-wing coalition, the Hungarian Democratic Forum (HDF), whose primary aim was to re-establish the continuity of Hungarian history and to carry on from where 'authentic Hungarian national history' had been artificially interrupted. The HDF, led by a failed historian, contended that after 19 March 1944, when German troops occupied Hungary, the country had lost its sovereignty, and had only regained it when the first post-Communist democratically elected government was sworn in. Hungary, consequently, could not be held responsible either for the Holocaust or for the Gulag; the Germans and the Soviets, respectively, were to blame.

Practical considerations were the main reason (though not the only reason) why the Socialist Party decided to move its central offices to the former Budapest Party Headquarters: it was the largest party property in Budapest except for the 'White House,' the former Central Committee building. The Socialist Party was not in a position to hold on to the White House: its location was too prominent at the time of the transition; it stands beside the Danube, near the Parliament House, and is too visible from everywhere in the city. The party wanted to normalize itself and project the image of a modest, almost invisible political organization that detested privilege.

The reburial of Imre Nagy, the executed prime minister of the 1956 revolution, was the single most important symbolic event of the transition. Resurfacing memories of the post-revolutionary terror proved to be decisive in delegitimizing Communist rule. When, in 1990, the successor party moved to the site of the bloodiest and best remembered anti-Communist atrocity, it was moving, not only to the scene of merciless slaughter but also to the specific place where the counter-revolution was 'invented.' The site was a reminder of the atrocities that perhaps justified post-revolutionary Communist 'justice.' Thus the party could evoke its victims, its victimhood, and its own pain when confronting the post-1989 discourse of nationwide suffering and mourning. In 1990 the enormous monument to the 'Victims of the Counter-Revolution' still overwhelmed the square, and the windows of the new central offices overlooked it; the new party headquarters incorporated the monument, the plaque at the entrance, and the notion of the place.

Footage from the newsreels shot on Republic Square during the days of the revolution introduced the two-part HNT film. It showed aerial detectors, microphones in the manholes on the square, the work of the excavators, and 20-metre-deep holes everywhere in front of the building. The director interviewed participants from both sides who had been present at the siege, as well as contemporaries who had worked either in various party offices or for the secret police, in buildings that without exception had underground cellars. A secretary who had worked at the Ministry of Interior, in the 'White House,' after 1956, recalled a frightening experience. One evening in 1959, she descended to the cellars to shred some papers and saw that the walls were covered with a brownish stain up to her chest. To her horror, she immediately concluded that the staining could only be dried human blood. She remembered the stories about a gigantic mincing-machine next to the shredder in the cellar. The mouth of the mincer – in the stories – was connected to the sewage system, which opened onto the Danube. (The White House stands on the bank of the river. It is the same building where the curly-haired officers were busy retouching the photographs.) The secretary, wearing a wig and facing away from the camera – she still feared the Communists – also recalled the bathtubs full of acid that provided an alternative technology for obliterating all traces of the prisoners.

In April 1993, the film crew commissioned a study by the National Geophysical Institute. The experts were asked to analyse the profile of the soil in front of the headquarters of the Socialist Party. The study discovered strange 'anomalies' in the ground: the antitypy (density) of the soil was higher at a depth of 30 to 40 metres than nearer to the surface. Strangely enough – concluded the professional analysis – the 'anomaly' was observable especially beneath the pedestal of the huge memorial that had been built in the early 1960s in memory of the defenders of the Budapest Party Headquarters. At this point the crew brought in oil drillers, who arrived with sophisticated equipment: drills fitted with exceptionally tough diamond bits.

On the back of the memorial's pedestal, which weighed many tons, there was a small iron door that instantly aroused the curiosity of the filmmakers. The bit was immediately positioned behind the door, and drilling started without delay through the strange opening. After days of work and fourteen metres of unimpeded drilling through the clay bank, the apparatus hit something solid, probably concrete. When the bit was pulled out, it was found that the mysterious material had eaten up the diamond. The result was the same after the second and third trials: the diamond bit was always seriously damaged. In the meantime, the mighty sculpture was removed and shipped to the outskirts of the city, to the 'sculpture park,' the ghetto of socialist memorials, where dead sculptures await their Last Judgment.

The unknown material under the ground supplied the *argumentum ex silentio*, the proof based on silence, with which the film concluded.[24] The anomaly that prevented the continuation of the search served as evidence that was difficult to refute: something must be there in the depths of the blood-soaked soil – something that even after long decades was keeping the secret that everyone already knew. In the elections, the socialists won an absolute majority; the HDF won only 14 per cent of the vote.

It was not the film that did not quite work, but the figure and the dystopia of the cellar prison. On top of (or beneath?) Stalin's underground – the utopia of both the underground movement and that of the Underground Railway – the post-1989 anti-Communists chose to superimpose the underground cellar. It proved difficult, however, to tie the Socialist Party to a representative, intense, compressed counter-figure of its past. Unlike the gas chambers of Auschwitz or the Gulag of Siberia – which, although tied to more or less concrete locations, denote a horrifyingly complex and wide-ranging historical figure – the underground prison is not sufficiently unique, nor does it seem capable of evoking and denoting an entire historical epoch beyond itself. The notion of the dungeon is more conveniently tied to medieval castles, to the torture chambers of the Inquisition, or to the tourist attraction of the Maison des Esclaves on Gorée Island, a short boat trip from Dakar in Senegal,[25] than to the location and notion of terror during Communist times.

Despite everything we know of the cellars of Ljubjanka Prison in Moscow (where, among thousands of other prisoners, Raoul Wallenberg was detained), the Communist regime cannot be evoked by a shorthand reference to the underground prison. By contrast, Auschwitz – at least in the West – unequivocally recalls Fascism, human horror, and the vulnerability of human beings, not just the Nazis. 'Why has Auschwitz become the universal exemplum with the stamp of eternal perpetuity in the European consciousness that embodies the whole world of Nazi concentration camps, together with the universal shock of the spirit over it, and with the mythical site, which should be preserved in order for the pilgrims to visit, like the Mount of Golgota?' So asked Imre Kertész, a survivor of Fascism and Communism, in one of his essays, 'What Makes Auschwitz so Perfect?' and in front of the audience that did not want to believe its ears:

> All truly great parables should be simple. And in Auschwitz, good and bad do not merge even for a single moment ... The picture is not distorted by a shade of alien color; the color, for example, of politics. The spirit of the narration here should not struggle with the fact that innocent – exclusively from the perspective of the movement, innocent – otherwise true believer Nazis had been locked in Auschwitz; this story is not complicated by such a fact ... Auschwitz is fully explored, and, in turn, it is both spatially and temporally a closed and untouchable structure. It is like a carefully prepared archeological find ... And we know all spatial segments of the story ... It stands in front of us as the Apocalypse, as one of Edgar Allen Poe's, Kafka's or Dostoevsky's horror-stories, narrated with uncomfortable details; its logic, its ethical horror and ignominy, the excess of torment, and the horrible moral of the story which the spirit of the European narration cannot leave behind, all these details are well-known.[26]

The right-wing historians and propagandists had no choice: the film had to be made. The world, the history that the Communists had created around Republic Square, the continuous deadly battle of the twentieth century – in fact, of modern times – between Fascism and Communism, the White Terror versus historical justice, Republic Square as just another instance of the White Terror of 1919 and of 1944, could not be undone without revisiting the underground, without arguing that what happened on the square had been justified. By holding up the underground, by bringing it to light, they could hope that the entire Communist historical construct, the world that the Communists made, could be undermined. Republic Square was the Archimedean point of the Communist interpretation of history, which the cellars could be expected to make both historically and morally untenable:[27]

In January 2002 (even before the museum was completed), the first paragraph of the introduction to the House of Terror's website stated this:

> Whoever has visited Budapest before knows that one of the most beautiful boulevards in the Capital is Andrássy Boulevard. The tree-lined street, with lavish villas and stately apartment buildings, connects downtown Budapest to Heroes' Square. It was named after one of the Austro-Hungarian Empire's greatest Hungarian statesmen, Count Gyula Andrássy. The Neo-Renaissance building at Andrássy Boulevard 60 was designed by Adolf Feszty in 1880. It is also notable that the 20th century terror regimes, the Nazis and Communists, both decided on a villa located on this boulevard for their executioners' headquarters. The fact that both regimes chose Number 60 Andrássy Boulevard as the scene of torture and interrogation, speaks for itself.[28]

According to the marble plaque at the entrance of the building, the 'inspiration' behind the House of Terror was 'the chief advisor to the Prime Minister in affairs related to history.' The original website introduction for the house[29] (as a result of professional and public outcry – arising mostly from the political left – the website has been slightly altered since) asserted that 'during World War II, Hungary found itself in the middle of the crossfire between the Nazi and Communist dictatorships. On March 19, 1944 the Nazis occupied Hungary and raised the representatives of the extreme right, unconditionally faithful to them, into power. The new, collaborating Hungarian government no longer guarded the life of its citizens with Jewish origin.'[30]

Historical statements, to paraphrase Ian Hacking, 'are words in their sites. Sites include sentences, uttered or transcribed, always in a larger site of neighborhood, institution, authority, language.'[31] The words about the recent tragic history of Hungary are uttered in the House of Terror. The site was intended to provide authority for the historical events being described. The chain that connects the self-description of the House of Terror with the documented traces of the past is irreversible and sometimes broken: moving backwards from the narrative through surviving historical records, individual brute facts, and isolated events, one cannot arrive at the 'total historical context' (in the sense of John Austin's 'total speech act context') of 1944. The contours of the sunken world that glimmers through the story presented by the House are essentially different from what – after an accurate and professionally responsible study – comes through the historical documents. There is no *real situation* behind the text – this is just text,[32] words, compromised by the site, by the House. Text that in turn, as an illustration of the possible consequences of the looping effect, is compromised by the words that the House of Terror was meant to authorize.

Linguistically, it would have been possible for Hungary to fight against both the Nazis and the Communists; it would have been imaginable – in a linguistic sense, outside the frame of Hungarian history – for Hungary not to have been Germany's last and one of its first allies; it would have been conceivable for Hungary not to have had anti-Jewish legislation already in the early 1920s. The execution of the Jews could have been postponed until after the arrival of the Germans, and even then the Hungarian authorities would have had the option of not actively and eagerly participating in the deportation of more than half a million Hungarian Jews. The House of Terror and the story it tells were presented as the embodiment of concrete, tangible, historically situated horror, as the only conceivable story to tell. Yet the concrete details of the terror it was meant to evoke was merely fictional.

The villa at 60 Andrássy Boulevard had been the 'House of Faith,' the headquarters of the Arrow Cross Party before the Second World War, and the Communists, partly for symbolic reasons, decided to move the headquarters of the secret police into the very same building. Immediately after the war, Fascist war criminals were kept and interrogated in their former House of Faith. Where Jews and Communists had been tortured and killed before 1945, their torturers and interrogators were tortured and interrogated in turn after the defeat of Nazi Germany and its Hungarian ally. (Not all the war criminals were taken to Andrássy Boulevard. Some of the perpetrators, who had been captured in Germany and deported back to Hungary – leaders of the Arrow Cross Party among them – ended up in the cellars of Military

Intelligence, in the building of the Central European University where I presently teach. When we purchased the building in 1992, the prison cells were still in the cellar, with the spyholes in the doors.)

The Arrow Cross leaders and war criminals were soon replaced in the cellars by political opponents of the emerging Stalinist regime, by critics of its oppressive measures, by innocent scapegoats, and by more and more former social democrats and former Communist comrades of the consolidating regime. All of the victims of the show trials spent time in the cellars under the AVH Headquarters. They included László Rajk, the former Minister of the Interior, and later on his interrogator and successor, János Kádár. In a reflection of the Stalinist logic of the exercise of power, most of those who at one time occupied leading positions and upper-floor offices at the secret police, ended up in the cellars of the same building: they either knew too much or had grown too powerful. Or perhaps a slot needed to be filled at the upcoming public show trial; the history of the past, of the illegal movement, needed to be rewritten in light of the fluid political situation; the country's alertness, its level of mobilization, needed to be maintained in the circumstances of the Cold War.

Without exception, the defendants in the show trials were accused of having collaborated with the secret police of the interwar years, a time when the Communists were underground. Just as in the Soviet Union with regard to the Bolshevik Party, the underground movement was considered to be not only the crucible of future victorious Communist parties, but also evidence of the sacrifices for which the Communists deserved their inevitable victory. In the Communist histories, illegality was described as something inherently superior, especially when compared with the 'collaborationist,' 'revisionist,' 'reformist,' and 'treasonous' practices of the legal social democratic parties. Those formative chapters in the histories of the Russian, Chinese, German, Rumanian, and Hungarian Communist parties were considered memorable and glorious because the founding members had to operate in extremely dangerous circumstances and under constant threat of exposure. The underground members of the illegal party operated in dangerous proximity to secret agents, who would try to recruit, bribe, or blackmail them or try to break their moral backbone. Irrefutable proof of the permanent danger was the high number of recruited agents and Communists who, having been detected, were sentenced to death or to long terms in prison. The rules and methods of illegal activity between the wars had been distilled from the hard-learned lessons of the victorious Bolshevik Party; in the resulting political climate, any mistake that led to discovery could not be anything but the outcome of some human weakness. Exposure could be only the consequence of the presence of agent provocateurs in the ranks of the underground.[33]

During the show trials of the late 1940s and early 1950s, the former Communist leaders in the dock were accused of having signed secret deals with right-wing and Fascist secret services, of having been recruited by the counter-intelligence agencies, and of having handed over 'illegal' party members. In the authorized versions found in the Communist history books, the heroic stories from the underground years highlighted the weakness and meanness of the accused. 'The only question for us here is whether you are just a wretched devil who has fallen prey to the enemy, or you have been a conscious and stubborn enemy of our movement from the very first moment on, when you set foot in the working class movement. This is the only question you must answer.' Thus asserted Kádár when, as Minister of Interior, he and the Minister of Defence went to interrogate Rajk.[34]

On 18 May 1951 it was Kádár's turn. The interrogation at 60 Andássy Boulevard was secretly recorded, and the Minister of Defence, with whom on 7 June 1949 Kádár had interrogated Rajk, listened to the loudspeaker from an adjacent room. Kádár's interrogator was a lieutenant-colonel in the AVH and, incidentally, the son of the defence minister. 'What do we call what you did in 1943?' the interrogation asked. (Kádár, who was the secretary of the illegal party that year, following the instructions of the Komintern, had dissolved the illegal party in order to reorganize it under a new name) 'It is called class treason,' answered the broken Kádár, after long hours of psychologically cruel interrogation. Interrogator: 'What kind of role did you play in dissolving the Party?' Kádár: 'My role was conscious.' Interrogator: 'Conscious what?' Kádár: 'Conscious class treason.' Interrogator: 'Why were you in the movement in the first place? ... What role can such a person play in the movement?' Kádár: 'I was recruited by the secret police ... Already in 1933, I was recruited; after my arrest, I had to sign.'[35]

Today, 60 Andrássy Boulevard is a UNESCO World Heritage site. Most of the palaces along the boulevard were built around the same time, in the latter decades of the nineteenth century, during the *Gründerzeit* era of Austria-Hungary. Around the completely grey facade of the House of Terror (even the glass of the windows is painted grey), the architect placed a black metal frame. The idea for these 'blade walls,' which isolate the building from the adjacent palaces, probably came from New York, where Marcell Breuer detached the Whitney Museum of American Art from its neighbouring buildings on Madison Avenue by means of the same design tool. Above the roof, as part of the black frame, there is a broad perforated metal shield with the word 'terror' inscribed backwards, the five-pointed star, and the Arrow Cross (fig. 2.1). Precisely at noon, the sun is supposed to shine through the perforations, so that the letters TERROR and the signs of autocracy cast a shadow on the pavement. All of this harks back to the Hungarian-born Arthur Koestler's Nicolas Salmanovich Rubashov, the show-trial defendant in *Darkness at Noon*. Rubashov, in that famous novel, is a Communist activist turned captive in Communist prison cells. The roof of the House of Terror points at what is under the ground: the cellar.

An English website summarizes the history of the House of Terror:

After the German invasion, the short and blood-thirsty Arrow-Cross rule began ... In 1945 Hungary was brought under the sway of the new conqueror, the Soviet Union. The Hungarian Communists who arrived in the Soviet tanks, in contrast to the short-lived Arrow-Cross rule, settled down for the long run. One of their first acts was to take over No. 60 Andrássy Boulevard, in order to signal to everybody that the moment of revenge has arrived. But that moment lasted but for very long painful years ... The museum wants to become a memorial dedicated to all those people who fell victim either to Arrow-Cross terror, which lasted for a few months, or to the decades long Communist rule.'[36]

The contrast between the duration of Nazi rule and that of the Communists (short months versus long decades) is noted at least four times in this brief text. It is as if the Arrow Cross never intended to settle down until the end of time ('resurrecting the thousand-year empire'), as if that party had been meant just as a short intermezzo, in contrast to the devious Communists, who intended to rule for long and painful decades. Incidentally, the text does not mention that there was a connection of sorts between the end of the Arrow Cross rule and the entry of the Soviets.

When the Hungarian Communists arrived from the East in the safety of the foreign armoured vehicles, they immediately signalled that the 'moment [albeit a very long moment] of revenge has arrived.' The text stipulates that the Communists who arrived with

2.1 The exterior of the House of Terror, Budapest, showing its 'blade walls' or black metal frame. (Photo: János Szentiváni)

the foreigners (thus they, just like the Nazi mercenaries the Arrow Cross, could not have been true Hungarians) settled in the House of Faith in order to take revenge for what the Nazis had done to them – that is to the Jews. The members of the AVH, the vanguard of the Communists – the Communists who were brought back by the conquerors – were Jews whose intention was to take revenge for the Arrow Cross rule and to punish all of Hungary for what had been done to them (by the German Nazis).

The Hungarian Communists who returned from Moscow had in fact suffered, not so much as Jews from the Nazis, however, but rather as Communists from the Stalinist purges. The Hungarian Communist movement had been decimated in Moscow, and most of those who had survived the purges had suffered long years of persecution either in the Gulag or in Soviet prisons, or had been subjected to humiliating punishments. Had they truly felt the need for revenge, the appropriate target of that revenge would have been their fellow Communists who had denounced their comrades to the Soviet secret agencies back in Moscow. It would thus be more plausible to attribute the urge 'to signal that the moment of revenge has arrived' to the Hungarian Communist show trials rather than to the anti-Communist atrocities.

According to the introduction on the House of Terror website, Hungary had tried to protect its Jews from the Germans, but the Bolsheviks – from whom Hungary had tried to save the blind West during the Second World War – with the help of their Hungarian agents, let the Communist terror loose for more than four decades.

> The *Sondereinsatzkommando Eichmann* – the deportation experts who came to Hungary with Adolf Eichmann after the German occupation in March 1944 – consisted of less than two hundred people. The guarantee of success could only be the collaboration of the Hungarian authorities ... As the events of the next months proved, Eichmann's original calculation had been well-founded ... The mass deportation of the Jews from the countryside started on May 15 in Sub-Carpathia, and ended on July 8–9 with the transportation of the Jews around Budapest. In 56 days [!] – according to German documents – 437.402 Jews were deported by 147 trains, with the exception of 15 thousands, to Auschwitz.[37]

This is what, contrary to the claims of the House, the archival records describe.

The Soviets left only after Imre Nagy's reburial, only after the first post-Communist democratic election, and this is the point where the story of the terror, as it is told in the House of Terror, comes to an end. The secret police used the building as their headquarters until 1956. The extremely cruel Communist terror stopped at the end of the 1950s with one final act of post-revolutionary retribution – the execution of more than two hundred people (a child among them), who had been sentenced to death for taking part in the 1956 revolution. After the early 1960s no one was sentenced to death for political reasons, and following the 1963 amnesty most of the imprisoned revolutionaries were freed. The story of the House of Terror is carved from one solid piece: it is the story of undifferentiated terror from the first moment of the German occupation until the summer of 1991, when, fifty-seven years later, the Soviet army left the territory of Hungary.

The building on Andrássy Boulevard is infamous for what has always been invisible to the public: the underground prison cells.[38] That which could not be seen was known to almost everyone. Even before the Communist regime collapsed, most adult Hungarians had heard horror stories about what went on in the cellars. The *idea* of the building and the general knowledge about its prisons were inseparable. The larger part of the introductory text on the House of Terror website describes the prison and torture cells under 60 Andrássy, where the resistance of the accused was broken, where a many died under interrogation, and where prisoners had to suffer 'the most horrible tortures one can possibly envision.

Of the twenty-seven rooms in the House of Terror dedicated to the double history of terror, two-and-a-half are devoted to the Arrow Cross years. The exhibition starts with the story of the 'double occupation':

Hungary emerged from World War I on the losing side. Once part of the Austro-Hungarian Empire, she had possessed a territory larger than Italy or England. However, under the terms of the Treaty of Trianon which settled the war, the empire was carved up, reducing its territory by two-thirds ... At that time the focus of politics was the implementation of a peaceful territorial revision ... In the mid-1930s, Hungary found itself in the crossfire of an increasingly aggressive Nazi regime in Germany, as well as a menacing and powerful Soviet Union. First allies then enemies, the Nazi and Soviet dictatorships began a life-and-death fight to create a new European system of client and subordinated states where there was no room for an independent Hungary. After the outbreak of World War II, Hungary made desperate attempts to hold maintain its fragile independence and democracy, and maneuvered to prevent the worst: Nazi occupation. Significantly, Hungary managed to resist occupation until March 19, 1944 in the fifth year of the war. On June 26, 1941, air raids bombed the city of Kassa in Hungary. Reports at that time indicate that it was the Soviet air forces which carried out the attack ... Regent Horthy announced Hungary's participation in the war against the Soviet Union ... Until the Nazi occupation in 1944, Hungary had a legitimately elected government and parliament, where opposition parties functioned normally ... With the cooperation of the puppet Hungarian authorities appointed by the Nazi occupiers, the National Socialists began their assault on western civilization's value structure through the horrific and so-called 'final solution program.' With record speed, the Nazi experts on Jewish persecution, the *Judencommando*, began to round up and capture Hungarian Jews and, on May 15, 1944, the deportation trains began running. In a period of two months, 437,402 Jews from the Hungarian countryside were sent to forced labor or extermination camps in the Third Reich. On August 27, 1944, Soviet troops crossed the Hungarian border. The country became the scene of life and death clash between the Nazis

and the Soviet Union. The short, yet extremely brutal Nazi occupation during World War Two was then replaced by two generations of occupation by
the Soviet Union. Hungary's sovereignty came to an end on March 19, 1944.
For more than four decades, Soviet occupation troops remained on her territory. The last Soviet soldier left Hungary on June 19, 1991.[39]

The tourist, walking through the maze of the House of Terror while
reading the syntactically inaccurate sentences and looking at the
photographs (some of which – but we do not know which – are 'real,'
that is, contemporary, war or documentary photographs, where as others are pseudo-documents or fictional reproductions),[40] is unable to see
through the (sub)text. The visitor cannot know that 'the peaceful territorial revision' meant that Hungary, in exchange for supporting Nazi
Germany, got back part of its lost territories from Hitler (as a consequence of the 'First Vienna Decision' of 2 November 1938, before the outbreak of the war, and the 'Second Vienna Decision' of 30 August 1940).
Most visitors have never heard of the 'numerus clausus' passed by the
Hungarian Parliament on 26 September 1920 (!), which restricted the
number of Jewish students at the universities. The 'first Jewish law,'
which sharply restricted the number of Jews in the public sphere and
professional occupations, was passed by Parliament in May 1938, before
the war. The 'second Jewish law' was ratified before German troops
invaded Poland in May 1939. And the Nazis' Nuremberg laws became
internal Hungarian law as a result of the 'third Jewish law' of August
1941, which forbade marriage between Jews and non-Jews.

Hungary did not join the war on Hitler's side in order to resist
Communism's advance or to 'save the blind West from the menace of
Bolshevism,' but for territorial gain. As Hitler's ally, Hungary attacked
Yugoslavia even before it formally entered the war. The Soviet military
did not threaten Hungary during the interwar years. Hungary
declared war not only on the Soviets but also on Canada, New
Zealand, South Africa, Australia, Great Britain, and the United States.[41]
At the end of the website's introduction, the Wagnerian leitmotiv of the
'short, yet extremely brutal Nazi occupation' versus 'the two generations of occupation of the Soviet Union' duly returns.

It was Admiral Horthy who, after the German occupation, appointed
a puppet government for Germany. It was he who handed over power
to the leader of the Arrow Cross. Had the Hungarian army not committed horrific war crimes in Ukraine and the Soviet Union, had it not
remained Hitler's ally until the war's bitter end, it would have been

difficult for the Soviet Union to occupy Hungary and place the Communists in power after the war.

In the brochure provided to visitors to the House of Terror, in the section on 'Hungarian Nazis' (by using the term 'Nazi' instead of 'Arrow-Cross,' the brochure is trying to stipulate that the Hungarian fascists – who in 1939 won about 20 per cent of the vote – were not really Hungarians), the text states: 'The Germans defended Budapest as a fortress, which gave the Soviet Army a long and brutal fight ... The siege lasted from Christmas, 1944, until February 13, 1945, resulting in great suffering and destruction. They reduced to ruin all bridges in Budapest ... More than a million people fled from the Red Army to the West and more than 100,000 never returned.' The third-person plural they is sufficiently vague to confuse the interested visitor who might think that it was the Soviets who destroyed the city. In fact, the bridges were blown up by the Germans, and Budapest was bombed mainly by Allied airplanes. A large number of the 'more than a million people' who fled from the Red Army were Hungarian soldiers, war criminals, and members of the political elite responsible for Hungary's participation in the war, who were fleeing from justice. Even so, once more, the sentence is more or less correct: they fled as long as they could, before the Red Army arrived.

The half-room, which is the threshold between the Nazi and Communist versions of terror, is dedicated to 'Crossdressing.' As the 'Changing Clothes' flyer explains:

After 1919 the communist party was organized illegally and, until the Soviet occupation, it had only a few hundred members. During the Second World War, only a few dozen communist activists could usually be counted on. When the Hungarian Communist Party was organized in the wake of the Red Army's s arrival, the growth of party membership became of decided importance. After the members of the Hungarian Communist Party succeeded to get their hands on the internal and military-political investigative organizations, they had access to the Arrowcross membership records as well. Following this, the Communist party was joined in great numbers by people who 'to a greater or lesser extent were infected by the counterrevolution and fascism epidemic,' said Mátyás Rákosi. The newly admitted 'small Arrowcrossers' in the communist party had to declare when and how long they had been members of the Arrowcross party, and state that this membership had been a mistake which they wanted to remedy. These declarations were sufficient no doubt to intimidate and blackmail those who signed them.

Communists and members of the AVH were thus either Jews who returned with the Soviets, or they were former members of the Arrow Cross – that is, Hungarian Nazis. Neither of the groups could be classified as native Hungarian. (Hitler's Germany, however, did not really support the Arrow Cross, which was somewhat suspicious about claims of German superiority. Germany provided neither political nor financial help to the Hungarian fascists and did not take the Arrow Cross seriously until 1944. Hitler stated openly in 1938 that the right-wing Hungarian government was doing a commendable job and should be taken more seriously than a would-be National Socialist administration.)[42] The Nazis simply changed uniforms. Displayed, in the exhibition hall are Arrow Cross uniforms that the 'small Arrowcrossers' left behind. In the photographs provided we see them posing in the pigeon-grey uniform, which later on was replaced by a sand-coloured one. The brochures also tell us:

> The director of the Soviet-style Political Security Department [later on the AVH] was a certain Gábor Péter, who had four years of primary school education and was trained, but never worked, as a tailor's assistant ... Gábor Péter himself could not avoid fate. The head of the AVH and more than a dozen of his uneducated officers ended up behind bars in January 1953, due to Stalin's pathological antisemitism ... The Soviet dictator had given the order for the construction of a so-called Zionist conspiracy. His most faithful student, Mátyás Rákosi [the Secretary-General of the Hungarian party], unhesitatingly gave up the mainly Jewish AVH officers, who for many years followed his inhuman orders, as prey.[43]

These statements are offered as if the world comes wrapped in a chain of isolated facts that have nothing to do with other facts with which they are strongly connected. As if the nature of the world can be unambiguously determined by a few facts taken in complete isolation; as if facts are not in part 'the consequences of ways in which we represent the world.'[44] ('Facts are not individuated before any inquiry, though that does not mean that the inquiry creates them out of nothing.'[45]) Some of the brute facts of these sentences, like some of the isolated data compiled in other brochures, should be accepted. As historical statements, however, they must not pass. History writing is not the morally uninformed art of chronicling isolated events of the past, understood as unrepeatable particulars located in space and time. An arbitrary selection (and omission) and sequence of a few disconnected brute facts in support of an obvious ideological preconception that aims at constructing a worldwide, racially grounded conspiracy theory, from the perspective of actual political needs, in order to stigmatize an all-too-well-defined group of people, is being offered by the House of Terror as history. A script – and a rather familiar one – is being put forward as a normal, normalized (that is, obvious) neutral presentation of history.

Taxpayers' money was used to construct the House of Terror as a 'memorial dedicated to the victims of both the Nazi and the Communist terror.' On the perforated roof of the House we see both the Arrow Cross and the five-pointed star. The ideologues and politicians who established this museum, and who have devoted only two rooms to the close to 600,000 Roma, Jewish, and left-wing victims of the Holocaust, needed the 'Hungarian Nazis' in order to place the Communist terror in context. The latter was longer-lasting and thus deeper and more devastating than the former. The Communist terror was tightly related to the Nazi terror, especially since later on, the victims of the Nazi horrors seized the first opportunity they could to perpetrate the devastating Communist dictatorship. The Jews were not only the victims of the Nazis, and not only the perpetrators of the Communist terror, but also their own executioners: they would not have been able to defend themselves from themselves. Only the Hungarians, the true victims, and the enemies of both kinds of terror, who found themselves in the midst of the crossfire of the life-and-death struggle between these terrorists, could finally put an end to the slaughter.

The last room of the House of Terror is dedicated to 'Farewell.' On one side of the door the visitor can watch a video of Imre Nagy's reburial ceremony from 1989, during which Viktor Orbán (who would be Prime Minister of Hungary in 2002), as a young radical politician, demanded the withdrawal of Soviet troops from Hungary. On the opposite wall, several television monitors follow the withdrawal of the last division of the Soviet army on 19 June 1991. And on the other side of the door, the very last image of the memorial is the opening ceremony of the House of Terror on 24 February 2002, on the eve of the 'Memorial Day Dedicated to the Victims of Communism,' less than six weeks before the Hungarian general election of April 2002. Thus the story comes full circle: the pilgrim who comes to visit the House of Terror reads on the marble stone at the entrance that it was the prime minister who had this museum built. And in the last image, the prime minister, in front of a crowd a hundred thousand strong and a forest of tricolours, announces the opening of the House of Terror. His word has become flesh: the Russians have cut and run, and the terror is over; it has been locked into the museum that he, the leader of the new right, has built.

The young leader, the youngest prime minister in Hungarian history, on the pedestal in front of this dreaded building, which he alone had the courage to tame, surrounded, on this festive occasion, by hundreds of thousands of his ecstatic adherents, under forests of the national tricolour, was rejuvenation incarnate. From the perspective of the opening, which then, inside, is turned into the very last image in the last room of the House of Terror, the story of end and beginning becomes unambiguously comprehensible: after the long decades of degeneration – starting with the German occupation on 19 March 1944 and terminating with the humiliating retreat of the Soviet troops on 19 June 1991 – the new era has begun. The leader and his native people under the flag have finally found each other, and are ready to embark on a smooth road leading to future, which can only be an extension of the present.

Critics of the House of Terror repeatedly pointed out that the Arrow Cross was being evoked only in order to implicate the Communists by association. They argued that the project was nothing but an ideological and political construct, that it was neither a memorial to the victims of Communism – who were being cynically exploited for base political propaganda – nor a monument to the hundreds of thousands who perished during fascist times, since they were barely visible. The chronological and the narrative frames of the museum had been carefully devised: the demonstration started with the 'double occupation' – as if the German and the Soviet occupations had overlapped strongly and the Arrow Cross rule had started immediately after the occupation, as if there had not been seven long months between the entry of the Germans and the Arrow Cross takeover, as if half a million Jews had not been deported during those months (in fact, in less than two months). In this way, Horthy's rule, which lasted until 15 October 1944, together with the deportation, was pushed back (or forward) in this phantasmagorical chronology and thereby excluded from the decades of decline and degeneration. Horthy's interwar Hungary could thus be incorporated into the mythic prehistory of the present. This criticism was partly mistaken, however: in fact, the House of Terror – in part as a consequence of the very invisibility of the victims of fascism and the grave asymmetry of the arrangement – is a proper memorial to fascism. The house in its context (the 'blade walls,' the prison-grey hue of the building, the televised and recorded opening ceremony, the film of the mass rally, shown in the last room, the blocked entry at the gate, which is meant to artificially produce a permanent queue visible from everywhere on busy Andrassy Boulevard), is almost a literal embodiment – and definitively, not just an illustration – of the emerging post–Cold War consensus on the definition of 'generic' fascism. In the words of Roger Griffin – probably the most prolific and certainly the most self-promoting exponent of this new consensus: 'Fascism is a genus of modern, revolutionary, "mass" politics, which, while extremely heterogeneous in its social support and in the specific ideology promoted by its many permutations, draws its internal cohesion and driving force from *a core myth that a period of perceived national decline and decadence is giving way to one of rebirth and renewal in a post-liberal new order.*'[46] (This insistence on a past of national decline and decadence versus the imminent rejuvenation that springs from the popular will of the people, sharply distinguishes Fascist and neofascist ideology from its suspected double, Communism. For the Fascist, freedom is the triumph of the will; in Communist ideology, it is recognized necessity. In the Communist imagination, the past is not decadence and degeneration; rather, it is the succession of necessary stages, which eventually, following the iron laws of history, should lead – via inevitable and revolutionary human intervention – to the ultimate end of history. This explains the lack of vitalism as an essential defining feature of Communism, the lack of eroticism in official Communist art, and so on.)

The House of Terror indulges in horror, in pain, in the suffering of victims – primarily the victims of the Communist terror. The distorted visual program (and the distortion is barely hidden), the deep and aggressive, mostly black-and-red colours, the surfeit of images, and the sensual, melodramatic music that surrounds the visitor cannot conceal the aesthetic pleasure taken by the curators and the designers: it aims at arousing weird fascination.[47] Through the layout, the design, the captions, the text of the flyers, and the museum's website, the visitor can memorialize the history, the words, and the world that fascism made. The House of Terror is a monument to Fascism.

Most probably, the precedents of the House of Terror cannot be found in Daniel Libeskind's Jewish Museum in Berlin, or in the U.S. Holocaust Memorial Museum in Washington, or in Yad Vashem in Jerusalem. It is advisable to look further, if not spatially then at least temporally. Almost seventy years before the right-wing Hungarian prime minister opened the doors of the House of Terror, on 28 October

1932, on the tenth anniversary of the March on Rome, the Duce opened the gates of the *Mostra della rivoluzione fascista* (Exhibition of the Fascist Revolution). The *Marcia su Roma*, Mussolini's entry to Rome in 1922, itself had symbolic meaning: it recalled both Caesar's crossing of the Rubicon and the march of Garibaldi's *Mille*. According to Margherita Sarfatti, one of the most important cultural ideologues of Italian Fascism, the exhibition 'for the first time in the modern world brings an event in recent history into the fervent atmosphere of affirmation and of a religious ceremonial ... [It is] conceived as a cathedral whose very walls speak.'[48]

This exhibition bombarded the lost and disoriented visitors with documents, objects, signs, symbols, images, facts, and artefacts. The distance between fact and fiction, construction and reconstruction, genuine historical documents and artistic recreation disappeared. The ephemeral ritual space swallowed up the attendees, who were denied the detachment required for contemplation or simply for understanding the sights. The ambition of the organizers, the architects, the historians, the curators, and the politicians who conceived the show was to build a total, self-contained environment, the apotheosis of the movement and the Duce – one that aimed at inspiring not rational but rather emotional reactions from the visitors and that immersed them in the flow of unexpected visual and rhetorical impulses.[49]

The exhibition made use of techniques refined by the futurists, by expressionist theatre, and by rationalist and constructivist architecture. The curators recruited *novecento* artists as well as supporters of the traditionalist order in art. The use of the so-called *plastica murale*, which turned flat surfaces into moving images, turned the *mostra* into a modern-day three-dimensional multimedia show. According to contemporary reports, descriptions, and photographs, documents were sometimes presented in anthropomorphic forms; at other times, documents were used as frames containing other documents or fictitious objects; immensely large-scale images alternated unexpectedly with surprisingly small-scale presentations.

The visitors had to follow a set route of pilgrimage, which led through nineteen chronological and thematic halls covering the period from the outbreak of the First World War to the victory and achievements (in five additional rooms) of the Fascist Revolution: from chaos through revolution to order. At the end of the pilgrimage the shaken visitor found herself in 'Room U,' the seven-metre-high Sacrarium of the Martyrs, designed, like the House of Terror, by a theatre designer.

2.2 Left, Mario Sironi's Gallery of Fasci. Exhibition of the Fascist Revolution, Rome, 1932. Mostra della Rivoluzione Fascista.

2.3 Right, Entrance to the House of Terror. (Photo: János Szentiváni)

The 'Hall of Tears' in the House of Terror is a clear reference to the shadowy 'Hall of the Martyrs' at the Exhibition of the Fascist Revolution: at both sites, the mixture of modernist and antique, Christian and profane elements, on which sound and music are superimposed, aim at overwhelming pilgrims. The cross is the central object in both cases (although the House of Terror was supposedly built – in part – to commemorate the victims of the Fascist *and* Communist terrors, among them the deported Jews).

At both sites, the dead are used as props. In Budapest, a sign assures the dead, mostly the anti-Communist martyrs (persecuted members of the higher clergy), but also including the victims of the Holocaust; that 'the sacrifice for freedom was not in vain.' In Rome, the victory of fascism was meant to provide retroactive meaning for all of the deaths in the trenches of the First World War. In both places, the senseless death of hundreds of thousands of mute victims was exploited for obvious and explicit political aims. In Washington and Berlin, notwithstanding the didactic and oversimplified presentations, there are solid bridges between the museum and the outside world, and both museums were built with the sincere and well-documented intention of respecting the available evidence, with the help of which the innocent dead could be recalled and remembered in a justified way. By contrast, in Rome and Budapest the victims were used cynically and for obvious political purposes. The House of Terror, like the Exhibition of the Fascist Revolution, is not meant to be a space of memory; the Budapest building, influenced by its predecessor in Rome, is a total propaganda space, one in which death and victims are used as rhetorical devices.

The *mostra* turned out to be a huge success: in two years close to four million visitors paid homage to Fascism at the Palazzo delle espozioni, the facade of which had been rebuilt in rationalist style. Besides Goebbels and Goering, Simone de Beavoir, Jean-Paul Sartre, Le Corbusier, and the students of a Hebrew school visited the exhibition. Pilgrims, two Hungarians and two blind men from the Dolomites among them, came on foot to see the *mostra*.

The Fascist exhibition was not without antecedents, either. Mario Sironi, one of the most noted *novecentista* painters, had designed the 1928 Italian press pavilion at the Cologne International Press Exhibition, where he became acquainted with the work of the Soviet constructivist artist El Lissitzky. It was Lissitzky who influenced Sironi's four rooms at the Fascist exhibition, among them 'The March on Rome' and 'The Hall of Honor, Dedicated to the Person, Ideal and Works of the Duce.' The Soviet material at the 1928 Venice Biennale and the 1929 Russische Ausstellung in Zurich also directly influenced the anti-Bolshevik Rome exhibition. Giuseppe Terragni, the greatest rationalist architect, the designer of 'Room O: The Year 1922 up until the Events of October,' the architect of the famous Casa del fascio in Como, borrowed from both El Lissitzky and Konstantin Melnikov.[50]

It is no wonder that some visitors found the Fascist exhibition so Bolshevik in spirit, to the point that 'with a change in emblems the pieces would bring applause in Moscow.'[51] The connection between Rome and Budapest is not accidental: the architect of the House of Terror, a well-known set designer who in past years had designed the sets of some Italian opera productions, had in the 1970s and 1980s worked with László Rajk on several neoconstructivist architectural and design projects. Rajk was one of the architects of the neoconstructivist catafalque for Imre Nagy's reburial in 1989.

The exhibition in Budapest starts on the second floor. After a labyrinthine descent, the visitor arrives at a glass elevator on the first floor. It takes three-and-a-half long minutes to lower the cabin two floors down, while a drooling unpleasant-looking elderly man, the former cleaning attendant at the executions, recalls at an extremely slow pace how the prisoners in the cellars were hanged. One has no choice but to stare at the repulsive face on the huge plasma monitor, which entirely covers one side of the elevator. At the end of the unbelievably slow descent, the visitor arrives in the cellars, the symbolic centre of the House of Terror. The long brochure that describes the 'Reconstructed prison cells' devotes four lines to the short Arrow Cross horror; the rest deals with the extreme brutality of the Communist terror, which used methods similar to those of 'the Middle Ages.' 'Based on recollections' – says the text – 'the building's cellar system had several floors. When the house was rebuilt, no signs of additional floors were found under the cellars. Nevertheless, it cannot be excluded that additional cellars of the labyrinth were dug into the earth.'

Underground, the organizers have reconstructed a 'water cell, where prisoners had to continually sit in the water,' a 'fox-hole, where there were no lights and the prisoner could not stand up,' and 'the guards' room,' where 'the ventilation system' from the reconstructed prison cell has been reinstalled (this was the tube through which, presumably, poison gas or some gas that could knock out the prisoners was blown in). A gallows has also been recreated in the cellars. Most of the objects on display do not carry the name of the donor or lending institution; in the case of the gallows, though, a small plaque authenticates the object. It was donated by the National Penal Authority, and according to the flyer it was used until 1985.

At the end of the long tour, for the first time since 30 October 1956, the underground becomes visible and identifiable: a real prison, with water in it, with real spyholes and a real gallows. Instead of a site where imagination resides, the underground is a concrete physical location where direct and personal encounter is offered to the visitors. The tube, the gallows, and the water cells are – in the context of the prison – objects of ritualized display: they serve as relics. The secret, the ultimate proof (although actually, it was another cellar) has come into sight, become physically perceptible to the pilgrims.

The House of Terror is not a marginal institution on the fringes of the city. It was built for close to US $20 million, a large amount of taxpayers' money in Hungary (the sum is almost twice what it cost to reconstruct the Budapest Opera, which incidentally is also on Andrássy Boulevard). The opening of the House of Terror was an integral part – and probably the most important event – of the 2002 election campaign. The principal aim of the governing radical right-wing party – the former Young Liberal Party, turned radical right – was to win over supporters of the Hungarian Truth and Life Party in order to avoid the need for a formal post-election coalition with the Hungarian Fascists. The opening was scheduled on the eve of the 'Memorial Day of the Victims of Communism,' a new remembrance initiated by the right-wing government to compensate for and balance 'Holocaust Memorial Day,' which had been introduced by the previous government.

Tens of thousands of active supporters of an extreme right-wing radical party assembled that day on Republic (Köztársaság) Square in front of the Socialist Party Headquarters, the site of the 1956 siege. The leader of the Hungarian Truth and Life Party pointed to the former Budapest Party Headquarters and baptized it the 'First House of Terror.' At the end of the rally, the demonstrators were instructed to bend down and press their ears to the pavement, to listen to the sounds from below, from the underground prison across the span of forty-six years. Then they stood again and marched to Andrássy Boulevard to unite with the other tens of thousands of supporters of the political right in power, who were waiting for the prime minister in front of the House of Terror, which was bathed in harsh red light. As the leader of the Truth and Life Party remarked, that day in front of the House of Terror, the forces of the Hungarian anti-Communist right had at last become visibly and firmly united. Referring to the upcoming election, the young prime minister declared: 'We have locked the two terrors in the same building, and they are good company for each other as neither of them would have been able to survive long without the support of foreign military force ... In the very last minute, before it could return, we slammed the door on the sick twentieth century.' (Six weeks later, a coalition of Socialists and Liberals won a narrow victory and returned to power.) At the opening ceremonies for the House of Terror, Orban noted that 'the evil promised to redeem the world but instead, it tortured the people under the ground in the cellars.'[52]

In July 1295, Pope Boniface VIII sent a mandate to the Bishop of Paris, Simon Mattifart de Bucy allowing him to build a chapel in the parish of St-Jean-en-Grève, on the site of what was probably the most famous case of host desacration accusation. The *capella miraculorum* emerged, which housed the *canif*, the knife, which became holy, as the miraculous consequence of the devious effort by a local Jew, who, not believing in the dogma of transubstantiation, tried to test the host by piercing it with the knife. The miraculous host was locked in the parish church of St-Jean-en-Grève. According to the *De Miraculo hostiae* (Of the miracle of the host), the Jew took out a knife and struck the host, which remained intact and began to bleed. He pierced it through with nails but the host continued bleeding. The Jew then threw the host into a fire, and finally into boiling water. The water turned red, and the host was transformed into a crucifix. A poor Christian woman gave up the Jew, who was tried, found guilty, and condemned to be burned. The Jew asked his executioners for permission to hold his book – that is, the Old Testament – while he was in the fire, in the hope that he would thus be saved. But both the book and Jew were burnt to ashes; as a consequence, his wife and children converted to Christianity.[53]

The story was thus converted, transformed into a concrete miraculous site: into a chapel on the site of the demolished house of the Jew, with elaborate rituals, into an order, the Brethren of the Charity of the Blessed Virgin charged with the guardianship of the chapel. It was no longer hearsay that fuelled the accusations; it was now possible and indeed sufficient merely to point without hesitation at the chapel; the solid structure provided concrete and inescapable evidence. 'The news from Paris very soon existed in Latin and in French, and travelled to the adjacent regions ... to the Low Countries, to southwest Germany and to northern Italy by the very late thirteenth and early fourteenth centuries.'[54] Visible facts, as Maurice Halbwachs reminded us in his *La topographie légendaire des évangiles en terre sainte*, 'are the symbols of invisible truth.'[55] 'No full-blown ... accusation which resulted in vindication and violence was complete without the creation of an enduring sign to mark the event ... Ruins were not allowed to stand as traces of a still open past, but were transformed into new, polished structures.' So concluded the historian from the lessons of the practices of the Middle Ages.[56]

The cellars under the House of Terror were neither invented nor recreated but finally found. The Communists had tried to cover all traces of their heinous acts, but the cellars could not be completely buried. The archaeologists of the Communist terror found them and bared them to the gaze of victorious posterity. The visitor turned witness who was finally confronted with unmediated truth now became entitled to provide an authentic account. The House of Terror is full of identifiable images (on the wall where the photographs of the perpetrators are lined up as if they had been assembled in a photo spread for an eyewitness test: a few Fascists are mixed with a large number of AVH officers and Communist officials), recognizable names, abundant dates, and concrete objects. The visitor is confronted with clear evidence that seems to be visibly objective, not invented, not made by the hands of the curators, but that unveils the so far invisible truths hidden in the depths.[57] The cellars have been turned into *sacramenta*, signs of (until now) hidden things.

Invisible truth argued Halbwachs, needs to find firm roots in concrete facts;[58] only claims that are based on concrete facts can leave long-lasting, persuasive impressions. Ideas must take on perceptible, concrete, tangible, localizable forms in order to find a firm place in memory: 'If a truth is to be settled in the memory of a group it needs to be presented in the concrete form of an event, of a personality or of a *locality*.'[59]

In an earlier version of her analysis of the host desecration accusation, Miri Rubin concluded: 'In those areas where the narrative had become most endemic ... it was a real presence, of atrocities remembered, commemorated in local shrines ... The tale ... grew in complexity and ambition, in size and ramification. No longer a single Jew, curious or malevolent, attacking a host with his kitchen-knife, but conspiracies of Jews ... The narrative evolved and converged with the growing desires for separation and excision of Jews from central European urban communities.'[60]

The architect and the interior designer of the House of Terror, Attila Ferenczfy Kovács, was the set designer of the Academy Award – winning film *Mephisto*, which deals with the dark relationship between the artist and the totalitarian state. The film's director, István Szabó, has recently been uncovered as a former informant of the Communist secret police. In an interview after the opening the House of Terror, he traced the influences that led to Kovács's design of the terror: 'My first serious film set design was *Dániel Szerencsés*, directed by Pál Sándor.' 'Quite a few elements from that film show up in the House of Terror too,' the interviewer noted. 'How were you able to study the atmosphere of the most brutal terror in the years of "soft dictatorship?"' 'There was an extremely depressing hotel interior in that film,' he replied, 'and when I was designing the set, the environment that had been so familiar from the Moscow Underground helped me in my work. That overdecorated, desolate, and unbearably gloomy underground space then found its way to the House of Terror.'[61]

NOTES

Another version of this text was published as 'Under Ground,' in *Retroactive Justice: Prehistory of Post-Communism* (Stanford: Stanford University Press, 2005).

1 When the British magazine *Picture Post* published an eleven-page photo reportage of the Spanish Civil War in December 1938, it called twenty-five-year-old Capa 'the best war photographer of the world' (3 December 1938, 13–24).

On 23 September 1936, the French journal *Vu* published a series of Capa's pictures, among them one of the most famous war photographs ever taken, *The Death of a Militiaman*, or *The Falling Soldier*, which Capa shot on 5 September 1936 at Cerro Muriano. In 1975 the British journalist Phillip Knightly published *The First Casualty: The War Correspondent As Hero and Myth Maker* (New York: Harcourt Brace, 1975), which alleged that *The Falling Soldier* had been staged. After a long investigation, Richard Whelan, Capa's biographer (*Robert Capa: A Biography* [New York: Alfred Knopf, 1985]), ascertained that Capa, born Ernő Endre Friedman in Budapest, had, in fact, photographed *The Falling Soldier* during the battle at Cerro Muriano on 5 September 1936. Whelan, relying on the testimony of an eyewitness, was able to identify the soldier in Capa's photographs as Federico Borrell Garcia, a twenty-four-year-old Republican volunteer from the village of Alcoy, near Alicante. In 'Proving That Robert Capa's "Falling Soldier" Is Genuine: A Detective Story,' written for *Aperture* (166, Spring 2002), Whelan reconstructed the likely chain of events that led to Borrell Garcia's death and to Capa's famous photograph: 'Capa encountered a group of militiamen ... from several units – Francisco Borrell Garcia among them – in what was at that moment a quiet sector. Having decided to play around a bit for the benefit of Capa's camera, the men began by standing in a line and brandishing their rifles. Then, with Capa running besides them, they jumped across a shallow gully and hugged the ground at the top of its far side, aiming and firing their rifles – *thereby, presumably, attracting the enemies attention* ... Once Borell had climbed out of the gully, he evidently stood up, back no more than a pace or two from the edge of the gully and facing down the hillside so that Capa (who had remained in the gully) could photograph him. *Just as Capa was about to press his shutter release, a hidden enemy machinegun opened fire. Borel, hit in the head or heart, died instantly and went limp while still on his feet, as Capa's photograph shows.* (The italics are mine. Whelan has published an online version of his *Aperture* article; see www.pbs.org/wnet/americanmasters)

In his biography, Whelan wrote: 'To insist upon knowing whether the photograph actually shows a man at the moment he has been hit by a bullet is both morbid and trivializing, for the picture's greatness ultimately lies *in its symbolic implications, not in its literal accuracy* as a report on the death of a particular man' (my italics). At that time, Whelan was unable to demonstrate the authenticity of the picture, so he opted instead for the idea that the issue was not how the picture was made, but rather what it wanted to communicate. A few years later, when additional information became available on the presumed specific circumstances of Capa's photograph, Whelan adjusted his strategy and took pains to prove that Capa's famous photograph was unquestionably authentic. Whelan did not seem to realize that in proving it he was claiming something much more serious: that Capa had been personally responsible for the death of Borrell Garcia. Whelan wanted to clear the photographer morally; he craved a picture that did not merely look like but in fact *was* a document. He now insisted on the specific circumstances of the event. For the sake of the morality of specificity, as opposed to the immorality of generalization, the detective turned biographer was ready to sacrifice Capa's integrity and to implicate him in the killing of the most important subject in the history of war photography (see Maria Mitropoulos, *The Documentary Photographer as Creator*, available at http://www.media-culture.org.au/0108/Photo/html.)

2 John Sadovy, 'The Fighting Really Began to Flare Up,' *Hungary's Fight for Freedom: A Special Life Magazine Report in Pictures*, 1956, 26–45.

3 On 'acheiropoietic' images – that is, images not by a human hand, such as the direct imprint of God on the Holy Shroud in Turin – see Marie Jose Mondzian, 'The Holy Shroud / How Invisible Hands Weave the Undecidable,' in *Iconoclash: Beyond the Image Wars in Science, Religion, and Art*, ed. Bruno Latour and Peter Weibel (Cambridge MA: MIT Press, 2002), 324–35.

4 Cf Latour, *Pandora's Hope: Essays on the Reality of Science Studies* (Cambridge, MA: Harvard University Press, 1999), 67.

5 Cf Ervin Hollós and Vera Lajtai, *Köztársaság Tér 1956* (Budapest: Kossuth, 1974), 168.

6 'In 1898 Secondo Pia, a lawyer and photographer, was instructed to take the first photographs of the [Holy] Shroud. On 28 May he exposed two 20 x 23.5' glass plates, which he developed the same night. The photographs were said to have revealed something new and unexpected: on the negative there appeared a positive image. It showed the front and the back of a male body, bright on a dark background, apparently three-dimensional as though lit from above. The brownish traces – hardly decipherable on the shroud itself – became a light and readable image ... The long history of the

shroud suddenly appeared as a prelude. In retrospect it became the history of a code, unlocked only in the age of photographic reproduction.' Peter Geimer, 'Searching for Something: On Photographic Revelations,' in Latour and Weibel, *Iconoclash*, 143.

7 Cf Loraine Daston and Peter Galison, 'The Image of Objectivity,' *Representations* 40 (1992): 81–128.

8 Budapest Military Court B. IV. 432/1958. sz. Quoted by Hollós and Lajtai, *Köztársaság Tér 1956*, 105.

9 Supreme Court of the Hungarian People's Republic. Tb. 46/1960/5. sz. Quoted by Hollós and Lajtai, *Köztársaság Tér 1956*, 111.

10 *Ellenforradalmi erők a magyar októberi eseményekben I. kötet* (Counterrevolutionary Forces in the Hungarian October Events, volume 1) (Budapest, 1957), 22.

11 Cf János Molnár, *Ellenforradalom Magyarországon 1956-ban* (Counterrevolution in Hungary in 1956) (Budapest: Akadémiai Kiadó, 1967), 184.

12 *Magyar Nemzet*, 3 November 1956.

13 Expert report; Supreme Court of the Hungarian People's Republic B.F.I. 461/1958/10. Quoted in Hollos and Lajtai, *Köztársaság Tér 1956*, 205–6.

14 George Mikes, *The Hungarian Revolution* (London: Andre Deutsch, 1957), 118–19.

15 Fonds HU 300-40-4 Hungarian Information Items (Police and Security), Records of the Research Institute of Radio Free Europe/Radio Liberty. Open Society Archives, Budapest, Hungary.

16 Ibid., 2–3.

17 Ibid.

18 Ibid. 3–5.

19 Ibid.

20 Ibid., 2.

21 'Images offering evidence that contradicts cherished pieties are invariably dismissed as having been staged for the camera. To photographic corroboration of the atrocities committed by one's own side, the standard response is that the pictures are a fabrication, that no such atrocity ever took place, those were bodies the other side had brought in trucks from the city morgue and placed about the street, or that, yes it happened and it was the other side who did it, to themselves. Thus the chief of propaganda for Franco's Nationalist rebellion maintained that it was the Basques who had destroyed their own ancient town and former capital Guernica, on April 26, 1937, by placing dynamite in the sewers (in a later version, by dropping bombs manufactured in Basque territory) in order to inspire indignation abroad and reinforce the Republican resistance.' Susan Sontag, *Regarding the Pain of Others* (New York: Farrar Straus Giroux, 2003), 11.

22 Fonds HU 300-40-4 (Police and Security), 3.
23 *Pincebörtön* (Cellar Prison). Two parts, 120 min. A film by Zoltán Dézsy.
   MTV (Hungarian Television), Budapest, 1992–4.
24 A classic example of proof firmly based on silence or on void is the trial of
   General Tomayuki Yamashita, held from October to December 1945 in
   Manila. The U.S. Military Commission there sentenced Yamashita, 'the Tiger
   of Malaya,' to death by hanging, for unlawfully disregarding and failing to
   discharge his duty as commander to control the actions of members of his
   command. Specifically, he had permitted war crimes and had failed to prevent atrocities from taking place. (The U.S. Supreme Court later upheld the
   sentence.) Most probably, Yamashita would not have been able to take
   action against the crimes that members of the Japanese Fourteenth Army
   Group were committing in the final phases of the war in the Philippine theatre. One Supreme Court Justice expressed in his dissenting opinion that it
   was not being alleged that General Yamashita had any knowledge of the
   crimes that the military under his command had committed. He could not
   have had any knowledge of what went on in the last phases of the war, since
   the advancing U.S. forces had disrupted communications between his
   headquarters and his battle forces. As Justice Frank Murphy put it: 'To use
   the very inefficiency and disorganization created by the victorious forces as
   the primary basis for condemning officers of the defeated armies bears no
   resemblance to justice or to military reality.' In *Re Yamashita*, 327 U.S. 1,
   quoted by Aryeh Neier, *War Crimes: Brutality, Genocide, Terror, and the
   Struggle for Justice* (New York: Random House, 1998), 230–1. For General
   MacArthur, who affirmed the death sentence, the ultimate proof was
   Yamashita's silence, his lack of communication, the non-existence of any
   documents to the contrary. On Yamashita's case, cf Law Reports of Trials of
   War Criminals: Selected and Prepared by the United Nations War Crimes
   Commission, vol. 4 (London: HMSO, 1948), case no. 21.
25 According to tourist guides, tens of thousands of slaves were gathered,
   incarcerated, and then shipped from the dungeons of the Slave House in
   the eighteenth and nineteenth centuries. However, 'despite the name, it's
   unlikely that the *Maison des Esclaves* was used to hold many captive slaves,
   apart from those who "belonged" to the merchant … In fact some historians have pointed out that although the island was a vital trading center and
   strategic port, and an important slave culture existed here, Gorée itself was
   never a major shipment point of slaves … Of the 20 million slaves who
   were taken from Africa, only 300 per year may have gone through Gorée.
   Even then, the famous doorway [of the dungeons] would not have been
   used: a ship could not get near the dangerous rocks and the town had a

perfectly good jetty a short distance away ... The historians who refute Gorée's connection with slavery are anxious to avoid accusations of revisionism, and emphasize that many millions of slaves were taken from West Africa in the most appalling circumstances ... But they see the promotion of Gorée as a site of significance to the history of slavery as a mere commercialism based on distortion, a cynical attempt to attract tourists who might otherwise go to Gambia's Jufureh or the slave forts of Ghana. Gorée's fabricated history boils down to an emotional manipulation by government officials and tour companies of people who come here as part of genuine search for cultural roots.' David Else et al., *Lonely Planet: West Africa*, 4th ed. (London: Lonely Planet Publications, 1999), 792.

26 'Táborok maradandósága' (The Perpetuity of Camps), in Imre Kertész, *A száműzött nyelv* (The exiled language) (Budapest: Magvető, 2001), 49–51.

27 After the Socialist Party returned to power in October 2002, its chair announced that the party would be changing its name to 'Social Democratic Party' and would be moving out of its building on Republic Square in order to leave the tragic past behind and emphasize the long road the party had travelled since 1989.

28 http://www.terrorhaza.hu.

29 Archived on 31 January 2002.

30 Cf András Mink, 'Alibi terror-egy bemutatkozásra' (Alibi Terror – on the Occasion of an Introduction), *Népszabadság*, 20 February 2002.

31 Ian Hacking, *Historical Ontology* (Cambridge, MA: Harvard University Press, 2002), 68.

32 Cf Latour, 'From Fabrication of Facts to Events,' in *Pandora's Hope*, 122–7.

33 'The Party can never be mistaken, said Rubashov. You and I can make a mistake. Not the Party. The Party, comrade, is more than you and I and a thousand others like you and I. The Party is the embodiment of the revolutionary idea in history ... History knows her way. She makes no mistakes.' Arthur Koestler, *Darkness at Noon*, trans. Daphne Hardy (London: Vintage, 1994), 40–1.

34 Magyar Országos Levéltár (Hungarian National Archive, hereafter MOL) M-KS 276.f. 62/2. őe. Cf László Varga, ed., *Kádár János Bírái Előtt Egyszer fent, egyszer lent 1949–1956* (János Kádár in Front of his Judges. Once Up, Once Down 1949–1956) (Budapest: Osiris–Budapest City Archive, 2001), 159.

35 The Interrogation of János Kádár [18 May 1951], MOL M-KS 276. f. 62/63.őe. Reproduced in Varga, *Kádár János*, 215–39.

36 *http://www.terorrhaza.hu*, accessed on 31 January 2002.

37 Gábor Kádár and Zoltán Vági-Krisztián, *Ungváry, Hullarablás. A magyarországi zsidók megsemmisítése* (Robbing the Corpse. The Economic Annihilation of the Hungarian Jews) (Budapest, manuscript, Vol. 3), 159–63.

38 One of my parents' best friends, István Gyöngyössy, a show trial victim
   himself, was sentenced to nine years at one of the follow-up trials of the
   Rajk case. In the 1960s, after being rehabilitated, he became the director of
   Chemokomplex, a foreign trade company. His office was on the second
   floor of 60 Andrássy. One man he interviewed for a job entered his office
   and told him: 'I have already been in this building, but four floors below.'

39 In each thematic room in the House of Terror there is a flyer in both Hungarian and English, which provides a narrative interpretation of the exhibition in that particular room. The text comes from the English version of the
   flyer in the Double Occupation room, which was in fact the first room of the
   exhibition. In this chapter I cite the text as it appears in the official flyer. I
   have not changed the spelling of the text.

40 'A photograph is supposed, not to evoke, but to show. That is why photographs, unlike handmade images, can count as evidence. But evidence of
   what? The suspicion that Capa's *Death of a Republican Soldier*, titled *The
   Falling Soldier* in the authoritative compilation of Capa's work – may not
   show (one hypothesis is that it records a training exercise near the front
   line) continues to haunt discussions of war photography. Everyone is liter-
   alist when it comes to photographs.' Sontag, *Regarding the Pain of Others*, 47.

41 As maintained by the contemporary anecdote, when, in the name of the
   Hungarian Kingdom, the Hungarian Ambassador handed over the document declaring war, the U.S. Secretary of State remarked: 'It was most certainly a hard decision by His Royal Highness, your King.' Where upon the
   ambassador noted that although Hungary was a Kingdom, she had no king.
   'Then who is the head of the Hungarian state?' asked the surprised secretary.
   'Admiral Horty is the Regent of the Kingdom,' came the historically correct
   answer. 'Don't you think, then, that your navy could be in grave danger during such a war?' came the sympathetic question from the Secretary. 'Let me
   remark,' responded the pedant ambassador, 'that, although Regent Horty is
   an admiral, Hungary does not have a sizable navy. In fact, Hungary, momen-
   tarily, does not even have a sea.' 'What happened to your sea, if I may ask?'
   the underinformed secretary continued politely. 'We lost it after the Great
   War to Italy,' was the enlightening reply. 'Then Italy should most certainly be
   your enemy in the ongoing war,' concluded the Secretary of State. 'Pardon
   me, Sir, but Italy is our ally,' came the matter-of-fact answer. And in this vein,
   the friendly chat went on for quite some more time.

42 Cf Krisztin Ungváry, 'Kik azok a nyilasok?'(Who Are the Arrow-Crossers?),
   Beszélő 3 (VIII) (IIIrd. Series) (June 2003): 58–9.

43 From the flyers *Anteroom of the Hungarian Political Police* and *Room of Gábor
   Peter, Head of the Hungarian Political Police*, respectively.

44 Cf Ian Hacking, *The Social Construction of What?* (Cambridge, MA: Harvard University Press, 1999), 33. See also Hacking, *Historical Ontology* (Cambridge, MA: Harvard University Press, 2002), esp. 1–26. As my argument shows, I do not fully subscribe to Latour's or even Hacking's somewhat milder constructivist position.

45 Bernard Williams, *Truth and Truthfulness: An Essay in Genealogy* (Princeton, NJ: Princeton University Press, 2004), 257.

46 Roger Griffin, 'Introduction,' in Griffin, ed., *International Fascism: Theories, Causes, and the New Consensus* (London: Arnold, 1998), 14 (emphases are mine). In *The Nature of Fascism* (London: Routledge, 1993, 23), Griffin provided a more concise core definition, which he repeated in 'Fascism's New Faces (and New Facelessness) in the "Post-Fascist" Epoch,' mimeo graph, for *Erwaegen, Wissen, Ethik,* published with twenty responses in 2005, 10. 'Fascism is a political ideology whose mythic core in its various permutations is a palingenetic [renewalist] form of populist ultra-nationalism.' The emergence of a 'fascist minimum' (Ernst Nolte's phrase), most probably began with the publication of Nolte's famous and infamous *Der Faschismus in seiner Epoche* (The Three Faces of Fascism) (Munich: Piper, 1993). See also Eugene Weber, *Varieties of Fascism* (New York: Van Nostrand, 1964); and George L. Mosse, 'Toward a General Theory of Fascism,' in G.L. Mosse, ed., *Interpretations of Fascism* (London: Sage, 1979). See also the entry 'Fascism,' in Griffin, *The Blackwell Dictionary of Social Thought* (Oxford: Basil Blackwell, 1993), 223–4.

47 'Between sadomasochism and fascism there is a natural link. "Fascism is theatre," as Genet said … Sadomasochism is to sex what war is to civil life.' Sontag, 'Fascinating Fascism,' *New York Review of Books* 22, 1, 6 February 1975. Reprinted in Sontag, *Under the Sign of Saturn* (London: Vintage, 1980), 73–105. The quote is from page 103. On fascination with fascism, see also Jeffrey T. Schnapp, 'Fascinating Fascism,' *Journal of Contemporary History* 31 (1966): 235–44.

48 Margherita Sarfatti, 'Architettura, arte e simbolo alla mostra del fascismo,' *Archittetura,* (January 1933), 10. Quoted by Emilio Gentile, *The Sacralization of Politics in Fascist Italy* (Cambridge, MA: Harvard University Press, 1996), 117.

49 Cf Carla Susan Stone, *The Patron State: Culture and Politics in Fascist Italy* (Princeton, NJ: Princeton University Press, 1998), 128–76.

50 See Thomas Schumacher, *Surface and Symbol: Giuseppe Terragni and the Architecture of Italian Rationalism* (New York: Princeton Architectural Press, 1991). On the *Mostra*, see also Giovanna Fioravanti, *Archivo centrale dello stato: Partito nazionale fascista. Mostra della rivoluzione fascista* (Rome: Archivo di Stato, Ministero per I Beni Culturali e Ambientali, 1990); Emilio Gentile, *The Sac-*

ralization of Politics in Fascist Italy, trans. Keith Botsford (Cambridge, MA: Harvard University Press, 1996), 109–21; and Jeffrey Schnapp, *Anno X. La Mostra della Rivoluzione fascista del 1932* (Rome and Pisa: Istituti Editoriali e Poligrafici Internazionali, 2003).

51 Quoted by Jeffrey T. Schnapp, in 'Epic Demonstrations: Fascist Modernity and the 1932 Exhibition of the Fascist Revolution,' in Richard J. Golsan, ed., *Fascism, Aesthetics, and Culture* (Hanover, NH: University Press of New England, 1992), 26.

52 *Orbán: rács mögé zártuk a múltat. Tizezrek a Terror Háza megnyitóján* (Orbán: We Have Locked the Past Behind Bars. Tens of Thousands at the Opening of the House of Terror), Index (on-line), 24 February 2002.

53 'De miraculo hostiae a Judaeo Parisiis anno Domini MCCXC,' *Recueil des historiens des Gaules et de la France*, ed. M. Bouquet and L. Delisle, vol. 22 (Paris, 1840–1904), 32, in Miri Rubin, *Gentile Tales: The Narrative Assault on Late Medieval Jews* (New Haven, CT: Yale University Press, 1999), 40–5.

54 Ibid., 45.

55 Translated by Lewis A. Coser, *The Legendary Topography of the Gospels in the Holy Land* (Chicago: University of Chicago Press, 1992), 224.

56 Rubin, *Gentile Tales*, 90.

57 On historic notions of objectivity, cf Lorraine Daston and Peter Galison, 'The Image of Objectivity,' and the essays in Lorraine Daston, ed., *Biographies of Scientific Objects* (Chicago: University of Chicago Press, 2000).

58 For an excellent theoretical reworking of Halbwachs's important insights, cf Jan Assmann, *Das kulturelle Gedächtnis* (Munich: Beck, 1997). I have consulted the Hungarian edition *A Kulturális Emlékezet*, trans. Zoltán Hidas (Budapest: Atlantisz, 1999), 35–49.

59 Halbwachs, *La topographie légendaire*, 200 (emphases added).

60 Miri Rubin, 'The Making of the Host Desecration Accusation: Persuasive Narratives, Persistent Doubts' (Paper given at the Davis Center Seminar, Princeton University, 15 October 1993), 31–2.

61 'A Mennyei Seregektől a Terror Házáig' (From the Heavenly Army to the House of Terror), *Magyar Nemzet*, 2 April 2002. 'Owing to its mysterious origins and the need people have to give history a meaning in our godless world, *The Conspiracy* soon became a kind of Bible, teaching that there is a "mysterious dark, and dangerous force" lurking behind all history's defeats, a force that holds the fate of the world in its hands, draws on arcane sources of power, triggers wars and riots, revolutions and dictatorships – the "sources of all evil." The French Revolution, the Panama Canal, the League of Nations, the Treaty of Versailles, the Weimar Republic, the Paris métro – they are all its doing. (By the way, métros are nothing but

mineshafts under city walls, a means for blasting European capitals to the skies.) ... *The informed reader will, I trust, have no trouble recognizing the famous* Protocols *in* The Conspiracy.' Danilo Kis, *Encyclopedia of the Dead*, trans. Michael Henry Heim (Evanston, ll: Northwestern University Press, 1997), 169, 198.

3 Putting Contested History on Display: The Uses of the Past in Northern Ireland

ELIZABETH CROOKE

Museums are one of the means for a community to interpret its history and present this history to itself and others. By putting the past on display, whether through objects, images, or text, a museum is committing itself to an interpretation. This interpretation is formed not only by what is included in the displays, but also by what is excluded. In Northern Ireland, many would expect the history presented in the local and national museums to include exhibitions on the conflict that has dominated the region over the past thirty years (often referred to as the 'Troubles'). Instead, that aspect of Northern Ireland's history and identity has been largely neglected by the museum sector and is generally presented only in occasional temporary exhibitions dealing with related issues, rather than head on.[1] More recently, however, a number of community-based groups have been adding a heritage dimension to their work. Groups have begun to collect oral histories of the conflict and to mount exhibitions of their local experiences, and they have proposed that museums be established that address how the conflict has affected their lives. The various approaches to the display of Northern Ireland's contested history taken by the state museum sector and community-based heritage initiatives reveal the complexity of dealing with contested histories, as well as the multiple agendas and purposes underpinning the creation of heritage.

Museums and history have been used for a range of purposes. This chapter discusses attempts to create public histories from the experiences of the conflict in Northern Ireland through the medium of the exhibition or museum. It considers the nature of the various examples, the groups developing the initiatives, their motives, and what all of this reveals about the purpose of (re)visualizing Northern Ireland's past. Just as the writing of history has a purpose, so too has the creation of museums. This chapter demonstrates the social and political nature of presenting history for the public through exhibitions and in museums. It begins by discussing the approach taken by the state museum sector and the difficulties that sector has identified with presenting the history of the conflict. The chapter then moves on to evaluate the agendas associated with a number of examples of more recent heritage activity based on the conflict experience. The purposes underpinning this activity are various: engagement with heritage can be an extension of forms of activism, a means to seek legitimization, and an approach to community capacity building. Display of the history of the conflict has been proposed as a means to bring about healing. This range reveals how the interpretation and display of history is never value free – it always has some contemporary social or political purpose.

Remembering and Forgetting

Most museums in Northern Ireland are either county museums, funded locally by county or district councils, or form part of the National Museums and Galleries of Northern Ireland group. The latter include the key national museums: the Ulster Museum, the Ulster Folk and Transport Museum, the Ulster American Folk Park, and W5, an interactive science centre. A tour of the permanent exhibitions in the museums of Northern Ireland will reveal little to inform the visitor of the dominant factor in the country's recent history. Instead, local museums are concerned mainly with displays of art, archaeology, natural history, and uncontroversial elements of local social history. This gap in representation could be interpreted as a defence mechanism, a means to put this past behind and learn about something more uplifting when we visit museums. Curators in Northern Ireland have often agonized over how they should tackle their recent history. What sort of history should be represented in museums? Should museums be expected to interpret a past that is so contested? Would it be responsible for them to comment on a political situation that is not yet by any means resolved?[2] The scale of the unknown and the unresolved is often mentioned as the reason why Northern Ireland's museums have not provided visitors with an interpretation of the conflict. It is because of the extremely varied and personal nature of the many experiences of the conflict, and the fact that one version of an event can differ greatly from another, that finalizing a narrative in a museum exhibition is so difficult. There are so many sides to the Northern Ireland conflict, so many different experiences, and so many unresolved issues, that most curators feel ill equipped to interpret the events in their exhibition spaces.

Evidence of the difficulties associated with displaying contested history is provided by some of the reactions to past attempts that have been made. The Tower Museum in Derry/Londonderry, opened in 1992, is the only museum in Northern Ireland that provides a permanent display on the conflict, which is represented in a film on the history of the city and in a small area of gallery space that displays photographs telling the story of the divided city. In the early years, the museum earned praise from the European Museum of the Year awards and the Gulbenkian Foundation;[3] however, it also received criticism from other circles and has been linked to public controversy. Three years after the museum opened, new exhibitions were criticized for including a former IRA gun as part of an exhibition on the conflict. The Northern Ireland newspaper the *Newsletter* ran the headline 'Museum Displays IRA Gun,' and a member of Parliament was quoted in the *Times* claiming that the display was 'perpetuating the propaganda of the IRA.'[4] The weapon was then removed from the museum. The museum sector seems to be more at ease with temporary exhibitions, which they have used to offer a more subtle interpretation of the issues that relate to the conflict, instead of trying to tell the conflict's story directly. For instance, in 1994 many museums hosted an exhibition on the use of symbols in Northern Ireland developed by the Community Relations Council, an agency established in the early 1990s with the aim of improving community relations.[5] The exhibition provided an interpretation of why symbols are needed and how they might be selected, and displayed the range of political and non-political symbols used in Northern Ireland. Visitors were told how symbols are developed and how objects, people, and places can take on iconic status. The meanings associated with colours, flags, and emblems were explored, illustrating how we build up a sense of identity through various codes that are recognizable to others. The theme of identity also dominated the exhibitions Local Identities, developed by the Northern Ireland Regional Curators Group, and Icons of Identity (figs. 3.1 and 3.2), created by the Ulster Museum, both in 2000. These exhibitions considered the shared experiences, contradictions, and inconsistencies common in our experiences of Northern Ireland. Icons of Identity reflected on the meanings ascribed to nine icons associated with life and politics in Northern Ireland and often used to fuel sectarianism. These meanings were explored, associated myths and contradictory interpretations were acknowledged, and examples were provided of when Republican and Loyalist communities share symbols, even if different messages are being portrayed. The mythical figure Cuchulainn (see fig. 3.2), for instance, is celebrated by Irish Republicanism for defending his land from invasion; in contrast, Loyalist communities remember him for defending Ulster. Visitor response to the exhibition, which was generally good, illustrated the inevitable difficulties of interpreting such history: some visitors found the exhibition sympathetic to loyalist interpretations of history, while others thought that in places it told a nationalist version of events. One visitor thought the exhibition was an inappropriate subject for the museum and wrote: 'Surely Northern Ireland gets enough exposure by media … We're very disappointed that the more orthodox viewing has been closed due to Icons which should remain in the past.'[6] The various reactions to the exhibition are examples of the differing opinions that exist concerning how such a difficult past should be interpreted in our local museums.

The appropriateness of displaying the contested history in Northern Ireland – the legacy of which, despite advances in the peace process, is ongoing for some and unresolved for many – relates not only to the approach taken to remembering and forgetting, but also to the role we ascribe to these processes. Memory can take many forms: it can be personal, individual, and private; it can also be collective, cultural, and public.[7] It is the complexity of memory that makes the representation of highly emotive and complicated experiences of contested histories so difficult. Adding to this complexity is the variable nature of our memory; memory is not fixed, it is context and audience dependent and can be triggered by any number of actions and objects. Our memory of past events changes with the context; our surroundings, and the people we are with at the time, influence our relationship with our past at that moment. When we move from one environment to another, our relationship with our history also shifts. Memories of events change over time, and we create alternative versions. Our memory has many layers: we don't totally forget and we don't totally remember. Our memory can also play tricks on us so that we have false memories. Gaynor Kavanagh noted in *Memory and the Museum*: 'We have a very personal stake in how we remember and are influenced by who, what and where we are at the moment of remembrance.'[8] The strongly

3.1 Section on the Virgin Mary in the Icons of Identity exhibition.

3.2 Depictions of Cuchulainn in the Icons of Identity exhibition.

private and individual nature of memory, and how memory becomes more emotionally charged when those experiences are placed on public display, is of major relevance when museums exhibit the Northern Ireland conflict. Fundamentally, the very act of displaying an object or event in a museum context will alter its impact on the individual. The act of display gives the past authority and force. Exhibition can suggest recognition and, depending on the display, may indicate a form of acceptance, tolerance, or legitimization. On the other hand, public criticisms of a group or person in a museum exhibition carry greater weight than they would in a private context. The contested history of Northern Ireland has become a burden for the region, and one that many museums in Northern Ireland have not been keen to carry in the present day. The established museums have been tentatively exploring how they might present the conflict; meanwhile, numerous community-based groups have begun creating collections, forming exhibitions, and proposing new museums based on their experiences of the past thirty years. The evaluation of a number of these examples that follows reveals the multiple purposes associated with interpreting the past within museums.

The Museum as Activist

A number of groups in Northern Ireland – groups more traditionally associated with various forms of local activism – have begun to include a heritage dimension in their work. Falls Community Council (FCC), for instance, was established in the 1970s to represent the needs and rights of people living in the mostly Republican area of Belfast. Recently the council created a heritage committee, which has proposed two flagship projects: the West Belfast Living History Museum, and a Conflict Resolution and Peace-Building Learning Centre. The museum is to include open access to an oral history archive, a personal reminiscence photographic archive, and an exhibition program. Already the council has developed an archive of oral testimonies of experiences of the conflict, chosen on the basis of their relevance to people of the Falls Road area. Since January 2002 a selection of these interviews has been made available to the public through an interactive computer archive in the FCC buildings. The interviews cover the following themes: the 1960s civil rights campaign, internment, the 1981 hunger strikes, and the experiences of women during the conflict. Visitors' responses to the archive have highlighted the value of sharing these memories and the importance of allowing those who have experienced the conflict to speak out. Visitors have welcomed the project as an opportunity to hear first-hand accounts of the conflict.[9]

In the City of Derry, the Museum of Free Derry in the Republican Bogside district opened in January 2007. The idea was first raised by the Bloody Sunday Trust, a group established to investigate the events of 30 January 1972, when a Republican civil rights march held in the city led to a confrontation with security forces and the death of fourteen people. The museum has taken its name from the now iconic mural painted with the words 'You are Now Entering Free Derry'; the mural, created in 1969, denoted the area of the city that was for a time a no-go area for British forces in Northern Ireland. The project coordinator forwarded the proposal on the basis that it will 'provide a positive legacy out of the whole issues and damage that has been done to the city.' He states that the history of the Bogside would be presented as 'a microcosm history of the entire troubles and the background to the troubles and the causes of the troubles.' The museum is being presented as a community project, as an opportunity for the people of the area to tell their own story. For the projector coordinator, this is 'the first step towards getting [each side] to understand each other.'[10] The proposal that has generated the greatest media attention, however, is the one calling for the Maze Prison outside Belfast – the place where many were imprisoned for terrorist activities – to be developed as a museum. The proposal came from Coiste na n-Iarchimi, an organization representing Republican ex-prisoners. This group has already begun collecting oral histories as material for such a museum, and has gained a high media profile through debates and publications. Coiste refers to the proposed museum as 'an icon and microcosm of the conflict,' with the potential to draw tourists and educate the public about ways to resolve differences.[11]

Some find it astonishing that Northern Ireland does not yet have a museum telling the story of the Troubles. Should the three projects noted above be welcomed as a means for filling that gap? Each raises many questions, such as these: How would the Troubles story be told? Whose version would be advocated? And what impact would the story have on other communities? All of these questions come back to a core issue: Why are the suggestions being made in the first place? The particular proposals outlined above have come from groups that are taking an active role in their community; they are perceived as reflecting a Republican approach to the political situation and as questioning the legitimacy of British rule in Northern Ireland. In each case the museum would reflect this approach. Each also claims to have a community relations agenda and to be making what could be a positive contribution to the peace process: the FCC refers to conflict resolution and peace building; the Free Derry Museum talks about creating understanding; and a councillor forwarding the Maze Prison proposal sees it as having the potential for 'cross community and cross party support.'[12] All three raise questions that could be asked of any exhibition of contested histories; these questions relate to the political aspects of ownership, space, and the construction of narrative. All three are based on the traditional divisions that have long dominated Northern Ireland: they are owned and promoted by groups that are very much the product of 'one side' of the political experience; they are located in parts of cities that represent the experience of only one community; and the narratives are to be constructed by groups that would be perceived as offering a partial version of events. It is questionable whether projects with these limitations could make a positive contribution to improving community relations in Northern Ireland. There is a risk that any of these projects could become an opportunity for one community to further embed and endorse a singular version of past events. Even in the very early stages these museums are already being used as political levers by agencies with sharply focused agendas. The centres are helping bring the experience of people in their areas into the public domain. They are broadening people's knowledge of their own past, and in this way that past will belong more of them, which will give these groups' other work greater authority and recognition.

Legitimization through Heritage

The three examples discussed above demonstrated how the collecting, writing, and displaying of history can be integrated into other political agendas. This is also the case in the example of recent heritage activity associated with the Orange Order; here the political message is one of legitimization. The Orange Order is a society established in the 1790s to sustain the memory of the victory of the Protestant King William III against the Catholic King James in the Battle of the Boyne (1690). Commemoration of the battle continues today in the form of annual parades held across Northern Ireland on 12 July. Always controversial, in recent decades the commemorations have been associated with sectarian clashes and widespread disruptions. To make their activities more acceptable to a broader range of people, the Orange Order has in recent years begun to promote more widely the historical and cultural dimensions of their activities. Thus each July the Order mounts exhibitions in Orange Halls across the province, hosts costumed re-enactments of the seventeenth-century battle, and promotes the com-memorations as festivals. In 2003 an exhibition mounted in an Orange Hall outside Belfast celebrated Orange Culture Week. Each Orange Lodge in the district had its own table on which objects associated with the lodges were exhibited, such as photographs, sashes, and drums. Samples of banners were hung on the wall behind; some of the banners were still being used in marches, while others, because of their age or fragility, were only for display purposes. The objects exhibited ranged from the bizarre, such as knitted Orangemen toys, to the expected, each Lodge displaying photographs of members from the previous cen-tury. One member proudly displayed his collection of Orange Order badges and pins from lodges in the Republic of Ireland, Scotland, and America and South Africa.

The marching season associated with the Orange Order is linked to ongoing controversy and objections, yet little reference is made to this in the exhibitions. Instead, the displays celebrate the material heritage associated with the Order – many of the banners illustrate the skills of craftspeople. The objects act as triggers to remind visitors of the rich-ness of this expression of Protestant heritage and the importance of its preservation. In this example, the exhibition is a form of cultural pro-paganda. The hope is that by emphasizing the historical and cultural dimensions of the Orange Order, it will be possible to preserve the annual marches as an expression of the heritage and traditions of the Orange community. Furthermore, the exhibitions promote Northern Ireland as a Protestant place, one that is loyal to the Crown and that defends the interests of the order. Together, the displays presented by the different lodges underscore the themes of unity, shared experi-ences, and common traditions. Some of this is achieved through the marches themselves; but the exhibitions are providing a new and alter-native means for promoting the idea of heritage associated with the order. The exhibitions serve as another means to emphasize the longevity of the order and its historical and cultural depth as an orga-nization. Like the examples discussed in the previous section, these exhibitions are being developed by a community for its members. The organizers may declare 'all welcome,' but in the main, only those who feel at ease with 'Orange culture,' the Orange Order, and its members would visit such exhibitions. They are a means for one community to further embed and endorse a singular version of its history.

Heritage and Community Capacity Building

Each of the examples discussed above can also be explained in relation to the practice of community capacity building. By selecting, interpreting, and displaying its heritage, a group can bind itself together and forge a sense of common experience and history. Some community groups develop a heritage dimension in order to communicate a message. It is not the heritage that is of value; of greater importance is what heritage can say about the community group. These points are well demonstrated by the activities of a community association based in Newry, a city near the border with the Republic of Ireland. This group's main aims are to provide new opportunities for young people, increase the sense of community spirit, and heighten community participation. Recently, the community association established a heritage committee. In 2003 this committee staged an exhibition of the history of the area that described its 'hopes and aspirations for the future' and emphasized the value of bringing people of the community together in order to achieve common goals. The exhibition consisted mainly of some two hundred photographs, most of them taken in the 1950s and 1960s. They depicted people outside their homes: children playing in the streets, teenagers engaged in music or sport, and families gathered together. Panels showed how the use of the buildings had changed over the years, the life of soldiers in the town, and the experiences of wives and families. The social housing of the early twentieth century was described as 'run down tenements,' which were dilapidated and 'virtually slums.' The impact of the conflict post 1960s was described as having taken 'the heart from the estate' and as resulting in high unemployment, low educational achievement, and a generally negative image of the area. The belief now was that 'community development has brought hope to the area.'

The exhibition in Newry was an exercise in community autobiography. It was an occasion when a local group could construct its own history and tell its story in its own way. It was an opportunity to construct a collective history and evoke shared memories. The exhibition did not go into details concerning the people in the photographs or the events they represented; instead, the photographs provided an idea of the past and acted as a trigger for reminiscence and the making of memories. The exhibition was an important act of community curation: members of the community selected the stories, objects, and images to place on display and provided their own interpretations. These community members made their own decisions regarding preservation, selection, interpretation, and display. For the community-based exhibitions discussed so far, the purpose is always to enhance community belonging. Some people consider this a very positive outcome of exhibition development. But in each case, it is essential to consider the *nature* of the community being expressed. The history on display may be meaningful only to a select few; others may find the exhibition exclusionary, intimidating, and isolating.

History and Healing

The display of history in Northern Ireland has also been associated with the potentially reconciliatory or curative impact of collecting stories and putting them on display. The powerful impact of memories associated with the conflict was recently demonstrated by the exhibition Every Picture Tells a Story, which toured public halls in Northern Ireland in 2004 (figs. 3.3 and 3.4). The exhibition displayed works of art created by children and young adults who had used the facilities of WAVE Trauma Centre, an initiative established in 1991 to help people bereaved and traumatized by the conflict. In their own words, and through simple images, the children told how the conflict had affected their lives and relationships. Through art and narrative, children shared memories of loved ones lost through the conflict and the sadness this had brought to their own lives and those of their family members. Visitor feedback repeated these adjectives: thought provoking, moving, and emotive. In this example, the process of creating the artworks and act of sharing the experiences with the public were both important. WAVE wants to help people rebuild their lives and explore their pasts, and art provides a means to do this. Placing some of the resulting work on public display in Every Picture Tells a Story has allowed others to learn of and acknowledge the experiences of the creators.

The idea that sharing these histories is beneficial both for those directly involved and for those who visit such exhibitions is being explored by the Healing Through Remembering Project. This agency

3.3 *Jigsaw of Peace* at the Every Picture Tells a Story exhibition.

3.4 Paintings on display at the Every Picture Tells a Story exhibition.

was established in Northern Ireland in June 2001 to 'identify and document possible mechanisms and realisable options for healing through
remembering for those people affected by the conflict in and about
Northern Ireland.' The project's board was building on the experience
of a visit to Northern Ireland in 1999 by Dr Alex Boraine, then Deputy
Chair of the South African Truth and Reconciliation Commission.
During his visit, Boraine found general support for mechanisms to
identify the truth in Northern Ireland and for finding ways to deal
with that truth in a more positive manner. The first task undertaken
by the board was to establish a consultation process. The principal
question was concerned with how people should remember the conflict in a manner that would contribute to healing; the subquestions
asked what should be remembered, what forms the remembering
ought to take, what the hurdles to such processes might be, and what
the implications and consequences could be of such processes. In all, 108
submissions were received. A report that outlined the findings of the
consultation projects, and that listed the board members' recommendations, was published in June 2002.[13]

Each of the forms of remembering identified in the submission, as a
means of addressing the legacy of the conflict, would affect our
understanding of the past, the construction of identities, and our relationships with one another. Three of the fourteen might be considered as likely to have a major impact on the creation of a public
history of the conflict: collecting oral histories; the creation of a
memorial; and the establishment of a museum. The physical record-
ing of stories and the development of an ongoing storytelling and
oral history collection process was the most frequent suggestion.
Wide support was shown for the creation of memorials, be they permanent or 'living' (perhaps in the form of festivals). A third popular
suggestion concerned the development of museums and exhibitions.
Numerous ideas of how such a museum could be established were
put forward: it could have separate spaces dealing with different
'sides,' so that people could visit the areas where they felt most com-
fortable and explore the others when they felt ready; it could be an
archive for oral histories; and it could serve as an education centre for
schools and local groups. Further suggestions could also be used to
shape the work of a potential museum. A desire was voiced for community and intercommunity dialogue, which could take place in a
museum space. Others called for a Centre of Remembrance containing a memorial room or memorial garden. Interest was shown in the

creation of a memorial fund to be used for financing community and individual memorials and projects.

Drawing from these proposals, the project board made six recommendations, each of which they considered would make a 'positive contribution to healing the wounds of the past.'[14] They were named as follows: a network of commemoration and remembering projects; the establishment of a Day of Reflection; the initiating of a collective storytelling and archiving process; the formation of a permanent Living Memorial Museum; the establishment of processes of acknowledgement; and the foundation of a long-term Healing Through Remembering Initiative. The recommendation for the Living Memorial Museum was that it should take the form of a 'dynamic memorial,' one that would collect memoirs and keep 'the memories of the past alive.'[15] Such a museum would provide a chronicle of the history of the conflict, increase public awareness of the impact of the conflict, and disseminate information and educational opportunities for the future. The museum would be a commemorative space, a space for different communities, and an educational space. The board also recommended that the museum be a safe space, one in which different perspectives could be 'housed together in a sensitive and tolerant way.'[16] In this way, the exploration of history could play a healing role.

Conclusion: The Multiple Uses of Heritage

In Northern Ireland, history plays an important role in the construction and definition of identity. People often refer to events from the past in order both to express who they are in the present and to justify or explain current actions. The selective display of history through the medium of the exhibition can be a means to forget certain aspects of the past and to emphasize others. With regard to experiences of the conflict, public remembrance through exhibitions, memorials, and monuments is now emerging as a general approach to dealing with this history. The various exhibitions discussed in this chapter each have their own version of the conflict, shaped by the varied past experiences and current needs of the authors. The exhibitions represent a form of commemoration, and the different approaches reveal the complexities of such activity. Some of the exhibitions act as a form of remembrance – a chance to remember lives lost in order to bring some solace in the present. Others are opportunities to celebrate, honour, and pay tribute. In Northern Ireland the construction of historical narratives around such accepted forms of remembrance is challenged by potential disagreements concerning who should be remembered, how past events should be interpreted, and whether tributes are appropriate.

The recent development of the exhibitions presented above, and the proposals to create new museums based on the conflict, reflect something of the identity of the region at this present time. One could argue that if Northern Ireland feels ready to place the story of the conflict in a museum, if communities are coming forward to publicly record their experiences, we must have entered a new phase. The positive interpretation is that the time has now come when people are prepared to reflect on the past in a more inclusive manner; indeed, some form of resolution, or end, to the conflict must have been reached in order for people to have the desire to represent these events. If it has been generally accepted that we must use our experiences and tell our stories in ways that contribute to healing, resolution, and the formation of good community relations, then a new cultural and political identity must be forming in Northern Ireland. However, the political process is fragile, and its lack of stability could well uproot the above proposals. Furthermore, even if the desire to represent the conflict exists, the subject matter is such that its representation will remain – for the immediate future at least – something that must be approached with caution.

The initiatives discussed in this chapter illustrate some of the characteristics and purposes associated with placing local and national histories on public display. As the examples discussed above demonstrate, our relationship with the past and the construction of heritage are associated with the political and social context of remembering. Remembering has a contemporary purpose; current events trigger, shape, and influence our memory, and there is often a deliberate reason why we want others to remember certain parts of our past. Therefore, the writing of history, the development of heritage awareness, and the creation of museums are all linked to contemporary needs. In Northern Ireland there are examples of how the recalling of events from the past has been tied to the legitimization of various social and political perspectives. The range of initiatives discussed in this chapter reveals how the region's history has long been visualized and revisualized according to varied and changing needs. In Northern Ireland, a place where issues of history and identity have been so closely tied to the conflict of the past thirty years, it is essential to be aware of the potential impact of such developments.

NOTES

1 For background, see Elizabeth Crooke, 'Confronting a Troubled History: Which Past in Northern Ireland's Museums?' *International Journal of Heritage Studies* 7, no. 2 (2001): 119–36.

2 These questions have been raised at museum conferences in Ireland, such as during the Can History Heal? Annual Study Weekend, hosted by the Social History Curators Group in Belfast in June 1999.

3 In 1993 it was 'specially commended' by European Museum of the Year Awards and was named Irish Museum of the Year.

4 *Newsletter,* December 1996, and the *Times,* 26 December 1996.

5 For further information on the Community Relations Council, visit http://www.community-relations.org.

6 Information gathered from visitor response cards, Icons Exhibition, Ulster Museum.

7 David Thelen (1990), cited in Gaynor Kavanagh, *Memory and the Museum* (Leicester: Leicester University Press, 2000).

8 Kavanagh, *Memory and the Museum,* 19.

9 Feedback from visitor questionnaires and interviews undertaken by Seana Toal as part of her research for an MA in Cultural Heritage and Museum Studies, University of Ulster (2003).

10 Adrian Kerr, project coordinator, in an interview for 24 Hour Museum by David Prudames, 'Free Derry Museum a Step Closer as Planning Application Is Lodged,' 10 June 2004, available at http://www.24hourmuseum.org.uk, accessed 18 June 2004.

11 Coiste na n-Iarchimi, *A Museum at Long Kesh or the Maze Report of Conference Proceedings* (Belfast: Coiste na n-Iarchimi, 2003).

12 Cited in Louise Purbrick, 'The History Block,' *Museums Journal* (July 2001).

13 Healing through Remembering, *The Report of the Healing through Remembering Project* (Belfast: Healing through Remembering, 2002). See also http://www.healingthroughremembering.org.

14 Ibid., 37.

15 Ibid., 46.

16 Ibid., 47.

PART THREE

Restoring National History with International Participation

4 Museums, Multiculturalism, and the Remaking of Postwar Sarajevo

EDIN HAJDARPAŠIĆ

Much discussion about recreating the multicultural, multiethnic Bosnia and Herzegovina after the 1992–5 war has revolved around the demographic and territorial representations of ethnic groups – that is, around census and map, two crucial institutions of political power that, as Benedict Anderson argued in the 'Census, Map, Museum' chapter of his *Imagined Communities*, help envision and construct modern nations.[1] Yet Anderson's third keyword – museum – has been overlooked by most observers and scholars in their explorations of the postwar reconstruction, even though the museum, like other national institutions (not only the census and the map, but the archive and the university as well), remains a relevant analytical category that offers insights into the complex political context in which these institutions operate.

Given the official partition of Bosnia into entities defined along ethno-confessional lines, the expectation that I will deal with separate nationalist museums that follow the pattern of political division is not unreasonable. After all, the wartime creation of the Museum of Republika Srpska in Banja Luka offers an excellent example of the institutionalization of invented national traditions.[2] Unfortunately, exclusive focus on nationalist cultural production would overlook one of the most significant postwar developments: the proliferation of discourses of multiculturalism and religious tolerance in Bosnia, and especially in Sarajevo. The cultivated image of the Bosnian capital as 'a crossroads of faiths and civilizations' where different nationalities can continue to live side by side appeared to defy the years of war that had effected ethnic apartheid elsewhere in the country (in Mostar and Stolac, for example).[3] The internationally sponsored reconstituting of Sarajevo's multiculturalism, however, has for the most part uncritically accepted the nationalists' insistence on the centrality of religious difference in the postwar remaking of culture and politics. In the first part of this essay, I will analyse how the discursive strands and the institutional setting of the 2002 Sarajevo Haggadah exhibit in the National Museum revealed the essentialist underpinnings of the politically dominant interpretation of multiculturalism as multiconfessionalism. The ethno-confessional order has prioritized certain symbols and venues over others. In the second part, I will argue that the Ars Aevi project for the creation of a new museum of contemporary art is attempting to introduce alternative ways of remaking public culture after the siege of the city. By discussing these two large museum projects, I aim not only to sketch out the major issues that have shaped cultural developments in postwar Sarajevo, but also to contribute a contextualized analysis of the interaction of what several scholars have called 'three closely related forces that are powerfully at work in the contemporary world: nationalism, globalization, and multiculturalism.'[4]

The National Museum and the Sarajevo Haggadah Exhibit

Under the auspices of the Austro-Hungarian government, the first museum in Bosnia and Herzegovina was officially established in Sarajevo in 1888, ten years after the Habsburgs acquired the province.[5] The institution's peculiar name – *Zemaljski muzej* (meaning regional or provincial, rather than national, museum) – was a literal translation of the German *Landesmuseum*, a term that points to the Habsburg view of Bosnia and Herzegovina as a single *region*, a territorial, social, and historical whole that could be analysed, classified, and displayed in proper scientific and educational institutions.[6] This totalizing vision of Bosnia, manifest in the museum founders' stated intent to preserve 'all that is archaeologically, culturally-historically, artistically, and craft-commercially significant for and characteristic of the region,' was an integral part of the Austro-Hungarian 'civilizing mission' that shaped new political and cultural institutions in the country.[7] During these formative years at the turn of the century, the Regional Museum acquired its basic structure: each unit, such as archaeology or natural sciences, was housed in a separate pavilion within the museum building complex. This arrangement was maintained as the museum's organizational basis over the next century.

In its early years, the museum happened to acquire a book that without question is today its most prominent holding: the Sarajevo

Haggadah. In 1894, as part of a policy of purchasing rare books (in addition to undertaking extensive archaeological research across the country), the curators bought a Jewish codex from the Kohen family of Sarajevo. After sending it to Vienna for a more detailed analysis, the curators concluded that the manuscript was not some rare copy, but an original, richly illustrated Haggadah from mid- to late-fourteenth-century northern Spain that found its way to Sarajevo with the Jews who were expelled during the Inquisition (see fig. 4.1).[8] The Sephardic family who owned it came to Italy by the sixteenth century, as notes in the book show; but it is not clear when or how the refugees and their Haggadah reached Bosnia. The book's condition, with wine stains and marks of a child's writing, attests that it remained in use and in the family's possession up until it was sold to the museum.

Thus the museum had obtained an extraordinary manuscript whose history paralleled the exile of Jews from Spain. Yet the Sarajevo Haggadah did not immediately attain the renown that it enjoys today. For most of its existence, the Regional Museum counted the manuscript as an important attraction, but certainly not as its main one. (Archaeological artefacts were most prominently displayed in the museum.[9]) Furthermore, because of the financial problems and political restrictions the museum faced in the interwar and sometimes in the socialist years, little was done to promote the manuscript as a separate exhibit; as a result, the Haggadah usually remained consigned to the library holdings.[10]

The framing of the Sarajevo Haggadah as the museum's most precious holding occurred only recently, during and after the 1992–5 war, when the manuscript's complex and ambiguous history – particularly the story of its survival of the Holocaust – was reinterpreted as a paradigm of the endurance of religious coexistence in face of war. Though it was well known that the Haggadah did not become a casualty of the Nazi purges because it was somehow hidden by the curators, this event gained special significance for those who were looking to protect and save the cultural heritage of Bosnia from the brutal campaigns of ethnic cleansing that followed the dissolution of Yugoslavia. Already in 1992, the year the war broke out, politicians, activists, and many public figures were beginning to compare the ethnic cleansing in Bosnia with the Holocaust.[11] Though such analogies were most often invoked to condemn the lack of international intervention to stop the war in Bosnia, stories told about saving the Sarajevo Haggadah in the 1940s and in the 1990s added different discursive dimensions. Those parallels focused not on the inaction of the world powers, but on the

4.1 Detail (illustrated page) from the Sarajevo Haggadah, anonymous.
(Image courtesy of the National Museum of Bosnia-Herzegovina)

recurring motif of the solidarity of Bosnia's religious communities – a solidarity heroically exemplified by people of different faiths risking their lives to safeguard a single Jewish prayer book.[12] At a time when extremist nationalists were murdering and persecuting entire communities and deliberately destroying all kinds of cultural objects (libraries, bridges, museums, mosques, schools), the symbolism of the Sarajevo Haggadah was easy to grasp. The book's survival held out the hope that some semblance of common life could be saved despite the intent of those who waged war to destroy all shared social spaces and thus create ethnically pure territories.

However, the underlying narrative of 'religious coexistence' that made the Haggadah such an appealing symbol was itself embedded in the broader nationalist discourse that made religious difference a key marker that set Bosnia's major ethno-confessional communities apart from one another. Precisely because it was formulated within familiar nationalist terms of reference, the symbolism of the Haggadah was appropriated during and after the war for the different agendas of the nationalist parties. The Bosnian government, besieged in Sarajevo by Serb forces and headed by president Alija Izetbegović, was in effect the legal guardian of the National Museum and thus of the Haggadah, which was often touted by Izetbegović and other leaders of the Bosnian Muslim Party of Democratic Action (SDA) as evidence of their commitment to religious coexistence.[13] Yet because the Haggadah was hidden in a secure bank vault during the war, the secrecy surrounding its whereabouts fuelled not only demands for accountability in its safeguarding, but also rumours (propounded by a few American journalists and Bosnian Serb politicians) that the precious Jewish book had been sold to buy weapons for the Bosnian Muslims.[14] The response of the Bosnian government was unequivocal: in April 1995, Izetbegović took the Haggadah out of hiding and brought it for Passover to a Sarajevo synagogue, where he made a brief speech about tolerance in front of the gathered journalists and Orthodox, Muslim, Jewish, and Catholic clerics.[15] More arguments over the book followed in late 1998, three years after the Dayton Peace Agreement partitioned the country into two entities and ended the war. Bosnian Serb nationalists, couching their demands for ethnic segregation in the language of fair multiethnic representation, argued that the Serb entity was entitled to one-third of the institutional possession of the Haggadah.[16] Despite such openly politicized disputes, the manuscript remained in Sarajevo the entire time and continued to be praised as 'the proof of multi-ethnicity in Bosnia.'[17]

But even as the book was fiercely argued over, the institution that housed it received very little public attention. The National Museum emerged heavily damaged from the siege, though most of its collections survived the war more or less intact.[18] The major problem it faced was the lack of funding to restore normal functioning of the institution – a problem epitomized and accentuated by bitter public quarrels between the museum, various ministries at different government levels, and the cantonal company providing heating in the winter. After the war, the museum had no heating, which it needed in order to sustain the reconstruction and the exhibits during the harsh winters, but for which it could not pay, since neither the cantonal nor the federal 'ministry for education, culture, and sport' agreed to subsidize those costs. Numerous international organizations donated urgently needed equipment and made several grants to secure crucial building repairs (most notably to the roof and the facade), but the persistent heating problem returned more and more acutely with each winter.[19] The institution's legal status, which is at the core of these disputes and problems that are impeding its full reconstruction, remains undefined (as of 2004–5).[20]

Any hopes to establish a museum program around the Haggadah faced not only this unwieldy institutional framework, but also the transformed political significance of the book after the war. With the enormous changes that the 1995 Dayton Agreement introduced in Bosnia, the ruling nationalist parties shifted their attention to new issues and political strategies. For instance, the SDA, which at one time had vigorously championed the Haggadah as evidence of its tolerance and openness, made little effort in the postwar years to maintain that discursive strand, preferring instead to sharpen its profile as a Bosnian 'Muslim' party.[21] At the same time, the institutions of the international community – such as the Office of the High Representative (OHR), and UN programs and offices – found in the Haggadah a useful symbol that vividly illustrated their newly minted slogans extolling multiethnicity and multiculturalism as the highest political and social ideals that Bosnians could achieve. The fact that the Haggadah was an emblem of the small Bosnian Jewish community, which was not one of the 'sides' that had waged war, made the prayer book all the more appealing, since in celebrating it, the international organizations did not need to worry about appearing to favour any one of the three larger confessions (the Orthodox, the Catholic, and the Muslim) in the country.

The new Haggadah exhibit announced by the UN Mission in Bosnia and Hercegovina (UNMIBH) and planned for 2002 thus represented an important undertaking for both the local institutions (the National Museum and the ministries of culture it dealt with) and the various international organizations that enthusiastically welcomed the event. Jacques Paul Klein, the UN special representative of the secretary-general and the head of the UNMIBH, personally intervened in several key areas. Besides helping arrange funding for the exhibit from a number of sources (various embassies, the World Bank, the UN, personal donations, charity organizations, and so on), Klein, as he himself put it, 'broke through' the ambiguous institutional jurisdictions that had been paralysing most activities in the National Museum. This set the stage for a grandiose return of the Sarajevo Haggadah.[22]

On 2 December 2002, in the National Museum, the UN special representative presided over the opening of the Haggadah exhibit before a distinguished audience of party functionaries, religious clerics, diplomats, academics, and many others. The unveiling of the specially constructed display in a secure, climate-controlled room was not only well attended by hundreds of guests but was also well covered by the media both in Bosnia and abroad.[23] For the principal theme of his opening speech, Klein focused on 'the journey' the book had made. He described the origins of the manuscript and the arrival of Sephardic Jewish refugees 'to a multicultural Sarajevo that was a beacon of tolerance in Europe.' Marring this image of 'intermingling of faiths and civilizations,' however, were 'tyrants of the past and the most recent purveyors of hatred in the Balkans.' They, asserted Klein, 'abhor culture ... The first targets of the recent violence were always the churches, mosques, and synagogues.' But despite these attacks on culture, the prayer book had survived, inspiring Klein to declare: 'Tonight the odyssey of the Sarajevo Haggadah has come to an end. It is home. It is safe ... It lives on, thanks to the courage and determination of people of all faiths.'[24]

The UN's involvement in the National Museum is illustrative of some broader patterns in the remaking of public culture after the war in Bosnia. In the first place, it affords insight into the pivotal role played by the international community, which, together with the nationalist parties, established a partition-based, multi-level system of government institutions through the Dayton Agreement, but which also occasionally intervened in the frequently deadlocked system to demonstrate how it should work. The ambiguous legal standing of the National Museum – various ministries claim or deny that it is under their jurisdiction – is indicative of the state of the country's postwar cultural institutions; so is the periodic involvement of the UN and other international organizations, both governmental and non-governmental. Without their immense financial resources and political influence, it would be extremely difficult for the local cultural institutions, devastated by war and severely neglected by state structures, to maintain their activities (let alone establish major new programs).

Yet direct international intervention has aimed not for a lasting, fundamental transformation of this disastrous framework, but for a series of short-term, superficial improvements symbolizing multiculturalism and religious tolerance. Klein's dramatic assertion that 'the odyssey of the Sarajevo Haggadah has come to an end' gains a different meaning when one considers that Klein's own mission in Bosnia ended just a few weeks after he spoke those words. As had long been planned, the UNMIBH mandate expired in December 2002. Its tasks were turned over to a number of authorities, and Klein, after a short break, moved on to serve as the UN Special Representative in Liberia.[25] Furthermore, the National Museum was forced to close its doors to visitors for several months in the autumn of 2004 because it could no longer afford to keep the institution, which kept an emergency working schedule even during the war, open to the public.[26] The closing of the National Museum less than two years after the opening of the Haggadah exhibit thus placed a fitting seal on the grandiose declarations of progress in postwar reconstruction. Outside the climate-controlled display of multiculturalism that the UNMIBH had left as its legacy, in the cold, dilapidated halls of the rest of the museum, were thousands of other artefacts, which would remain without heating in the winters that followed. Kemal Bakaršić, former curator of the museum and professor of library science at the University of Sarajevo, pointed out that the exclusive focus on the Haggadah was 'not good policy for the Museum ... All the other collections' – items from Habsburg archaeological expeditions, natural science collections, ethnographic research records, rare books in the library – also needed 'some kind of care, some kind of reconstruction,' which the postwar political institutions were bestowing only on certain cultural objects.[27]

The essentialist interpretation of the *cultural* as a derivative expression of the *religious* – and the corollary positioning of multiculturalism as multiconfessionalism – is the second and the most significant postwar pattern that the Haggadah exhibit reveals. The priorities of the reconstruction undertaken by the international community and by the nationalist parties help clarify how religion became the keyword for understanding discourses of culture and multiculturalism in the postwar years. Besides an immediate end to the fighting, the Dayton Agreement declared its primary aim to be the reconstitution of prewar Bosnia, which has been fashionably described as a multiethnic and multicultural haven of peaceful coexistence. At the same time, the Dayton framework officially sanctioned the partition of the country into ethnically cleansed territories, thus immediately precluding any real possibility of undoing the segregation and devastation that the war had inflicted. The postwar reconstruction therefore entailed, not a reversion to the prewar Bosnia, which international organizations like the OHR and the OSCE invoked as an ideal, but an endorsement of 'partition albeit in the name of "multi-ethnicity,"' as David Campbell observed. The world view underpinning this peculiar vision of multiethnicity, propagated 'by both the peacemakers and the paramilitaries,' is based on several essentialist assumptions about

4.2 The reconstructed National Museum in Sarajevo, 2005. The facade has been reconstructed with international aid, but the museum has no heating inside during the harsh winters. The institution – and its Haggadah exhibit – were closed to the public in 2004–5. (Photo by Edin Hajdarpašić)

national identity in Bosnia.[28] That cultural differences in Bosnia are only a reflection of the basic religious divisions among its constituent communities – Muslim, Catholic, Orthodox, Jewish – is one of those assumptions. The restoration of multiethnicity and multiculturalism conceived in such reductionist terms has consequently meant the resurrection of each confession's religious symbols, the convocation of clergy representatives, and the reconstruction of the religious buildings themselves.

In this regard, there are hundreds of examples of the remarkably fast pace of the reconstruction of existing religious objects and the building of new ones; both local authorities and governments of various nations have insisted that those tasks take priority. In Sarajevo alone, several new mosques have appeared thanks to funding from the governments of Indonesia, Saudi Arabia, and Jordan.[29] Many older churches and mosques have been restored through the joint sponsorship of individual countries (Greece, Turkey, Italy) and EU and UN restoration programs. New religious schools and faith-based NGOs, and various clerical assemblies have been formed across the country.[30] These developments are providing concrete physical representation to the nationalist imaginary; they are also furnishing the pieces that the international community has uncritically embraced for its mosaic-like image of multicultural Bosnia and particularly of Sarajevo, 'where the main Orthodox church, Catholic cathedral, Islamic mosque and Jewish Synagogue are within a few hundred meters of each other.'[31]

The Haggadah exhibit, though praised by the UN special representative as the multicultural antithesis to (presumably monocultural) nationalism, underscores the dominance of the ethno-confessional principle in Bosnia. Klein's speech to inaugurate the exhibit, which he delivered on a stage flanked by the highest-ranking clerical leaders in the country, made the conflation of cultural and religious symbols exceptionally clear: those who 'abhor culture … always [targeted] the churches, mosques, and synagogues.' The remaking of this 'culture' after the war, whether by the nationalists or by the international organizations, invariably emphasized religious objects, from new mosques to Jewish prayer books to restored Catholic and Orthodox churches. In relation specifically to museums, the UNMIBH not only intervened in the Haggadah exhibit but also initiated the renovation of the Old Orthodox Church Museum in Sarajevo, which reopened in December 2001.[32] Just as at the opening ceremony for the National Museum, Klein and the clerical representatives from the Inter-Religious Council appeared before diplomats, politicians, and journalists as the guardians of Bosnia's cultural – that is, religious – traditions.[33] Because of the extremely politicized role of the Serb Orthodox Church during the war, the restoration of the Church Museum in Sarajevo was publicized far less heavily by the UN than the Sarajevo Haggadah – a Jewish symbol that nearly all parties could, for the sake of appearing tolerant and generous, politely embrace. In the broader postwar context, the climate-controlled room in the National Museum and the Old Orthodox Church Museum are the only two *museum* sites that the UNMIBH directly sponsored and restored; both interventions have been described as major achievements in 'peacekeeping.'[34] They remain as the legacy of a particular reconstruction policy that ultimately worked to celebrate rather than undermine the nationalist divisions in Bosnia.

The emphasis on the central place of religion in culture and politics also plays into the ambitiously global 'clash of civilizations' stereotype, most famously propagated by the political scientist Samuel Huntington at the end of the Cold War, but also tacitly adopted and popularized (particularly in the United States) by other scholars, intellectuals, and politicians in recent years. Underpinning these world conflict theories is the notion that 'great civilizations' and 'cultures' are defined by monolithic and supposedly mutually incompatible *religious* blocs that spark clashes where they overlap, as in Kashmir, Chechnya, and Bosnia.[35] On the one hand, the nationalists in Bosnia, keen to legitimize the positions of power that they won through war, have welcomed views and theories that affirm the pivotal importance of the religious structures on which they rely for political mobilization. On the other hand, some recent scholarship has emphasized the potential that faith has for bringing different communities together after violent conflicts. Nonetheless, these works also tend to reinscribe the essentialist idea that in 'non-Western cultures, religion is a primary motivation for political actions.'[36] A number of recent books on Bosnia, such as *Islam and Bosnia* or any of the several works by Rusmir Mahmutčehajić, similarly argue against the harmful effects of confessional divisions; yet in proposing their own agendas, they also uncritically accept the conflation of religion and culture, one of the foundation blocks of the partition.[37]

These developments offer several insights into the workings of multiculturalism today. In Bosnia itself, the war and the postwar partition have helped reduce the extraordinarily complex history of the Haggadah to a politically convenient symbol in the service of (inter)nationalist reconstruction. They have also entrenched the view that *culture* is something so ancient and so deeply spiritual that present and future generations of a particular community have no choice but to carry on or in some way honour the venerable traditions. Moreover, the celebration of the survival of a Jewish prayer book in a city that experienced the systematic destruction of almost its entire Jewish community during the Second World War reveals how certain histories – like the Holocaust in Yugoslavia – have been divested of their disturbing implications for contemporary Bosnia and incorporated into the affirmation of

Sarajevo as a 'beacon of tolerance in Europe.' The international community's organizations, such as the UNMIBH and the OHR, could articulate and endorse such multiculturalism only from a privileged universalist position that, in Slavoj Žižek's words, 'condones the folklorist Other deprived of its substance' and 'treats *each* local culture ... as "natives" whose mores are to be carefully studied and "respected."'[38] The reconstructive intervention that made the Haggadah exhibit possible in 2002 helps render visible such assumptions about culture and multiculturalism.

Yet museum exhibits, no matter how convincingly presented, can also generate unintended 'distortions' – that is, profoundly different reactions that hinge on divergent institutional images and personal memories of the past.[39] From this open-ended perspective, it is possible to draw out alternative interpretations of the Haggadah's history, even within that climate-controlled space which asserts a unidimensional reading of multiculturalism. Finally, if one wishes to understand the complexity of disparate contexts and interpretations, it is crucial to emphasize that museums themselves are not just about representations of the past. As Dipesh Chakrabarty has argued, museums, 'more than archives and history departments, have travelled the distance needed to keep up with changes that mark late democracies,' especially in cases where museums are dealing directly with major *contemporary* events, political processes, and social dynamics.[40]

At a time when nationalist partition and its underlying premises came to be sanctioned by all political authorities in Bosnia, what hope remained that alternatives not complicit with the ethno-confessional conception and propagation of 'culture' could, after all, be possible and viable in postwar Sarajevo?

The Ars Aevi Museum of Contemporary Art

Next to the National Museum, on the upper floor of the former Museum of Revolution, the temporary exhibition depot of the Ars Aevi project opened in the summer of 2000. Works by Michelangelo Pistoletto, IRWIN, Sophie Calle, Dennis Oppenheim, Ilya Kabakov, and scores of other contemporary artists were arranged throughout the makeshift gallery space. Outside the building, past rows of Daniel Buren's tall green-and-white-striped flags, a new bridge across the Miljacka River was constructed in 2002 near a place that had been a front-line checkpoint during the war. All of these pieces, including the bridge (designed by Renzo Piano), represent parts of a long-term international collaborative effort by contemporary artists, museums, galleries, curators, and architects to establish the Museum of Contemporary Art in Sarajevo.

The idea for this project arose in the summer of 1992, at a time when Serb paramilitaries were laying siege to Sarajevo and beginning to devastate the city through nearly constant shelling and sniping, which would go on for three years. Proposed by a group of intellectuals and based on 'the conviction that the artists of this age feel and understand the injustice done to our city,' the endeavour sought to make Sarajevo 'an open city once again' by calling contemporary artists 'together to create a unique museum, one which will, even in its initial steps, announce the superiority of spirit and art over the forces of evil and destruction.'[41] During the wartime years of project development, coordinated by the director Enver Hadžiomerspahić in Sarajevo and in Italy, it became clear that cooperation among European contemporary art centres and collective donations of artworks would be the organizing principles for the formation of the proposed museum. Once it attracted the attention of artists appalled by the siege of Sarajevo, the project grew rapidly to include several museums in Italy, Slovenia, and Austria; meanwhile, it gathered hundreds of works by prominent contemporary artists. Yet precisely because of the siege, the donated exhibits could not be displayed in Sarajevo; thus 'it was necessary to create temporary centers abroad,' first in Milan, Prato, and Ljubljana, and later in Venice, Vienna, and Bolognano.[42]

The resulting art collection was first fully presented to Sarajevo's public in 1999. By that time, however, the original Ars Aevi concept had begun to reflect the changing circumstances of the postwar years. The project, which functioned across several cities from its outset, also worked with several galleries (such as the Obala Art Center and the Collegium Artisticum) within Sarajevo itself. The sites of individual exhibitions included unusual urban spaces such as the partly reconstructed Vijećnica (the former National Library) and the vacant grounds behind the former Museum of Revolution (which housed the previously mentioned temporary depot). Though this kind of flexibility is not surprising for a project that emphasized openness and exchange, the various Ars Aevi endeavours also highlighted two interrelated and somewhat paradoxical factors that shaped its development. First, the project was continuing to grow, as evidenced by the expansion of its collection (for example, it acquired the Rendez-Vous series of works in

2001) and of its activities (for example, it offered art seminars and museology courses in 2002). Second, Ars Aevi still had no permanent place
of its own where it could organize and display the entirety of its impressive collection, which includes works by Michelangelo Pistoletto, Anish
Kapoor, Marina Abramović, Joseph Kosuth, Dmitri Prigov, Jannis
Kounellis, Bizhan Bassiri, Gloria Friedmann, Bill Viola, Mona Hatoum,
Komar & Melamid, Juan Muñoz, and many others. At the same time,
the foundational aim of building a 'museum of contemporary art' was
evolving to include ambitious new plans for the construction of 'a number of different locations or modules dispersed across the urban space
of Sarajevo, forming an architectural complex that will connect the old'
and new parts of the city.[43] The expansion of the Ars Aevi project was
made possible in large part by increases in funding. These came not
only from the European partner museums and centres (especially from
those in Italy), which helped start the venture during the war, but also
from much larger international organizations – most notably UNESCO
– that had joined the project as sponsors by 2000.

Yet the influx of international support failed to change the ruinous
political framework with which Ars Aevi – like so many other cultural
institutions in Sarajevo and across Bosnia – struggled during the first
postwar decade. It managed to avoid the problems of the sort confronting the National Museum; however, it faced different problems, most
of which centred on its interim locations and its activities. For instance,
the federation's culture ministry served an eviction notice to the collection's temporary depot inside the Historical Museum (the former
Museum of Revolution) in 2002 because, it contended, no one was pay-
ing the rent for the space.[44] Yet this same governmental institution had
at one time been a supporting member of Ars Aevi and was listed as
one of its sponsors. Itself poorly financed and under pressure from
international organizations to streamline its operations, the culture
ministry repeatedly reduced funding for the Historical Museum and
demanded payment for the use of some spaces, thus exacerbating the
plight of both the museum and the art depot inside it.[45]

The problematic relationship between state institutions and cultural
organizations also became apparent during the organization of Bosnia
and Herzegovina's participation at the 2003 Venice Biennale. Though
Bosnian artists had presented their works at this prestigious event in
the past, in 2003 Bosnia was for the first time represented as a sover-
eign state among the fifty-two other national pavilions at the Biennale.
The Ars Aevi project and its staff were commissioned to organize the

exhibit, with Hadžiomerspahić as the commissioner and Asja Mandić as the curator; meanwhile, UNESCO volunteered to house Bosnia's pavilion in its Zorzi palace. The result of these efforts, which were coordinated almost entirely through the Ars Aevi project, was a remarkable event at the Biennale. Bosnia's pavilion avoided some of the problems inherent in the Biennale's nationalistic structuring of representative country shows by highlighting four artists – Nebojša Šerić Shoba, Maja Bajević, Edin Numankadić, and Jusuf Hadžifejzović – whose pieces, absent from the Biennale in previous years because of the war, offered a provocative commentary on a variety of issues instead of posing as authentically Bosnian works.[46] But the political significance of Bosnia's first national appearance at this major international gathering sometimes overshadowed the artistic merits of the exhibit. For most ministers and other officials in Sarajevo, Bosnia's debut at the Biennale was an opportunity to make yet more public appearances and speeches about the importance of nurturing culture, education, and the arts. Among the many declarations was the pledge by the cantonal and federal authorities to provide funding and land for a future Ars Aevi Museum. Needless to say, not one of these promises bore fruit, and no ground was broken for the new museum. More strikingly, the government's assurances of support often turned into serious obstacles for the functioning of cultural institutions. For instance, the state authorities, who had previously agreed to commission the Biennale exhibit in the first place, later forgot their promises and covered only a small part of the costs incurred by Ars Aevi for the organization of the event. This lack of concern among the state institutions for the welfare of cultural organizations, even when they represented the state at major international events, meant that some basic conditions – such as regular salaries and working telephone lines – were not secured for the Ars Aevi's work at the Biennale.[47]

Regarding both the art depot eviction and the Biennale organization, UNESCO assistance was able to alleviate the immediate problems by supplying some funding or arranging for provisional solutions. Nonetheless, UNESCO's involvement did not contribute anything towards resolving the ongoing institutional predicament that was keeping many war-damaged cultural establishments so incapacitated that they could barely function. Given this broader context, the Ars Aevi project has fared extraordinarily well since the war, despite being compelled to wait for a museum building of its own. Throughout this liminal time, the Renzo Piano bridge has been the only completed element of the ambitious architectural project that will at some future point house the growing art collection.[48]

The Ars Aevi exhibit Between (June 2003), organized as a showcase for young artists from Bosnia (and partly as a tribute to World Refugee Day), offered an intriguing reflection on the postwar social and political milieu. The installations, raised on the empty parcel of land marked for the future complex, consisted of rows of UN High Commissioner for Refugees (UNHCR) tents, in which young artists' works were displayed. Asja Mandić, the curator of the exhibit, offered an insightful interpretation that was acutely attuned to the political underpinnings of that event: 'The idea of exhibiting artworks on the grounds of the future museum in UNHCR tents; designed for refugees, for people living temporarily in tents, suspended in between-space and between-time while their houses are not being built, is symbolic of the situation and atmosphere of the Ars Aevi Project, and of the position of young artists who have nowhere to show their works, as it is of the reality of Bosnia and Herzegovina in which life as a refugee is part of everyday experience.' Permeating the exhibited works was 'the overall socio-political situation of international isolation, destitution, spiritual and physical deracination' that left a deep imprint on most artistic and cultural production after the war.[49] The pieces of some of the eighteen participants further developed the explicit and often ironic criticisms of the Dayton accord's political impact.[50] By foregrounding the refugee camp as its site, the exhibit also called attention to the enormous political violence and the patterns of persecution that were continuing to displace millions of people around the world every year. Furthermore, by juxtaposing the position of young artists from Bosnia – a country devastated by so much political violence – with the position of refugees, the exhibit offered a trenchant commentary on the postwar marginalization of social groups and cultural issues that did not fit into the ruling principle of partition and segregation. Between thus presented opportunities to discuss the practical problems that contemporary artists were facing in Bosnia and to voice bitter grievances against the entire nationalist political order.

Yet the provocative parallels drawn between the contemporary art museum and the refugee camp in the postwar context are blurred and complicated by the presence of international organizations – particularly UN programs – across those spaces. Both the makeshift refugee tents with their visible UNHCR logos, and the future Ars Aevi Museum, for which UNESCO has pledged long-term aid, have come within the reach of various organizations' global enterprises, which together cover an immense range of political, social, and cultural issues worldwide. Though many of these organizations (UNESCO, UNHCR, UN missions to specific regions) share the same institutional basis, their disparate interventions point to an equally diverse field of definitions of 'culture' deployed by these organizations. When dealing with, for example, the idea of 'cultural heritage,' it is clear that even within the UN's own statutes 'there is no single concept of "cultural heritage"': each UNESCO instrument gives a different definition.'[51] The wide-ranging and wildly divergent programs have not propagated some all-encompassing notion of 'culture,' and as a consequence, the constantly evolving work of disparate international organizations (UN missions, but also numerous NGOs, EU institutions, and regional partnerships) has left that field broadly conceived and open to changes with respect to particular regional situations.[52]

In the case of the Ars Aevi project, the varying levels of international involvement contribute additional insights into two closely related developments already mentioned in the discussion of the Haggadah exhibit: the emergence of a complex relationship between locally based cultural institutions and international donors, and the inordinate proliferation of discourses of multiculturalism. Ars Aevi has grown from a relatively small collaborative undertaking (coordinated among art centres in individual cities) into a large-scale endeavour that is increasingly oriented towards UNESCO sponsorship. This tells us that while the project was 'international' from its very inception, the nature of its involvement with international organizations changed profoundly after the war. The postwar reconstruction established the presence of numerous programs funded by individual states and regional and global organizations; together, they promised immense resources for the renovation of many institutions across the country. As noted above, in this process these international organizations largely adopted the ethno-confessional premises on which the postwar partition was based, but did so under the pretence of multiculturalism as multiconfessionalism.

The insistence on multiculturalism as the highest cultural ideal in Bosnia also provided the impetus for the proliferation of these same terms of reference among countless local institutions, which increasingly and indiscriminately began to praise their own projects and values as 'multiethnic' and 'multicultural.'[53] The rapid spread of this new discourse occurred partly because of attempts by local institutions to curry favour with those international donors that extolled and funded examples of multiculturalism (such as the Sarajevo Haggadah). Efforts to engineer multiculturalism and multiethnicity were also powerfully reinforced by the quota system (another Dayton scaffold), which sought to create a numerically balanced representation of each nationality within some organizations.[54] But calculated decisions to use the new terms in order to gain international sponsorship contributed only slightly to the widespread adoption of discourses of multiculturalism. The burgeoning 'civil society initiatives,' cultural programs, youth forums, NGO activities, political debates, film, theatre, and music festivals, media reports, and academic conferences kept reiterating the multicultural mantra, to the point where references to multiculturalism outgrew their initial, informal fashionableness and became almost mandatory for any broader cultural institution in postwar Sarajevo.

Reiterations of typical multicultural phrases are present within Ars Aevi as well. In its early catalogues this group made very little use of the term, preferring instead the term 'International Cultural Project' and the idea of 'intercultural dialogue.'[55] However, its more recent promotional materials (especially those published after 2000) have stated that the evolving objective of Ars Aevi is 'to create an International Multicultural Center,' one that among other things will organize 'Multicultural Seminars' on art in 'Sarajevo, Multicultural Capital.'[56] Furthermore, even some methods for selecting new works specify that 'no more than two out of ten artists forming [an additional collection] nucleus should be from the same country.' As Hadžiomerspahić has put it, the point of this is to 'preserve the multicultural character of the Collection.'[57] Ars Aevi began to increasingly espouse these terms after the project began 'expanding the network of its promoters and supporters' to include UNESCO, the Council of Europe, and the European Commission.[58] The involvement of international organizations in the sponsorship of the contemporary art museum is so closely intertwined with the project's adoption of multicultural references that the two developments cannot be clearly distinguished or disentangled. Indeed, together they illustrate a crucial postwar dynamic that has characterized the flowering of multiculturalist discourse at a time of triumphant nationalist division.

Yet the all-encompassing reach of that discourse has, at the same time, slightly diffused both its multiconfessional underpinnings and almost any distinct meaning that the expression 'multicultural' might have in postwar Sarajevo. Through constant yet widely differing usage (associated with the Sarajevo Haggadah, different program descriptions, park statues, various gatherings, and countless other events and places), 'multicultural' in many instances now serves as a trite, unimaginative reference that can be applied to almost anything that is not overtly characterized by extremist nationalism. Nonetheless, the most frequent usage – 'multicultural' as a synonym for 'multiconfessional' – continues to keep tacit references to the ethno-confessional partition always present in the postwar background. Furthermore, given the international endorsement of nationalist divisions, the multiconfessional interpretation of multiculturalism has remained the most widespread and politically the dominant one, particularly with regard to the Bosnian capital. Indeed, tributes to the stereotypical image of Sarajevo's religious mosaic – complete with recycled symbols of its 'Muslim mosques, its Orthodox churches, its Hebrew temples, its Catholic churches and Cathedral' – appear in varying forms in most descriptions and visual representations of the city, including in occasional Ars Aevi promotional materials.[59] This kind of internationally sponsored propagation of multiculturalism has also meant that some of the project's events, just like other OHR or UN affairs, are attended by party functionaries, diplomats, and various political officials, who are eager to appear as generous patrons of the arts and 'multiculture.'[60]

Ars Aevi has thus found itself in a paradoxical situation. It is one of the few institutions to bring together artists who articulate far-reaching criticisms of the nationalist political order (as in the Between exhibit and in other events); yet in order to secure a viable place of its own after the siege, it has had to adopt one of the chief postwar conventions: the discourse of multiculturalism. But even though the project has partly complied with these conformist codes, Ars Aevi's substantive contributions have nonetheless created a small but significant institutional setting for contemporary art and incisive political critiques. Among the many pieces in the collection that open up questions about art, culture, and politics, the works by Maja Bajević and Jusuf Hadžifejzović present perhaps the most direct and most trenchant commentaries on the postwar situation in Bosnia.[61] In Double-Bubble, a video work, Maja Bajević nonchalantly recites phrases describing different religious practices and horrific expressions of violence; in this vein, she presents TECHNO and TURBO, two new forms of religion fittingly captured by statements and acts such as 'I go to church; I rape women.'[62] Contemporary creeds also constitute some of the subtexts of Jusuf Hadžifejzović's opus, in particular one of the pieces from his Cetinje-Sarajevo Depot. Working with found objects (as he has for most of his career), Hadžifejzović displays several wrapped – or veiled – Barbie dolls whose torsos, tightly enveloped by white gauze, are stuck in intricately engraved bullet casings, popular post-war souvenirs made by artisans in the old quarter of Sarajevo (see fig. 4.3). The works by Bajević and Hadžifejzović, both parts of the Ars Aevi collection, exemplify the kinds of artistic engagement that not only address contemporary social problems, but also confront the very structures – such as those of religion, gender, and nation – that repro-duce injustice and violence. Furthermore, these pieces point to the range and endurance of such creative work, which existed well before the war and which continues to develop with the times. Bajević's career and Hadžifejzović's works, such as his 1990 performance From Kitsch to Blood Is Just One Step, are particularly important if we are to understand that diverse, politically engaged cultural movements in the former Yugoslavia continued to advance provocative and innovative works even as these alternative scenes were devastated by the wars of the 1990s and marginalized by the postwar political order.[63] Ars Aevi, as one of the gathering places of those cultural forces, inhabited that marginal space for the entire first decade of its existence.

Nonetheless, the Ars Aevi project will likely, at some future point, achieve its original aim of establishing a permanent museum of con-temporary art in Sarajevo; or, to return to the parallels drawn by the Between exhibit, it may finally be able to leave the temporary UNHCR tents and secure a roof over its head. Yet which other 'refugees' will be left behind in postwar poverty?

Loose Ends

The destroyed and unreconstructed Museum of the 1984 Winter Olym-pic Games, the Museum of Literary and Theatrical Arts, and the former Museum of Revolution, are examples of cultural institutions that are being entirely neglected by the existing political system. Before the war, those places were living, functioning parts of city life; they reflected his-torical influences and cultural experiences that could not be categorized solely in religious terms, no matter how flexible those terms might be. Since the war, those places – even though they could represent perhaps some of the closest approximations of prewar Sarajevo – have been left shattered and have been struggling to maintain a semblance of periodic activity despite receiving little or no reconstruction funding.

4.3 Jusuf Hadžifejzović. Detail of engraved bullet casing from the Sarajevo/Cetinje Depot. (Image courtesy of Ars Aevi)

In sharp contrast, sacral buildings and religious objects, including the Sarajevo Haggadah, have occupied the most visible positions on the list of cultural reconstructive priorities of both the nationalist parties and the international organizations. The success of this particular program of reconstruction is in large part due to the world views and political agendas, shared and implemented by both nationalists and internationalists in Bosnia, that asserted religion as one of the commanding keywords in postwar culture and politics. The flourishing manifestations of multiculturalism have in effect furnished apparently unobjectionable illustrations of the basic principles of ethno-confessional partition couched in terms deemed acceptable and even desirable by the international organizations in charge of peacekeeping and reconstruction. The artists and intellectuals gathered around the Ars Aevi project have tried to confront and overcome the problems inherent in these postwar political structures, yet Ars Aevi's own success in securing international donations for the creation of a permanent museum of contemporary art also greatly depends on its adoption of the multiculturalist terminology.

Both the Sarajevo Haggadah exhibit and the Ars Aevi project have, in different ways and with different aims, become included in the post-war reconstruction. This raises further questions about the exclusion, neglect, and intolerance of other social and political issues. Indeed, the inspiring stories told about Sarajevo's famous multiculturalism and religious tolerance often stand in stark contrast to everyday life in the city since the war. In that environment – which is characterized by traumatic memoirs of the siege, high levels of permanent unemployment, a frustrating educational system, widespread suspicion against 'newcomers' from Sandžak and Kosovo, pervasive bigotry against non-heterosexuals, growing apathy towards political activism, and so on – it is not the ideals of multiculturalism, but the pressing problems perpetuated by the continuing rule of nationalists and internationalists alike, that dominate the lives of most Sarajevans.

NOTES

1 Benedict Anderson, *Imagined Communities: Reflections on the Origins and Spread of Nationalism* (London: Verso, 1983, rev. ed. 1991); the influential chapter 'Census, Map, Museum' was also reprinted in Geoff Eley and Ron Suny, eds., *Becoming National: A Reader* (Oxford: Oxford University Press, 1996), 241–58.

2 The Museum of Bosanska Krajina (or the Museum of Vrbaska Banovina, as it was called in 1930 when it was founded) was renamed the Museum of Republika Srpska at the outset of the war in 1992 and was supposed to become – as an article in *Patriot Magazin* put it – 'an institution of significance for the preservation of Serb identity.' Since its inception, however, it has been mired in serious financial troubles. Eleonora Trivunović, 'Na vidiku stalna postavka,' *Patriot Magazin*, 13 October 2003. Also see Goran Tarlać, 'Rođendan pod najlonom,' *Reporter*, 19 July 2000, 22–3.

3 Nirman Moranjak-Bamburać, 'Povlaštena raskrsnica: metafora raskrsnice & jezik prostora i njegovi efekti,' *Forum Bosnae* 5 (1999), 47–58.

4 Sheldon Pollock, Homi K. Bhabha, Carol A. Breckenridge, and Dipesh Chakrabarty, 'Cosmopolitanisms,' *Public Culture* 12, no. 3 (2002): 577–89.

5 However, this was not the first attempt to establish a museum in Bosnia. Ivan Franjo Jukić proposed (but did not manage) to found a 'Bosnian

museum' several decades earlier; see his 'Molba I' at the end of *Bosanski Prijatelj* I (Zagreb, 1850).

6 Even though the meaning of *Zemaljski* is much closer to 'Provincial' or 'Regional,' today the museum's name is most frequently translated as 'National.' For example, see the official website of the Zemaljski muzej/ National Museum: http://www.zemaljskimuzej.ba (accessed 15 June 2004). Following official usages of both terms, in this paper I use 'Regional' to refer to the museum up to 1992, and 'National' for contemporary usage.

7 Almas Dautbegović, 'Uz stogodišnjicu Zemaljskog muzeja Bosne i Hercegovine u Sarajevu,' in *Spomenica stogodišnjice rada Zemaljskog muzeja Bosne i Hercegovina* (Sarajevo: Svjetlost, 1988), 12. Benjamin von Kállay, the finance minister and chief official in the region, nicely summed up the Habsburg colonial aspirations in Bosnia: 'Austria is a great Occidental Empire, charged with the mission of carrying civilization to Oriental peoples'; quoted in Robert Donia, *Islam under the Double Eagle: The Muslims of Bosnia-Herzegovina, 1878–1914* (Boulder, CO: East European Monographs, 1981), 14–15.

8 Svjetlana Papo, 'Sarajevska Hagada,' *Bibliotekarstvo: Godišnjak društva bibliotekara Bosne i Hercegovine* 43–6 (1998–2001).

9 Following Anderson, it could be suggested that the colonial legacy in archaeology deeply influenced and shaped the later Bosniac nationalist movement in Bosnia, especially in the logoization of *stećci*, or medieval tombstones that grace the front garden of the Zemaljski muzej, and of fleur-de-lis regalia that appeared in the 1990s on various army and militia uniforms, publication names, office logos, and currency imprints.

10 On the interwar period, see Ladislav Šik, 'Zašto skrivamo sarajevsku Haggadu,' *Jevrejski glas*, 1 April 1931, 2; also Dušan Marinković, *Sarajevske muzeje treba pomoći!* (Sarajevo: Obod, 1926). See Dautbegović, 'Uz stogodišnjicu,' 18–34, for an overview of museum activities in the past century.

11 In an address to the academic gathering that marked the five hundredth anniversary of the coming of Sephardic Jews to Bosnia (1492–1992), the then-president Alija Izetbegović wrote that 'today the people of Bosnia and Herzegovina experience a genocide, such as was done to the Jews in World War II.' 'Pozdravna riječ,' *Oslobođenje*, 12 September 1992; reprinted in *Sefarad 92: Zbornik radova* (Sarajevo: Institut za istoriju, Jevrejska zajednica, 1995). For the appeal made by religious leaders gathered at the U.S. Holocaust Memorial Museum, see Judith Weinraub, 'Never Again, Religious Leaders Protest Carnage in Bosnia,' *Washington Post*, 4 August 1995, D1.

12 The most common version of how the Haggadah was saved from the Nazis generally involves the museum director, Jozo Petrović, improvising a lie

about the manuscript's whereabouts to the German general who attempted to seize it; meanwhile the curator Derviš Korkut arranged to hide the Jewish prayer book at a Muslim cleric's house in a mountain village. Vlajko Palavestra, 'Pričanja o sudbini sarajevske Haggade,' in *Sefarad 92*, 305–312. Variations on this version were almost always cited in major journalistic reports (see below for reports in the *New York Times*, the *Jerusalem Post*, the *Washington Post*, ABC's *Nightline*, *The Village Voice*, Associated Press releases, and so on). Yet as Kemal Bakaršić convincingly demonstrates, proving exactly what happened with the Sarajevo Haggadah during the Second World War is extremely difficult; while it is reliably certain that Petrović and Korkut did something to hide the manuscript from the Nazis, both the prevalent 'mountain village' story and existing archival documents are so ambiguous and riddled with contradictions that they cannot adequately explain exactly where the Haggadah was between 1941 and 1945. 'Gdje se nalazila sarajevska Haggada u toku II svjetskog rata,' in *Sefarad 92*, 285–303.

13 See Izetbegović, 'Pozdravna riječ' for an early mention of safeguarding 'multiculturalism.' As for the Haggadah during the 1992–5 war, some stories, circulated in the press during the siege, have the museum director Enver Imamović and 'a few soldiers' risking their lives to rescue the manuscript from imminent disaster in 1992: 'Had they come just a few minutes later, they would have found nothing because water was already up to their knees in all the Museum premises.' Mirsada Bosno, 'Umiranje Nacionalnog muzeja u Sarajevu,' *Alternativna informativna mreža*, 2 February 1995. A later account mentions the danger of a fire breaking out in addition to the threat of the flood. Vildana Selimbegović, 'Tajna austrijske kase,' *Dani*, 13 December 2002, 40–1. It is difficult to confirm details of these stories, but two things are clear. First, Enver Imamović played some part in getting the Haggadah out of the museum and into the much safer bank vault in 1992. Second, the same museum director who claimed to have heroically saved the embodiment of Bosnian multiculturalism authored several chauvinistic history books during and after the war; see Imamović, *Korijeni Bosne i bosanstva* (Sarajevo: Međunarodni centar za mir, 1995), and his *Historija bosanske vojske* (Sarajevo: Art 7, 1999). For a critique of Imamović's work, consult Jon Kvaerne, 'Da li je Bosni i Hercegovini potrebno stvaranje novih historijskih mitova?' in *Historijski mitovi na Balkanu: Zbornik radova* (Sarajevo: Institut za istoriju, 2003), 95–107. At the opening of the 2002 Sarajevo Haggadah exhibit, the UN special representative Jacques Klein thanked 'the good men ... who risked their lives to save the Haggadah in 1941 – and people like Enver Imamović who did the same thing to save this precious work in 1992.'

14 As one 1994 letter to the editor in The *New York Times* asked, 'Does anyone who reads this know the fate of the Sarajevo Haggadah? Safely hidden, as it was in World War II? Disappeared? Destroyed?' Francis B. Randall, 'Sarajevo Haggadah,' *New York Times*, 8 March 1994, A20. Also see Strajo Krsmanović, "Afera Hagada," *Alternativna informativna mreža*, 18 April 1995. The allegation that received the widest exposure was made by the American journalist Thom Shanker in 'Missing Pages,' *New Republic*, 13 February 1995, 14–15.

15 After making the speech, however, Izetbegović did not stay for the seder. Roger Cohen, 'Bosnia Jews Glimpse Book and Hope,' *New York Times*, 16 April 1995, A10. For media coverage of this Passover and the following one in 1996, see 'Medieval Haggadah opened for Sarajevo's Pesah,' *Jerusalem Post*, 16 April 1995, 2; Vince Beiser, 'In War and Peace, One of Europe's Oldest Jewish Communities Celebrates Passover,' *Village Voice*, 2 April 1996, 34. Also, a full-hour *Nightline* program dedicated to the Sarajevo Haggadah aired on ABC on 2 April 1996.

16 The Bosnian Serb proposal was that the Haggadah should rotate between Banja Luka, Mostar, and Sarajevo (that is, supposedly Serb, Croat, and Muslim cities, respectively). Aida Čerkez-Robinson, 'Bosnia's Nationalists Argue over Jewish Relic,' Associated Press, 22 December 1998.

17 Quotation from Jakob Finci, the leader of the Jewish community in Bosnia. Marcus Tanner, 'Bosnia's Serbs and Muslims Wrangle over Jews' Holy Book,' *Independent*, 23 December 1998, 8.

18 Rizo Sijarić, 'World of Museums,' *Museum Management and Curatorship* 12 (1993): 195–201.

19 As of winter 2004–5, the museum still had no heating. The little funding it once had had been gradually reduced in recent years. See Vedrana Seksan, 'Muzeje u muzej!' *Dani*, 9 November 2001, 45–7; 'Finansiranje smanjeno za 60 procenata,' *Oslobođenje*, 16 March 2002, 18; 'Bosanski barometar,' *Dani*, 1 November 2002, 7; 'Čuvarima baštine BiH prijeti gašenje,' *Oslobođenje*, 10 November 2002, 7; 'Muzej u ledenom dobu,' *Oslobođenje*, 24 December 2002, 14; 'Gavrilovic: Heating Problem in National Museum Unresolved,' ONASA News Agency, 1 October 2003.

20 'Urušavanjem zidina muzeja urušava se naša istorija,' *Oslobođenje*, 9 January 2002, 23; 'FBiH Govt. Demands Resolving of Legal Status of Cultural Institutions,' ONASA News Agency, 23 July 2003; 'Intervju s federalnim ministrom Gavrilom Grahovcem,' *FENA*, 19 June 2004.

21 As one report put it: 'Even though Bosniac [Bosnian Muslim] leaders have been the greatest proponents of a multiethnic Bosnia, their leadership has largely failed to foster conditions that welcome minorities.' Furthermore, in regions where the SDA received a majority or ruling plurality of votes

(including Sarajevo), minorities faced 'a variety of problems, including discriminatory property legislation; administrative obstacles; threats to personal security; discrimination in employment and a hostile school curriculum.' International Crisis Group, 'Rebuilding a Multi-Ethnic Sarajevo: The Need for Minority Returns,' *ICG Report no. 30*, 3 February 1998, i, 1. See also Esad Hećimović, "Biti musliman na državni način," *Dani*, 26 October 1998, 17–21.

22 Quotation from Klein interview with Ramona Koval, 'The Sarajevo Haggadah Story,' Australian Broadcasting Corporation Radio National, *Books and Writing* program, 10 February, 2002. This radio broadcast is also available via the Internet: http://www.openbook.ba/news/abc/koval.htm (accessed 26 June 2004). Ramona Koval's article 'The Sarajevo Haggadah' (based on the broadcast) also appeared in *Brick: A Literary Journal* 70 (2002): 28–38.

23 'Sarajevska Hagada se vraća u Zemaljski muzej,' *Oslobođenje*, 29 November 2002, 10; Mile Stojić, 'Hagada,' *Dani*, 6 December 2002, 15; Vildana Selimbegović, 'Tajna austrijske kase,' *Dani*, 13 December 2002, 40–1; Viola G. Gienger, '"Small Miracles" Save Jewish Text,' *Washington Post*, 14 December 2002, B9; Associated Press, Agence France Press, Deutsche Presse-Agentur, and the ONASA News Agency also carried press reports on the opening of the exhibit in early December 2002.

24 Jacques Paul Klein, 'Inauguration of the Vault Room for the Sarajevo Haggadah and Other Cultural Artifacts,' National Museum of Bosnia and Herzegovina, 2 December 2002. The full text of the speech was released by the UNMIBH and at one time was accessible via their official website: http://www.unmibh.org/stories/view.asp?StoryID=247 (accessed 14 March 2003). Sometime after the UNMIBH mandate ended, the website shut down as well.

25 'UN Forces Take Over Peacekeeping Roles in Liberia,' Associated Press, 1 October 2003.

26 'Zemaljski muzej pred zatvaranjem,' *Oslobođenje*, 12 October 2004, 2; 'Zemaljski muzej 15. oktobra zatvara vrata,' *Oslobođenje*, 14 October 2004, 2; 'Čuvari nacionalnog blaga,' *Oslobođenje*, 25 November 2004, 22; Saida Mustajbegović, 'BiH ostaje bez blaga neprocjenjive vrijednosti,' *Dani*, 26 November 2004, 62–4.

27 Bakaršić interview with Koval, ABC National Radio *Books and Writing* broadcast.

28 David Campbell, 'Apartheid Cartography: The Political Anthropology and Spatial Effects of International Diplomacy in Bosnia,' *Political Geography* 18 (1999): 395–435.

29 Mladen Paunović, 'Gdje god nađeš zgodno mjesto džamiju sagradi,' *Alternativna informativna mreža*, 22 April 1998; Dženana Karup-Druško, "Gladnom narodu raskošne džamije,' *Dani*, 22 October 1999, cover page and 16–

18. The erection of enormous new religious buildings, such as the King Al Fahd Mosque in Sarajevo, could be constructively compared with similar endeavours in Mostar (the new St Peter and Paul Church) and Belgrade (the new St Sava Church).

30 Selma Hadžihalilović, 'Nevladine organizacije u BiH,' *Alternativna informativna mreža*, 23 September 1999; Irham Čečo, 'Vjera za treći milenij,' *Dani*, 6 December 2002, 42–4; David Smock, 'Divine Intervention,' *Harvard International Review* 25, no. 4 (Winter 2004): 46–51.

31 From the statement by Jacques Paul Klein, presented at Religious Communities and Democracy in Bosnia and Herzegovina at the Beginning of the 21st Century conference, Banja Luka, 22 March 2000.

32 The Museum of the Old Orthodox Church (Muzej Stare Crkve) was founded by Jeftan Despić in 1889, only a year after the establishment of the Landesmuseum; see *Stara Crkva u Sarajevu i njen muzej* (Sarajevo: Srpsko-pravoslavna crkvena opština, 1940), 10–32.

33 In an address to the Republika Srpska National Assembly, Klein pointed out that he 'worked closely with the BiH Inter-Religious Council to establish "the four religious sites project." … This initiative will seek simultaneously to reconstruct religious and historic structures that are symbolic to each of the main religious groups in this country. We are currently examining several projects, including the completion of the restoration of the main Serb Orthodox Church in Sarajevo as well as restoration of the Old Orthodox Church Museum in that city.' Jacques Paul Klein, Address to the Republika Srpska National Assembly, Banja Luka, 3 July 2001.

34 'Peacekeeping' reference made by Klein in Koval interview; also see the achievements report issued by the UNMIBH, available at http://www.un.org/Depts/DPKO/Missions/unmibh/Achiv.pdf (accessed 29 June 2004).

35 Samuel P. Huntington, *The Clash of Civilizations and the Remaking of World Order* (New York: Simon and Schuster, 1996). Also see the introductions to separate Croatian and Serbian translations of Huntington's work: *Sukob civilizacija i preustroj svjetskog poretka* (Zagreb: Izvori, 1997); and *Sukob civilizacija i preoblikovanje svetskog poretka* (Podgorica: CID, 1998).

36 Douglas Johnston, ed., *Faith-based Diplomacy: Trumping Realpolitik* (Oxford: Oxford University Press, 2003); statement quoted from front flap.

37 Maya Shatzmiller, ed., *Islam and Bosnia: Conflict Resolution and Foreign Policy in Multi-Ethnic States* (Montreal: McGill-Queen's University Press, 2002); Rusmir Mahmutćehajić, *Bosanski odgovor: o modernosti i tradiciji* (Zagreb: Durieux, 2002); Mahmutćehajić, *Sarajevo Essays: Politics, Ideology, and Tradition* (Albany: State University of New York Press, 2003).

38 Slavoj Žižek, 'Multiculturalism, Or, the Cultural Logic of Multinational Capitalism,' *New Left Review* 225 (September/October 1997): 28–51.

39 Susan Crane, 'Memory, Distortion, and History in the Museum,' *History and Theory* 36, no. 4 (1997): 44–63.

40 Dipesh Chakrabarty, 'Museums in Late Democracies,' *Humanities Research* 9 (2002): 5–12.

41 Enver Hadžiomerspahić, 'Generalna koncepcija,' *Ars Aevi Catalogue of the Collection of the Museum of Contemporary Art (1994–1997)* (Sarajevo: Ars Aevi, 1999, 4th ed.), 10–11.

42 In the project's catalogue, each of the directors of contemporary art museums in Milan, Prato, Ljubljana, Venice, and Sarajevo wrote prefaces for the exhibits (Enrico Comi, Bruno Corá, Zdenka Badovinac, Chiara Bertola respectively, with Azra Begić and Muhamed Karamehmedović for Sarajevo exhibits). Ibid., 26–33, 58–66, 106–13, 166–73, 186–97, 210–17. For the Vienna exhibit, see the catalogue *Sarajevo 2000: Schenkungen von Künstlern für ein neues Museum in Sarajevo* (Vienna: Museum Moderner Kunst, 1998). The project, originally called Sarajevo 2000, was renamed Ars Aevi, Latin for the Art of the Age, in 1996. Besides its Latin meaning, the name represents an anagram of Sarajevo, with the letter O signified by the circle in the project's logo.

43 Quotation from the promotional catalogue *Ars Aevi Collection: Museum of Contemporary Art Sarajevo* (Sarajevo: Ars Aevi, 2004), 14. On new activities, see 'Strategija rada u muzejima,' *Oslobođenje*, 25 November 2002, 11.

44 'Ugroženo 300.000 izložbenih eksponata,' *Oslobođenje*, 3 December 2001; 'Poduzet ću sve da dug Ars Aevi bude izmiren,' *Oslobođenje*, 12 October 2002, 10; 'Bosanski barometar,' *Dani*, 18 October 2002, 7.

45 'Great Interest in Construction of Ars Aevi Museum,' ONASA News Agency, 1 July 2002; 'Conditions for Implementation of Ars Aevi Project Created,' ONASA News Agency, 27 May 2004; 'Ko je potrošio milion namijenjen muzejima?' *Oslobođenje*, 18 November 2004, 8.

46 In addition to the four artists in the pavilion, the artist Damir Nikšić, also from Bosnia, participated in the Biennale outside of the national pavilion section. See *50th International Exhibition La Biennale di Venezia: Pavilion of Bosnia and Herzegovina* (Sarajevo: Ars Aevi, 2003). On some of the political implications of national divisions and exclusions at the Biennale, see Christopher Hawthorne, 'The Venice Biennale's Palestine Problem', *New York Times*, 1 June 2003, 36.

47 See: 'Bh. umjetnici na bijenalu u Veneciji,' *Oslobođenje*, 6 March 2003, 10; 'Djela bh. umjetnika u renesansnoj palaci Zorzi,' *Oslobođenje*, 4 April 2003, 19; 'Otvoren bh. Paviljon,' *Oslobođenje*, 14 June 2003, 10; 'Bh. umjetnici

zadovoljni prezentacijom na Bijenalu,' *Oslobođenje*, 17 June 2003, 17; Vedrana Seksan, 'Pući od ponosa,' *Dani*, 20 June 2003, 44–7.

48 Speaking on one of the attractions of undertaking the Ars Aevi project, the architect Renzo Piano said that 'it is more usual to have a building without [an art] collection. But a collection without a building is a real rarity, which was fantastic for me ... The fact that the museum is being made in progress is such thanks only to the lack of money ... But we did not accept the lack of money as a limitation. We accepted it as a our chance and we based our entire project on the fact that we do not have the money.' Vedrana Seksan interview with Renzo Piano, 'Uspomene su važnije od srušenih zgrada,' *Dani*, 28 June 2002, 50–1.

49 Asja Mandić, 'Between ...,' in *Ars Aevi: izložba Između ... / exhibition Between ... Art Camp* catalogue (Sarajevo: Ars Aevi, 2003), 9–11.

50 For example, see works by Anur, Andrej Đerković, Lala Raščić, ibid., 14, 18, 36. A number of these and other young artists from Bosnia (such as Šejla Kamerić) were included in a similar Ars Aevi undertaking a year earlier in the exhibition 'U potrazi za identitetom'; see the catalogue *U potrazi za identitetom / Searching for identity* (Sarajevo: Ars Aevi, 2002), 6–9, 32–3, 36–7.

51 Jiri Toman, *The Protection of Cultural Property in the Event of Armed Conflict* (New York: UNESCO, 1996), 40.

52 Also see Thomas Hylland Eriksen, 'Between Universalism and Relativism: A Critique of the UNESCO Concepts of Culture,' in *Culture and Rights: Anthropological Perspectives* (Cambridge: Cambridge University Press, 2001), 127–48.

53 See Elissa Helms, 'The Nation-ing of Gender? Donor Policies, Islam, and Women's NGOs in Post-War Bosnia-Herzegovina,' *Anthropology of East Europe Review* 21, no. 2 (2003): 85–93.

54 The Bosnian presidency, for instance, consists of three members: a Croat, a Serb, and a Bosniac. Other political institutions also have provisions for numerically fixed representation of each nationality. See Sumantra Bose, *Bosnia after Dayton: Nationalist Partition and International Intervention* (Oxford: Oxford University Press, 2002), 41–142.

55 Hadžiomerspahić, 'Generalna koncepcija' (a reprint of the original text that was distributed from 1992 to 1997 at various Ars Aevi events).

56 Quotations are from the 2004 edition of the promotional catalogue, 10, 18; the phrasing 'Sarajevo – Multicultural Capital' is included in the Ars Aevi Manifesto, 345.

57 Hadžiomerspahić, *Ars Aevi Informator* (Sarajevo: Ars Aevi, 2003) 10.

58 Hadžiomerspahić, 'Činjenice o projektu "Kounellis u Sarajevu"' in *Projekt Ars Aevi: Kounellis u Sarajevu* (Sarajevo: Ars Aevi, 2004), 9.

59 Full-page image with the caption 'Sarajevo – Multicultural Capital,' inset in *Ars Aevi Informator*, 2. Quotation by Hadžiomerspahić, 'Loving the Differences,' in *Ars Aevi Catalogue: Eventi Tellurici: Bizhan Bassiri* (Sarajevo: Ars Aevi, 2004), 93.

60 For instance, the opening of the Ars Aevi bridge in September 2002 was attended by a number of international community officials and local politicians (however, unlike the events sponsored by UNMIBH, religious clerics were not in attendance). At the occasion, Paddy Ashdown (OHR) remarked that 'with this deed, we are closer to ending the past and entering the future'; the constant repetition of such inane statements by international officials, similar to Klein's speech about 'the end' of the Sarajevo Haggadah narrative, often served to underline the idea of ending the international work of reconstruction within the first postwar decade. 'Umjetnost spojila obale,' *Oslobođenje*, 30 September 2002, cover page and 15; 'Opservatorij,' *Dani*, 3 October 2002, 48.

61 Renata Salecl offers an intriguing discussion of the relationship between art and war, with specific reference to Marina Abramović and Anish Kapoor (whose works are featured in the Ars Aevi collection), in 'Umjetnost rata i rat umjetnosti,' *Protiv ravnodušnosti* (Zagreb: arkzin, 2002), 172–87.

62 Also see 'Maja Bajević: Black on White,' *n.paradoxa: international feminist art journal* 7 (2001): 26–7, 44.

63 For prewar background, see Ješa Denegri, 'Sarajevske umjetničke priredbe u drugoj polovini osamdesetih godina,' *Novi izraz* (1998): 163–8. For more on both artists, see Asja Mandić, 'Maja Bajević' and 'Jusuf Hadžifejzović,' *50th International Exhibition La Biennale di Venezia: Pavilion of Bosnia and Herzegovina* (Sarajevo: Ars Aevi, 2003), 28–47, 48–67.

5 Building a Jewish Museum in Germany in the Twenty-First Century

BERNHARD PURIN

Postwar West Germany had difficulty dealing with its anti-Semitic past. In the 1950s, there was no public interest in the history of the Nazi period, nor was there interest in dealing with the history of Jews in Germany. *The Diary of Anne Frank* was published in German in 1950, but its preface mentions only the 'fate of a girl during the war,' and it found only a limited market (Gilman 1988). The first postwar attempts to display Jewish history and culture can be traced to the 1960s. The major Jewish exhibitions in those years were Synagoga, which was organized by the municipal museums in Recklinghausen and Frankfurt in 1960–1 and Monumenta Judaica – 2000 Years of Jewish History and Culture on the Rhine, at Cologne's municipal museum (Stadtmuseum) in 1963–4 (see fig. 5.1). These exhibitions presented a broad overview of Jewish history in Germany from the Roman era to the early 1930s. The Holocaust was not featured as an issue for discussion, but it should be noted that the term 'Holocaust' was not widely used in Germany until the late 1970s. The catalogues of both exhibitions mention only 'das Schicksal der Juden am Rhein im Nationalsozialistischen Einheitsstaat' (the fate of the Rhineland Jews in the unified National-Socialist state) (Düwell 1963, B730–B791). And, in his preface to the Synagoga catalogue, the mayor of Frankfurt referred to the 'Greueltaten, die im Namen des deutschen Volkes an Juden verübt wurden' (atrocities that were committed against Jews in the name of the German people) (Historisches Museum Frankfurt/M 1961, 7).

In the 1960s, the main events dealing with the 'Shoah,' – the Eichmann trial in Jerusalem and the Auschwitz trials in Frankfurt – did not initiate new discussions regarding Germany's Nazi past. It was in 1979 that the

5.1 Visitor viewing ritual objects at the exhibition Monumenta Judaica Cologne, 1963. (Konrad Schilling, ed., *Monumenta Judaica – 2000 Jahre Geschichte und Kultur am Rhein* [Cologne: Fazit, 1964])

American television miniseries *Holocaust* changed this situation. The broadcasting of the experiences of the fictitious Weiss family during the Shoah marked the first time that the Nazis' persecution of European Jewry became visible to large numbers of people in an individualized way, and this event made the term Holocaust common in the Federal Republic of Germany.

In those years, the 'barefoot historians' of the Dig Where You Stand school were beginning to do local research on the workers' movement. It was they who did the first research on local Jewish history, with a special focus on the Holocaust.[1] Many titles of their early publications illustrate the astonishment they felt about the fate of the Jews after decades of silence and repression: *Sie waren unsere Nachbarn* (They were our neighbours) (Sessinghaus-Reisch 1989), *Sie lebten unter uns*

(They lived among us) (Rübsam 1988), or *Plötzlich waren sie alle weg* (Suddenly they were all gone) (Streibel 1991.)

This development reached its peak in 1988, when Germany remembered the fiftieth anniversary of *Kristallnacht* (the Night of Broken Glass, 9 November 1938). As part of the commemoration, approximately four hundred books on local Jewish history were published in cities and towns throughout both Germanies. But this type of historical research also came under criticism. Monika Richarz, former director of the Hamburg-based Institute for the History of the Jews in Germany, examined most of these publications and concluded: 'As a result of local patriotism, there is often an unconscious apologetic attitude in these publications. They support a common thesis that, before 1933, there was no anti-Semitism in the community studied, and that, during the Nazi period, the perpetrators came from outside, but not from the local population' (1991, 32).

In addition to this historical work, more and more 'Jewish sites' came into the local historians' view. Jewish cemeteries, former synagogues, schools, and ritual baths were rediscovered, and many were renovated for use as small museums and memorial sites. The exact number of these small sites open to public is still unknown, but it can be assumed that there are roughly one hundred of these 'places of remembrance' all over Germany. Besides these small memorials, a few large Jewish museums were established in western Germany, starting with the opening of the Jewish Museum of Frankfurt in 1988, the Jewish Museum of Franconia with its two branches in Fürth and Schnaittach in the late 1990s, and finally, in 2001, the Jewish Museum Berlin, which has become one of the most successful and most-visited museums in Germany.[2] Recently it was followed by the Jewish Museum Munich, which opened in spring of 2007.

Conflicts in and around Jewish Museums

There is a major difference between Jewish museums in Germany and those elsewhere. Sabine Offe, a German scholar who recently published a book on Jewish museums in Germany and Austria (Offe 2000), wrote: 'Jewish Museums in Germany differ from those in the United States in that they are not embedded in contemporary Jewish life. They have been established for a largely non-Jewish public, mostly lacking in knowledge and experience of Jewish history, culture and religion. Those who conceive of, establish, and work within these museums are mostly non-Jewish Germans' (1997, 78–9). Germany's difficulties in dealing with its past and the different, non-Jewish, staff and visitors framed the controversies that surrounded nearly every Jewish museum in Germany during its development.

One of the first of these conflicts erupted in Rendsburg, a small town north of Hamburg. In the early 1980s, a former synagogue and its out-buildings which until the 1930s contained an apartment for the rabbi and his family and a kosher butcher, were rediscovered. Desecrated but not destroyed during *Kristallnacht*, they were renovated by the local historical society. Later, a regional museum, the Schleswig-Holsteinische Landesmuseum Schloss Gottdorf, became involved, and developed a concept for a permanent exhibition. The absence of objects related to the local Jewish history, and the personal interests of the curators as well, resulted in an exhibit of paintings, drawings, and sculptures by persecuted Jewish artists. The museum started to collect works by artists such as Jankel Adler, Max Liebermann, Felix Nussbaum, and Jakob Steinhardt. The opening of this museum with a permanent exhibition of persecuted art in 1988 sparked an emotional debate involving historians, art historians, and museum professionals. Some art historians questioned whether 'Jewish art' still exists, and warned about the dangers of defining art as 'Jewish' or 'persecuted.' Some historians criticized the exhibit's lack of historical background, while others noted the absence of documents directly related to the Holocaust.[3]

Another conflict arose in the early 1990s, when a Jewish museum was founded in the Austrian city of Hohenems. This museum was located in a building that had been the home of a Jewish textile factory owner, and its permanent exhibit focused on the relationship between Jews and non-Jews in Hohenems. The former Jewish population of this area lived in a Catholic environment, one in which Christian anti-Juda-ism as well as a Catholic anti-Semitism became integral components of the Christian Social Movement, which became significant starting in the 1860s. This movement became an important theme in the perma-nent exhibition. The focus on Catholic anti-Semitism provoked heated debates when local Catholic groups criticized the exhibition as an impediment to Christian-Jewish reconciliation (Greussing 1992).

But the main controversy in Hohenems centred on whether and how to display Jewish ritual objects. Before a group of museum profession-als started to develop the permanent exhibit, a society calling itself 'Friends of the Museum' began to buy Judaica for the museum's collec-tion on the antique market. They bought, among other items, Polish

Chanuka lamps, a pair of Hungarian *Rimonim* (Torah ornaments), and a wedding canopy with inscriptions in Hebrew and Romanian. In the early 1990s, no one problematized these kinds of acquisitions. The worldwide discussions around 'looted art' began only in the late 1990s. And from a museological point of view, no one discussed whether it was appropriate to visualize the culture of an Austrian Jewish community with objects from Romania. Hohenems was no exception. At that time, many small and large Jewish museums, including those in Frankfurt and Berlin, were purchasing ceremonial objects on the market. In one case – the Jewish Museum of Westphalia, in Dorsten – this acquisition policy was even visualized in one of the museum's publications, which features a photograph of the board of governors on a shopping tour in Amsterdam (Stegemann and Eichmann 1992, 16).

When the Jewish Museum of Hohenems opened its permanent exhibition in 1991, these acquisitions were not displayed, but left in the storage rooms. The museum's supporters who had purchased these objects did not understand the curators' decision and criticized it in a highly emotional way.[4] A genuine discussion of this issue was not possible at that time. As in the renovation projects in former synagogues which began in the 1980s, the main agenda of this group was to reconstruct a Jewish culture that could not be reconstructed and to heal wounds that could not be healed. Offe (2000) describes how, for some Germans, creating a Jewish museum was a way of rescuing and rebuilding the Jewish culture that had been destroyed by the Nazis, and in this way finding redemption. It was anticipated that buying and displaying beautiful Jewish ceremonial objects would accomplish this goal. *Festschriften* (commemorative volumes) published on the inauguration of former synagogues that became memorial sites or small museums often reveal this motivation. 'With the renovation of this former house of worship we hope to heal the wounds of the past' is one of the typical statements to be found in such publications (Landkreis Dillingen 1996, 7). The exhibit designed by the museum professionals in Hohenems, though, was anti-redemptive. On the basis of documents and local photographs, it displayed the persecution of the Jews of Hohenems. The display's effect was heightened by its portrayal of the local Austrian citizenry. Showcasing the beautiful objects bought abroad would have reflected the generosity of the Austrian donors; instead, the local photographs displayed in the permanent exhibit in Hohenehms identified these same citizens and/or their relatives as former Nazis and as modern-day Austrians living and working on property confiscated from their Jewish neighbours.

5.2 Members of the board of the Jewish Museum of Westphalia after a successful shopping trip to Christie's in Amsterdam. (Wolfgang Stegemann and Johanna Eichmann, *Jüdisches Museum Westfalen. Ein Beitrag zur Geschichte der Juden in
Westfalen. Katalog* [Dorsten, 1992], 16)

It was the Jewish Museum in Vienna, founded in 1895, closed by the Nazis in 1938, and reopened in 1996, that became an example for a new generation of Jewish museums in the German-speaking countries. The City of Vienna provided the Palais Eskeles (an urban villa that from 1823 to 1827 belonged to Eskeles, a Viennese court Jew) to house the museum. This elegant structure in the city centre, a stone's throw from St Stephen's Cathedral, situates Vienna's Jews and their culture in the heart of the city's historical and cultural heritage. But Felicitas Heimann-Jelinek, chief curator of this Jewish Museum, pointed out in the catalogue of the opening exhibition: 'Above all, the main interest of a post-1945 European Jewish museum should be to motivate its visitors to ask themselves the right questions' (Heimann-Jelinek 1996a, 129). And the Jewish Museum in Vienna attempts to offer a new perspective on Viennese Jewish history and the Holocaust, one that contradicts the impression made by the elegant, Old World *palais*. For example, in the permanent exhibition, ceremonial artefacts are displayed, not only in a religious context, but also as reminders of the Holocaust. The displays dealing with the Jewish holidays and the Jewish life cycle display ceremonial objects from the collection of Max Berger (1924–88), a Holocaust survivor who became a successful entrepreneur after the war. In addition, New York artist Nancy Spero created the installation *Remembrance*, comprising a series of block prints on the white walls of the ground floor exhibition hall. These prints, based on images from Austrian Jewish history and tradition, visualize aspects of remembrance and memory, including the Holocaust (Hanak and Widrich 1996, 44–9).

But the most unusual section of the museum is the historical exhibition marked by a total absence of objects. Visitors are confronted only with eighteen holograms depicting aspects of Vienna's Jewish history: 'Out of the Ghetto,' 'Enlightenment,' 'Zionism,' 'Anti-Semitism,' 'From *Zedaka* to Welfare State,' and others. In the words of Heimann-Jelinek, the exhibit 'raises doubts about the absolute expressive value of the historical items and about the concept of 'true "historical reconstruction"' (1996b, 62). Reesa Greenberg argues that 'at the Jewish Museum in Vienna, the fundamental concepts associated with modernist museums have been jettisoned and a new museum paradigm, more in keeping with the post-Holocaust era, has been created' (2003, 248).

Vienna's Jewish Museum served as a template for the Jewish Museum of Franconia in Fürth, near Nuremberg, not only because I moved from the former to the latter museum project, but also because the Fürth project was designed by Martin Kohlbauer, a Viennese architect who drafted the exhibition design for the Vienna museum as well. But in contrast to the Jewish museum in Vienna, and like other German Jewish Museum projects, the opening of the Jewish Museum of Franconia has generated debates, especially around how the museum displays the Holocaust and how it presents local Jewish history. The permanent exhibition does not include a special section on the Holocaust, but in each section of the exhibition, Holocaust-related aspects – that is, the history of the displayed objects during the Nazi period – are explained and refracted by passages from *My Life as a German and a Jew* (1933) by Jakob Wassermann (1873–1934), a Jewish writer born in Fürth. This autobiography, first published in 1921, 'was possibly the strongest expression of the anguish German Jews felt in the face of the growing tide of anti-Semitism' (Friedlander 1997, 1: 73–112).

In this way, in contrast to the Jewish Museum Berlin, for example, the museum in Fürth offers its visitors more than one way of looking at history. The display strategies employed in Fürth led to controversy in 2002, when an exhibition by a young German Jewish artist dealing with stereotypes about Jews today became a nationwide scandal, similar to the debates around the exhibit Mirroring Evil: Nazi Imagery/ Recent Art, mounted the same year at the Jewish Museum in New York.[5]

Looking back on my years in Fürth, I would argue that these controversies arose out of a misunderstanding, and out of the excessive demands made by Germans who support Jewish museum projects. Most of Germany's museums, including its Jewish museums, are established by the state, by municipalities, or by foundations, and are subsidized with public money. These museums attempt to teach about the past, and also to bring about reconciliation with the Jews. Thus Jewish museums in Germany, even the smallest ones, are expected to do the following: teach young people and adults Jewish history, be it local or broader; explain three thousand years of Jewish culture and religion in a concise manner; and document and remember the Holocaust. And they are expected to do so not only as educational institutions, but also as sites of remembrance both for the victims and for the descendants of the perpetrators. These museums are intended to express the will of German society to fight racism, and to serve as political statements of responsibility. Faced with all these expectations, they are bound to fail.

5.3 The Jewish Museum of Franconia in Fürth, located in an early eighteenth-century house of a court Jew. (Jewish Museum of Franconia, Fürth)

The Future of Jewish Museums in Germany

With the opening of the Jewish Museum of Munich in 2007, the years of establishing Jewish museums in Germany will probably come to an end. Some existing museums, especially smaller ones, may close in near future for lack of visitors. Many small Jewish museums in former synagogues are open only the first Sunday of every month and host fewer than three hundred visitors a year. Other Jewish museums, including the major ones, will change their profiles and their programs, partly because they will be working with a different kind of public. Before I discuss some of the main challenges and changes that will affect Germany's Jewish museums over the next few years, let me describe briefly the museum project in Munich, of which I am the director (Fleckenstein and Purin 2007).

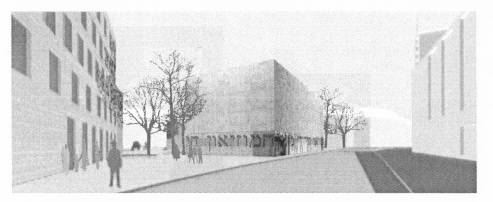

5.4 Artist's rendition of the Jewish Museum Munich, part of the New Jewish Centre. (Photo by Wandel-Hoefer-Lorch Architects, Saarbrücken)

With nearly nine thousand members, the Jewish community of Munich is the second-largest Jewish community in Germany. And it is still growing, due to a large, ongoing Jewish immigration from Eastern Europe. Because Munich's Jewish population is not concentrated in one neighbourhood, but is spread out over the entire city and its surroundings, a strong spiritual and administrative centre is needed to link together the scattered members of this community. This is the mandate of Munich's New Jewish Centre. In 2003, the Jewish community of Munich, the State of Bavaria, and the Municipality of Munich established the New Main Synagogue of Munich, the New Jewish Centre, and the Jewish Museum on one of the central squares of the city, St-Jakobs-Platz. The cornerstone was laid on 9 November 2003, exactly sixty-five years after *Kristallnacht*. The Jewish Centre St-Jakobs-Platz is the largest non-commercial project in the State of Bavaria, and probably in Germany. And it represents the largest investment of the State of Bavaria and its capital Munich in a non-commercial project. The Jewish Museum on St-Jakobs-Platz will become part of the ensemble. The City of Munich will assume responsibility for constructing the museum building, which opened in 2007, as well as the operating costs of the museum, which will have an exhibition space of approximately 930 square meters, a study area, a library, a cafeteria, and a bookshop. This Jewish museum will attempt to explore and engage the public with the Jewish past and present in Munich and in Germany.[6]

Three major challenges and changes will confront Germany's Jewish museums over the next few years. Working with these challenges could result in a new paradigm for Jewish museums, one that will inform the concept for the new Jewish museum in Munich. First, like most German museums, Germany's Jewish museums are affected by the question of how to deal with 'looted art,' that is, art appropriated from Jewish collectors during the Nazi years. For Jewish museums, this is an especially difficult problem, because they are more deeply involved in it than other museums. Nearly every Jewish museum collection item more than sixty years old was touched by the Holocaust in one way or another. These objects are silent witnesses to the Holocaust, and as the last survivors who are able to narrate their own experiences disappear, these objects will become more important for Holocaust education. Most German museums see the problem of looted art and Holocaust-related assets only as a legal issue; that said, Jewish museums can set an example by developing new ways to display these objects.

Pioneering work in this area has already resulted in a few exhibitions. In the mid-1990s I curated an exhibition on the history of Vienna's pre-war Jewish Museum during the Holocaust. It was called *Beschlagnahmt: Die Sammlung des Wiener Jüdischen Museums nach 1938* (Confiscated: The Collection of the Vienna Jewish Museum after 1938). In 1938 this Jewish museum's collection was appropriated by Adolf Eichmann. A year later, Vienna's Museum of Natural History used parts of it for an anti-Semitic exhibition titled *Das körperliche und seelische Erscheinungsbild der Juden* (The Physical and Psychological Appearance of the Jews). This exhibition displayed, not only artefacts from the confiscated collection of this Jewish museum, but also mugshots of Jews that had been taken by the Gestapo in Vienna in 1938. This exhibition, which included with statistical material and quotations from Hitler and others on the 'Jewish question,' attempted to demonstrate the alleged inferiority of the Jewish 'race' in a pseudo-scientific manner.

When this exhibit closed, the collection was parcelled out to the Museum of Natural History, the Museum of Ethnology, the Museum of Ethnography, the National Library, and the University Library in Vienna. In 1995, we (the curators of Vienna's new Jewish museum) placed vitrines containing these objects and photographs from the Nazis' exhibit in the foyers of each of these museums and libraries. In this way, we confronted not only the visitors, but also each institution with its own history, in its own building.

Some years later, when I was working at the Jewish Museum of Franconia, I became personally involved in a case of looted art, when I realized that one of our collection's highlights, an early-eighteenth-century silver Torah breastplate, was a looted artwork. This valuable piece had belonged to a South German Jewish family until 1938, when it was stolen by a Nazi stormtrooper. In the early 1990s, when the plans to establish a Jewish museum in Fürth became public, the son-in-law of the thief donated the breastplate to the city of Fürth, but without giving any information about it, or its provenance. After nearly two years of research, I found the heirs of the object's prewar owners, living in New York, and returned the piece to them. This was one of the first cases of returned Holocaust assets that was not mediated by the courts (Bohlen 2002; Purin 2001, 106–17).

In the Jewish Museum of Franconia, this act of restitution became incorporated into a section of the permanent exhibition. At a growing permanent display, visitors were informed about the current status of the research and, later, about the return of the object. Through this process, we learned that a museum's loss of an object can also be a gain. Thanks to the generosity of its current owners, the breastplate remained in Franconia's Jewish museum, on loan, until 2003, when it was moved to the local museum in Gunzenhausen, the family's place of origin, where it is now displayed. Through restitution, the breastplate has become more valuable, in a broader sense, in that its story is known and is being transmitted to the museum's visitors. Ever since the restitution in 2001, the rightful owners have 'visited' their Torah breastplate in Germany every year. The older daughter has started to learn German, and last year she visited the local school in Gunzenhausen for six weeks. The breastplate, in turn, was brought to New York in 2003 and was used at the bat mitzvah (coming-of-age ceremony) of the younger daughter. In this way, a Jewish museum display object has assumed an important function connecting past, present, and future; linking two countries; and creating community.

In Munich too, we will confront our visitors and the broader public with the issue of looted art. The opening exhibition will deal with Jewish collections and Jewish collectors in Munich (in the same way as the Thannhauser collection at the Guggenheim and the Feuchtwanger collection of the Israel Museum). We hope to bring a number of magnificent works of art to Munich to illustrate the important role played by Jews in collecting and dealing in art in a city that, from the late nineteenth century to the Second World War, was one of the most important art centres in Europe. The exhibition will not only present an art-historical view of these collectibles, but will also communicate the untold stories behind these objects, including their fate during the Nazi era when they were looted. In this way, it will become an exhibition, not only about Jewish collectors and collecting, but also about the expulsion and annihilation of the collectors and the confiscation of their collections.

A second important new development that has affected Germany's and Austria's Jewish museums in the past few years is the growing interest of descendants of German and Austrian Jewish families all over the world in becoming a part of these museums' communities. In Hohenems, for example, in 1998, the first meeting of descendants of emigrated local Jews was held. This event, initiated and organized by the descendants themselves, was attended by approximately 250 people from the United States, Great Britain, Israel, and Australia. Most of them had never visited Hohenems before. None of them was born in Hohenems, no one's parents were born there, and fewer than five of those who attended had grandparents who were born in Hohenems. Most interesting is at least half of those present at this three-day meeting were no longer Jewish. In the United States, a Society of Friends of the Jewish Museum Hohenems has been established. This group has its own website and publishes a newsletter twice a year. For the members of this society, a visit to Hohenems has become a 'must' on every trip to Europe. They also support the museum financially (Inama 1999).

In the village of Creglingen, 80 miles east of Stuttgart, a small Jewish museum was opened in 2004. Arthur Obermeyer, a philanthropist from Philadelphia, whose grandparents immigrated from this German village to the United States at the turn of the twentieth century, is the museum's main sponsor. On his website, Obermayer (2000) explains his motives:

> One of the most appealing aspects of this museum is that it represents a joint project of Germans and Jews. So many individuals from the community and region have given generously of their time and their support. The city as well has been a major donor to this project and the board has devoted countless hours to its success. This symbolizes the kind of healing process that the museum is intended to foster. What was not even an idea two years ago is now becoming a reality, and what started out as a genealogical venture is now turning into an important source of reconciliation between Germans and Jews.

In the 1980s and 1990s, many Germans became interested in building Jewish museums as a step towards German–Jewish reconciliation. In the new millennium, some descendants of emigrated German Jews seem to have also become interested in this project. This new development recalls Vera Zolberg's discussion of the wave of museum building in late-nineteenth-century North America as a measure to help heal the deep social divisions and ethnic and racial tensions of those decades and to renew national feelings and commitments (1995, 5–16).

In other places, too – for example, in Halberstadt in the former German Democratic Republic, and in Fürth – there are indications of these kinds of relationships between Jewish museums and the descendants of emigrated local Jews all over the world (Fleckenstein 2004, 19–30). At the Jewish Museum of Munich, involving the descendants of Munich's prewar Jewish emigrants will be an integral part of the concept. We will have an information and study area with special facilities for them, including databases on Shoah victims, genealogical materials, and the like. The museum will also become something of a visitors' centre for descendants who are visiting Munich, and it will develop online resources for virtual visits as well. The new communication technologies open the possibility of building a museum community whose members can participate in the museum's activities and offerings from anywhere in the world.

Third, the dramatic changes within Germany's Jewish communities since the collapse of the Iron Curtain have affected its Jewish museums. When Germany's major Jewish museums were planned in the 1980s, the country's Jewish population was less than 30,000, and the outlook for this community was bleak. Most of its members were ageing, and many of the younger generation were leaving Germany. Jewish museums were seen as a substitute for a lost culture that was no longer visible. But since the collapse of the Eastern Bloc beginning in 1989, approximately 100,000 Jews from the former Soviet Union have immigrated to Germany and changed the structure of its Jewish communities dramatically. For example, the Jewish community of Munich had 3,000 members in 1989, but, today, with nearly 9,000 members, it is the second-largest Jewish community in Germany (Berlin, with 12,000 members, is the largest). Even smaller Jewish communities, such as the one in Fürth, are growing. By the late 1980s, Fürth had formed a small Jewish congregation with fifty members. Over the past fifteen years, this group has expanded tenfold to approximately five hundred.

As a result of this development, Jewish culture in Germany has become more visible. Furthermore, for the first time in postwar Germany, the diversity of Jewish cultures has become more apparent. Until the early 1990s, Germany's Jews spoke 'with one voice,' that of the Central Council of Jews in Germany. This tradition derives from Germany's prewar *Einheitsgemeinde* (unified community), which had a single, all-inclusive local synagogue and a strong board of community leaders that represented all religious groups (Brenner 1997). But today, new Jewish groups with alternative orientations are forming, and they are clamouring for recognition. Especially in cities like Berlin, many new Jewish subcultures are thriving, from the fundamentalist Lubavitchers to the organization of Jewish gays and lesbians. But the Jewish Museum Berlin, for example, is not dealing with these new developments. Although the permanent exhibition claims to narrate the history of Jews in Germany from Roman times till today, visitors will find little information about the immigration of Jews from the former Soviet Union to Germany. I would argue that Jewish museums in Germany should be, not only places to remember German-Jewish history, but also places where the majority of Jews living in Germany can find their roots, even if these roots are linked, not with German-Jewish history, but with Russian Jewish history.

Another phenomenon that can be observed in recent years is a change in the staff of Jewish museums in Germany. Even a few years ago, no more than a handful of Jewish curators worked in Jewish museums. But today, more and more well-educated young Jewish professionals are starting to work in Jewish museums, and they will also change the profiles of these institutions. Germany's Jewish museums will probably become more 'Jewish,' in that they will no longer be German cultural-historical museums that display a lost culture. Unlike American Jewish museums, which are embedded in an elaborate Jewish infrastructure and are visited mainly by Jews, in Germany there will be an opportunity to create a new type of Jewish museum, one where Jews and non-Jews can think together about their past, present, and future and where visitors, Jewish and non-Jewish, are encouraged to deal with their common questions. But these challenges can be met only if Jewish museums in Germany cease to be understood as 'places of remembrance' and sacred spaces of memory, and come to be seen as laboratories where past, present, and future can be discussed among the curators and the visitors.

NOTES

1 Since 1956, the annual *Leo Baeck Institute Year Book* (New York: Leo Baeck Institute) has been giving the most comprehensive overview of these publications in a bibliographic appendix.
2 For an overview, see Grossman, (2003).
3 The controversy is documented in Frank Trende, (1991).
4 Offe analysed this controversy in *Ausstellungen, Einstellungen, Entstellungen* (2000, 239–85).
5 For further details of this controversy, see Kleeblatt (2002, 21–6), and Bohm-Duchen. (2002, 21–6).
6 For further details on the project, see Sachs and van Voolen, (2004, 132–5).

BIBLIOGRAPHY

Bohlen, Celestine. 2002. 'Museum Helps Jewish Family Regain Relic Nazis Stole.' *New York Times*, 28 August.

Bohm-Duchen, Monica. 2002. 'Too Fascinated by Fascism? A Response to the "Mirroring Evil" Exhibition.' *Jewish Quarterly* 49, no. 3: 21–6.

Brenner, Michael. 1997. *After the Holocaust: Rebuilding Jewish Lives in Postwar Germany.* Trans. Barbara Harshav. Princeton, NJ: Princeton University Press.

Düwell, Kurt. 1963. 'Das Schicksal der Juden am Rhein im nationalsozialistischen Enheitsstaat: Die Jahre 1933–1945.' In *Monumenta Judaica – 2000 Jahre Geschichte und Kultur am Rhein. Katalog*, edited by Konrad Schilling, B730–B791. Cologne: n.p.

Fleckenstein, Jutta. 2004. 'Nachkommen jüdischer Emigranten – Interessenten oder Akteure in jüdischen Museen?' In *NURINST – Jahrbuch 2004. Beiträge zur deutschen und jüdischen Geschichte*, 19–30. Nuremberg: Nuremberger Institut für NS-Forschung und jüdische Geschichte des 20. Jahrhundert.

Fleckenstein, Jutta, and Bernhard Purin, eds. 2007. *Jewish Museum Munich.* Munich: Prestel Verlag.

Friedlander, Saul. 1997. *Nazi Germany and the Jews*. Vol. 1. *The Years of Persecution, 1933–1939.* New York: HarperCollins.

Gilman, Sander. 1988. 'The Dead Child Speaks: Reading the Diary of Anne Frank.' *Studies in American Literature* 7: 9–25.

Greenberg, Reesa. 2003. 'The Jewish Museum, Vienna: A Holographic Paradigm for History and the Holocaust.' In *Images and Remembrance: Representations and the Holocaust*, edited by Shelley Hornstein and Florence Jacobowitz, 235–50. Bloomington: Indiana University Press.

Greussing, Kurt. 1992. *Die Erzeugung des Antisemitismus in Vorarlberg um 1900.* Bregenz: Studien zur Geschichte und Gesellschaft Vorarlbergs 10.

Grossman, Grace Cohen. 2003. *Jewish Museums of the World.* Westport, CT: Hugh Lauter Levin Associates.

Hanak, Werner, and Mechthild Widrich. 1996. 'Nancy Spero – Remembrance/ Renewal.' In Heimann-Jelinek and Sulzenbacher, *Jewish Museum Vienna.* 44–9.

Heimann-Jelinek, Felicitas. 1996a. 'Memoria, Intelligentia, Providentia.'In Heimann-Jelinek and Sulzenbacher, *Jewish Museum Vienna*, 129.

– 1996b. 'On the Historical Exhibition at the Jewish Museum of the City of Vienna.' In Heimann-Jelinek and Sulzenbacher, *Jewish Museum Vienna*, 62.

Heimann-Jelinek, Felicitas, and Hannes Sulzenbacher, eds. 1996. *Jewish Museum Vienna.* Vienna: Jewish Museum of the City of Vienna.

Historisches Museum Frankfurt/M. 1961. *Synagoga: Jüdische Altertümer, Handschriften und Kultrgeräte. Katalogue zur Ausstellung*, 7.

Inama, Johannes, ed. 1999. *Hohenems Revisited / Begegnungen in Hohenems: Meetings of Descendants of Jewish Families from Hohenems / Treffen der Nachkommen jüdischer Familien aus Hohenems.* Hohenems: Jüdisches Museum Hoherems.

Kleeblatt, Norman, ed. 2002. *Mirroring Evil: Nazi Imagery/Recent Art.* New York: Jewish Museum; New Brunswick, NJ: Rutgers University Press.

Landkreis Dillingen. 1996. *Alte Synagoge Binswangen: Eine Gedenkschrift.* Dillengen.

Obermayer, Arthur S. 2000. *Talk at Dedication of Creglingen Jewish Museum (November 19, 2000).* Available at http://www.obermayer.us/museum/ aso_speech_eng.html.

Offe, Sabine. 1997. 'Sites of Remembrance? Jewish Museums in Contemporary Germany.' *Jewish Social Studies* 3, no. 2: 78–89.

– 2000. *Ausstellungen, Einstellungen, Entstellungen: Jüdische Museen in Deutschland und Österreich.* Berlin: Philo Verlag.

Purin, Bernhard. 2001. 'Das Toraschild von Gunzenhausen.' In *Beiträge öffentlicher Einrichtungen der Bundesrepublik Deutschland zum Umgang mit Kulturgütern aus ehemaligem jüdischen Besitz*, edited by the Koordinierungsstelle für Kulturgutverlust, 106–17. Magdeburg.

Richarz, Monika. 1991. 'Luftaufnahme – oder die Schwierigkeit der Heimatforscher mit der jüdischen Geschichte *Babylon: Beiträge zur jüdischen Gegenwart* 8, 27–33.

Rübsam, Rolf. 1988. *Sie Lebten unter Uns: Zum Gedenken an die Opfer der 'Reichskristallnacht' 1938 in Bremen und Umgebung.* Bremen: Hauschild.

Sachs, Angeli, and Edward van Voolen, eds. 2004. *Jewish Identity in Contemporary Architecture.* Munich: Prestel, 132–5.

Sessinghaus-Reisch, Doris. 1989. *Sie Waren unsere Nachbarn: Spuren jüdischen Lebens in Mönchengladbach. Katalog zur Ausstellung 1989.* Mönchengladbach.

Stegemann, Wolf, and Johanna Eichmann, eds. 1992. *Ein Beitrag zur Geschicte der Juden in Westfalen. Katalog.* Dorsten: Jüdisches Museum Westfalen.

Streibel, Robert. 1991. *Plötzlich waren sie alle weg: Die Juden der 'Gauhauptstadt Krems' und ihre Mitbürger.* Vienna: Picus Verlag.

Trende, Frank, ed. 1991. *Streitfall Kunstgeschichte: Jüdische Museum Rendsburg.* Kiel: Veröffentlichungen des Beirats für Geschichte des Arbeiterbewegung und Demokratie 8.

Wassermann, Jakob. 1933. *My Life as German and Jew.* Trans. by N.S. Brainin. New York: Coward-McCann.

Zolberg, Vera. 1995. 'Culture and the Threat to National Identity in the Age of the GATT.' *Journal of Arts Management, Law and Society* 25, no. 1: 5–16.

6 Remusealizing Jewish History in Warsaw: The Privatization and Externalization of Nation Building

ROBIN OSTOW

Since the mid-1980s, but particularly in the 1990s, large, state-of-the-art Jewish museums have opened in many of Europe's capital cities. In Paris and Amsterdam, Jewish collections that had been housed in national and municipal museums have become autonomous institutions and moved into quarters of their own. In Vienna and Berlin, new museums have been built and new collections (and installations) have been acquired.[1] Bennett (1995), Zolberg (1995), and others have pointed to the traditional role of museums in nation building. Anderson (1991) describes museums as sites where states demonstrate their role as guardian of the national heritage.[2] These Jewish museum projects, realized with considerable state and municipal funding, have appeared in the context of national processes of working through histories of participation in the Nazi genocide against the Jews of Europe.

Today, with Western Europe's individual states moving towards a larger union, Jewish museums are showcasing each country's commitment to racial tolerance and displaying the kinds of minorities it will integrate. Proponents of these museums have emphasized their pedagogical role, arguing that they will prevent another Holocaust. But, ironically, as these Jewish museums were being planned and built, genocides were taking place in parts of Africa and in the former Yugoslavia, with little effective European interference. Bunzl (2004) comments that Vienna's Jewish museum showcases, not the overcoming of racism, but rather the redrawing of the fault lines separating the groups that will and will not be included in the new Europe.

After the Cold War, the states of the former Eastern Bloc also came under pressure to publicly acknowledge their role in the destruction of European Jewry under Hitler. But to date, with the important exception of Hungary in the early 1990s (discussed in István Rév's contribution to this book), their relative poverty has made it difficult for them to commit themselves to musealization, even of their own histories. Prague's enormous Jewish Museum was privatized and returned to its Jewish community in 1993. It was only the size, the quality and the decay of its inventory that attracted private, public, and international funding for its restoration (Ostow 2003). As of this writing, a major Jewish museum project is in the works in Warsaw, launched and fuelled less by developments internal to Poland than by the renewed contact of Polish Jews with Jewish organizations based in the United States. This chapter will trace the history of this initiative. It will then explore the master plan for the permanent exhibit, the discourses and debates surrounding the planned museum, and the team working towards its realization. Finally, it will place this museum project in the broader context of nation building in post-Communist Poland.

The Museum of the History of Polish Jews: The Inspiration and the Vision, 1993–2004

The museum project in Warsaw is actually a late result of what has been called the 'Americanization of the Holocaust.'[3] Though Warsaw had been home to two previous Jewish museums,[4] the impulse for this new one grew out of the establishment of the U.S. Holocaust Memorial Museum in Washington, DC, which opened in 1993. Jerzy Halberstadt and Grażyna Pawlak, both secular Jews, had grown up in postwar Poland. In the late 1980s they were working at Warsaw's Jewish Historical Society (ŻIH).[5] After the collapse of Communism, they were recruited by American Jewish organizations. Halberstadt joined the team that organized the permanent exhibit of the Holocaust Museum in Washington, and Pawlak worked with the Ronald S. Lauder Foundation, which supports Jewish religious and cultural initiatives in several European countries, including Poland. This was the time of what has been called the 'Jewish rebirth in Poland' (Gruber 1996, Gebert 2000): many Polish citizens were '(re)discovering' their Jewish identity and were beginning to 'reinvent' Jewish traditions and to reconstitute Jewish life in Poland (see Hobsbawm and Ranger 1983).

Inspired by the success of the U.S. Holocaust Memorial Museum, Pawlak thought of building a similarly impressive museum in Warsaw, but one that would exhibit Jewish life – rather than death. She obtained seed money from the Lauder Foundation and brought Halberstadt into the project. For the first couple of years, progress was slow at best. In 1996 a committee was formed to develop a plan for what would be called the Museum of the History of Polish Jews. This name was chosen to indicate that the museum would adopt a broad definition of Polish Jewry, one that would extend beyond Poland's current borders. In this museum, 'Poland' would refer to 'everything that was or is Polish,' and the category 'Polish Jews' would include 'Jewish inhabitants of Polish territory at a certain moment.'[6] A year later the city donated to the museum 13,000 square metres of land directly opposite the Warsaw Ghetto Memorial. By this time it was clear that a large, state-of-the-art museum was being envisioned. Donations were trickling in, but they were in no proportion to the dimensions of the proposed museum. By 1998, Pawlak had grown quite frustrated with the results of the fund-raising. Shortly afterwards, she left the project and Halberstadt took over.

The museum began to look financially viable once an American Jewish organizer and fund-raiser named Stephen Solender committed to it in late 2001.[7] Solender saw this museum as an important counter-balance to the concentration camp memorial culture that informs Poland's Jewish landscape. He felt that Polish Jews should not be culturally reduced to a population that had perished in the death camps. Rather, their thousand-year history in Poland and their contributions to Western democratic traditions – including the leadership of the state of Israel – should be showcased in a major way in Warsaw. But mobilizing the financial support to realize this museum proved complicated. Polish Holocaust survivors in the United States were unresponsive. Solender found that they had only bitter memories of Poland: 'They can't accept the changes at the top and the fact that anti-Semitism in Poland is now secondary.'[8] Equally important, many had already donated their money to Holocaust museums and/or memorials in the United States and Israel. Solender's target group was wealthy American Jews between forty and fifty years old and he began organizing them into groups of Founding Friends, who would donate $1,000 each. This generation, which had been seeking its 'roots,' listening to klezmer music and visiting Jewish museums since the 1980s, seemed more receptive. However, as of December 2003, funding was still far short of the museum's goal of $63 million. It was not even clear how much had been raised. In the summer of 2003 the director of development, Ewa Junczyk-Ziomecka, indicated that as donations came in they were being spent on development activities, and that as a result no money was accumulating.[9]

To suggestions that the museum be reduced to a more modest scale, Solender replied that it was important to build 'a sophisticated, high-quality product.' According to his plan, the Polish government would assume 25 per cent of the costs, American Jews 20 per cent, and European foundations and businesses the remaining 55 per cent. To achieve this goal, Solender began placing direct pressure on the Polish government; at the same time, he approached major foundations for 'conditional gifts,' which would depend on other philanthropies and on the Polish government. A major stumbling block to his campaign was that construction had not yet begun. Worse, in late 2003 the architect, Frank Gehry, left the project. The public explanation for his departure was his dissatisfaction with the amount budgeted for his fees. Privately, people close to the project attributed the disagreement to the costs of the materials he wanted to use.

By 2004 the project had half a dozen staff, who worked out of a small house in Warsaw's Marymont district when they were not on the road, raising money. In the absence of an architectural design, the museum's permanent exhibit was developed – in the parlance of the publicity brochure – 'from the inside out.'[10] The exhibit design firm Event Communications, based in the United Kingdom, was awarded the contract.[11] Together with a team of historians from Poland, the United States and Israel, it prepared a 125-page master plan. The following section examines some key portions of the March 2003 version of this document, which is still evolving.

The Master Plan: March 2003

This museum is about literally filling in a void in Warsaw's landscape. It is being built on a large empty space that was once a vibrant, densely populated Jewish neighbourhood. Like Washington's Holocaust Museum, the Museum of the History of Polish Jews will be a 'narrative historical museum.' This means that instead of displaying a collection, it will use its exhibits as building blocks in a continuous storyline. Narrative museums address visitors intellectually but also emotionally. They encourage visitors to project themselves into the story and experience it as insiders, while at the same time keeping a distance (Weinberg and Elieli 1995, 49–52). The first narrative Jewish museum was the Diaspora Museum that opened in Tel Aviv in 1978. Jeshajahu (Shaike) Weinberg, who designed this museum, was appointed director of the U.S. Holocaust Memorial Museum in the early 1990s. Before coming to the museum world, Weinberg computerized the offices of Israel's prime minister; then, for fifteen years, he served as director of Tel Aviv's theatre. His personal style fused high technology with drama to deliver a 'straightforward narrative at the expense of ambiguity, and this … precluded sustained focus on controversial issues' (Linenthal 1995, 215). In the late 1990s, Weinberg spearheaded the team planning Warsaw's Jewish Museum. His death on 1 January 2000 removed him from the project.

In contrast to the U.S. Holocaust Memorial Museum, which used largely authentic materials, the permanent exhibit in the new 'multimedia narrative museum'[12] in Warsaw was originally slated to be entirely virtual. But in response to objections from would-be supporters of the project, it was decided that 'some' (it's still vague how many) authentic objects would be displayed. Most of the installations, though, will consist of TV monitors, models, images projected against walls, replicas, voices, sounds, and smells. Some objects in the exhibits will be called 'authentic replicas' to differentiate them from more impressionistic props. The permanent exhibit is to be interactive, and the walk through the museum is described as 'edu-tainment' (Junczyk-Ziomecka and Rudzińska n.d., n.p.). 'Visitors will be taken on a virtual journey to a lost world' (ibid.). This declaration is loaded. It implies that Polish Jewish culture no longer exists, and it repeats the widespread Polish perception that Jewish culture is a sunken Atlantis. Both of these assumptions are offensive to many people who are trying to live as Jews in Warsaw today.[13]

According to this plan, the *marche* through Polish Jewish history will take the form of a large circle, with many small galleries branching off at various points. The main path will lead visitors through six major historical eras and offer a variety of experiences and opportunities for 'interaction.' Visitors will enter the exhibit through an artificial forest, which is intended to remove them from the everyday world and to show how the first Jews arrived in Poland in the Middle Ages, when most of Europe was covered in forest. The trees in this forest will not be naturalistic. Rather, they will suggest a Shakespearean forest in which humans are likely to become lost and enchanted.

The first (so to speak) human-made object in this forest will be a gravestone, a replica of a medieval tombstone from Breslau. Medieval tombstones are often exhibited in Europe's Jewish museums. The permanent exhibit in Paris's Jewish museum begins with medieval gravestones, and medieval gravestones were also on display in the Jewish museums of prewar Vienna and Prague. Rév points to the importance that nationalist groups in Eastern Europe today place on being able to document a continuous history dating from the Middle Ages.[14] Gravestones also serve to root the Jewish population in national soil. Malkki (1992) describes the rooting of peoples in the soil of their countries as part of a 'national order of things' that informs the Western imaginary. Interestingly, though, the Warsaw exhibit has also come under criticism for starting with an image of death.[15]

A large area of the permanent exhibit will display the 'Golden Age of Polish Jewish History,' the sixteenth and early seventeenth centuries. Between 1500 and 1648, Poland's Jewish population rose from 30,000 to 500,000, which made it the largest concentration of Jews in the world. During this time, Poland became the world's major centre of Jewish learning and culture. Many of Poland's most important synagogues date from this period. The exhibit will feature a model of sixteenth-century Kazimierz, the Jewish district of Cracow. Photos and blow-ups of oil paintings will be projected against the walls, and interactive monitors will allow visitors to summon details and images of Jewish life in this era. The visitors in the master plan's graphic seem to be playing, delighting in the virtual richness around them.

A side gallery will contain an 'interactive library.' Although this particular one will be a new, high-tech variation, the library, too, is a common installation in Jewish museums. Library installations can also be found in the Jewish museums in Vienna, Prague, and Amsterdam. They document the Jews' self-definition as 'the people of the book.' In another gallery, 'a larger than life Jewish wedding canopy (chupah) floats in the air. Images of a wedding are projected onto a screen (mostly from the golden age, but some from other periods too).' And sounds will be piped in (Master Plan, 52). Here, visitors will be able to play at getting married or stage their own version of *Fiddler on the Roof*.

The next historical exhibit is the small town, or 'Stetl.' This area also has a canopy – a model of the vault of an eighteenth-century wooden synagogue from the town of Wolpa. As visitors walk through this gallery, they will see images of *stetl* life projected against the walls – a marketplace, houses, fields. These images too will be enhanced by sounds, voices, and smells. From the *stetl*, the tour will head towards the city installation, which will showcase the role of Jews in modernizing Poland: 'The city bombards visitors with fast changing images, sounds and graphics in a number of languages' (ibid., 75).

Visitors will exit the city through a passage that is a reconstruction of Nalewki Street in the Jewish section of Warsaw, based on photos from the 1920s and 1930s. This section, too, will features film footage, sounds, voices, and panoramas: 'Nalewski Street suggests the potential for mutual co-existence in a reborn, democratically run Poland, and its displays aim to capture the spirit of vibrancy and confidence that marked the period.' But 'it quivers under the sense of impending doom ... Nazi bombers over Warsaw ... can just be glimpsed' (ibid., 89).

In this museum, the Holocaust will be represented by a reproduction of the Warsaw Ghetto, a rhetorical strategy of pars pro toto. This is intended to foreground local history and the tropes of resistance and martyrdom that inform Polish historical narratives. The installation will be a stage set: 'The surrounding wall will be an authentic replica of the wall built around the Warsaw Ghetto' (ibid., 95). In fact, the museum and the installation are to be constructed on the ground where the ghetto once stood. Also, this installation will reference an older exhibit on the Warsaw Ghetto, on display just a few hundred metres away at Warsaw's Jewish Historical Society. This earlier exhibit, which was mounted in 1948 and has been reorganized a number of times, displays largely authentic objects. One of the key objectives of the Warsaw Ghetto installation at the new museum will be to display 'the *shared* experiences of Poles and Jews in this period' (ibid., 97, my emphasis). 'It is important to show that this war was one of the few occasions when Poles and Jews truly identified with each other: about 10% of the Polish army was made up of Jews, and Jewish civilians engaged in wartime efforts' (ibid., 99). This message, which informed the recent film *The Pianist*, supports the museum's mandate of 'improving relations between Poles and Jews.'[16] But it is a contested position among those who experienced the Nazi invasion of Warsaw, and among historians as well (Zimmerman 2003). It is also a point of disagreement among the staff of the museum.[17]

The Master Plan sketches show how visitors will walk through the reconstructed ghetto (see fig. 6.1). 'Passageways will be narrow, more restricted than would be expected in a museum. The alleys will always appear crowded ... *Projections (images) will also inevitably fall across the visitors. They will become part of the presentation*' (My emphasis). This strategy of integrating visitors into the exhibit represents 180 degrees of difference from classical museum displays, in which vitrines distance viewers from artefacts that, in some cases, had once been part of their own or their ancestors' daily life.

At another level, while walking through what looks like a stage set with film footage projected against the walls, visitors are likely to feel

6.1 The Warsaw Ghetto installation. (Property of the Museum of the History of Polish Jews, Warsaw and Event Communications, London)

like extras in the crowd scenes in movies such as *Schindler's List* or *The Pianist*. And, like Wladyslaw Szpilmann, the protagonist in *The Pianist*, they will survive the Nazi occupation of Warsaw and walk out of the ruins. In the U.S. Holocaust Memorial Museum, visitors are encouraged to personally engage with the narrative by carrying through the exhibit a card they have been given. On this card are the name, photograph, and biography of a Holocaust victim. In the planned exhibit in Warsaw, references to popular films such as *Schindler's List* and *The Pianist* will recall to visitors real and fictional people with whom they have already imaginatively engaged, and briefly bring the visitors into the film.[18]

The sketch of the final installation shows visitors walking through a passage whose walls bear images of the piles of rubble that constituted Warsaw's cityscape after the war. From the walls protrude TV monitors with talking heads – survivors telling their stories (see fig. 6.2). The section on Jewish life in postwar Poland is still being developed. Some of the challenges involve dealing with the relationship between Poland's Jews and the Communist government and contextualizing postwar Polish anti-Semitism (official and popular), including the expulsion of 25,000 Jews in 1968.

The visit will end at another wall. But this one will be of transparent glass. Nothing will be projected against this surface. Rather, it will offer departing visitors a view of a real monument – Nathan Rapoport's Warsaw Ghetto Memorial (fig. 6.3), the first major Holocaust memorial in Europe. This massive, sculpted piece of granite, designed by a Warsaw Jew who spent the Second World War in the Soviet Union, draws heavily on the Polish discourse of heroes and martyrs and on Delacroix's romantic images of the French Revolution (Young 1993, ch. 6). It fuses the tropes of resistance and death. And it will, most likely, be the only authentic artefact displayed. It will constitute an external object that has been appropriated into the exhibit.

Today, the Holocaust memorial is a standard component in Europe's Jewish museums. These museums differentiate themselves from Holocaust memorials by setting out to display Jewish 'life,' but each one includes a major installation that functions as a kind of internal Holocaust memorial. In Prague's Jewish Museum, the empty Pinkas synagogue, with the names of 77,297 Czech and Slovak Holocaust victims inscribed on the walls, serves this function. In Paris it is Boltanski's installation – the Inhabitants of the Hotel de Saint-Argnan in 1939 – which names the deported residents of the building that

6.2 Postwar passageway. (Property of the Museum of the History of Polish Jews, Warsaw and Event Communications, London)

currently houses the Jewish Museum; and in Vienna, the *Schaudepot* (viewable storage area) on the top floor of the Jewish Museum showcases the possessions that the victims left behind.

This virtual journey through Polish Jewish history, then, will begin with a replica of a medieval tombstone in an impressionistic forest, and end with a real memorial to the heroes and martyrs of the Warsaw Ghetto. Walking through this exhibit of Polish Jewish history as a series of simulations and special effects will be like walking through and being part of a movie. In her contribution to this volume, Mieke Bal points to the present-day convergence of museum exhibits and film.[19] She sees cinematic techniques as underlying structures that shape visitors' experiences of the sequence of displays. In the Museum of the History of Polish Jews, films – especially popular films about the Holocaust in Poland – will serve to link visitors to the history of Jewish life in Warsaw, and to its original sites, which the Nazis reduced to rubble. The films, then, become hyperfacts refering to other, less visible facts.

In his chapter in this book István Rév describes the more duplicitous use of hyperfacts in the House of Terror in Budapest. In the Warsaw project, such hyperfacts are part of the legacy of the U.S. Holocaust Memorial Museum. Martin Smith was chosen as Exhibition Department Director at the museum in Washington on the basis of his television film *The Struggles of Poland*, and filmmakers worked with curators on designing the permanent exhibit (Linenthal 1995, 140–1, Weinberg and Elieli 1995, 52). If the technology of the exhibit plan in Warsaw is cutting-edge, the narrative will be a traditional epic in linear time, with moments of national grandeur and tragedy. It will focus on the richness of Jewish life in Poland and on the parallel courses of Polish and Polish Jewish history, in particular the common tropes of resistance and martyrdom. The exhibit will also be traditional in its unquestioning representation of Poles and Polish Jews as mutually exclusive categories.

The Promotional Discourses around the Museum

In addition to a master plan, the staff of the Museum of the History of Polish Jews have generated a considerable amount of promotional literature, beginning with a short article by Grażyna Pawlak outlining the ideas she was working with 1996: 'Our museum presenting the wealth of intellectual and cultural accomplishments of Polish Jews will be testimony that the Holocaust could not have been related to the manifestations of anti-Semitism in our country, but that the extermination

6.3 Frontal view of the Warsaw Ghetto Memorial's fighters. (Photograph courtesy of the Estate of Nathan Rapoport. Source: James Young, *The Texture of Memory: Holocaust Monuments and Meanings*. New Haven: Yale University Press, 1993. 173)

camps were built by the Nazis in Poland because it was the center of Jewish Europe' (1996, 108). The museum she envisioned would demonstrate that Poland was the centre of Jewish Europe and the site of cultural accomplishments. More important, it would demonstrate that the Germans, not the Poles, were responsible for the Holocaust. These are messages from Polish Jews and non-Jews to Jews in the United States and Israel, who tend to foreground Polish anti-Semitism.

Endorsements from prominent supporters of the museum have appeared in the Newsletter that is produced twice a year in Polish and English by the museum's staff. American promoters see the museum as a means to address contemporary and historical concerns of American Jews regarding Poland. Solender, the major fund-raiser, writes: 'This project has appeared at a very significant moment. In Europe, anti-Semitic tensions are on the rise; the Museum of the History of Polish Jews is a powerful statement against anti-Semitism ... The knowledge that is to be gained from our history will be presented at the museum, and will protect us in the future.'[20]. For him, the museum will serve as a cultural Maginot Line. Wiktor Markowitz, chair of the museum's American support committee, refers to the wartime failures of American Jews: 'The vast majority of American Jews – almost 80% – have Polish roots ... During the Nazi genocide, America's Jews did not help the dying Jews of Poland sufficiently. Now they should help recover the memory of their ancestors' lives which were lived on Polish soil for almost 1,000 years.'[21]

To Israeli supporters, the project looks somewhat different. Shimon Peres, then Israel's Minister of Foreign Affairs and Deputy Prime Minister (as well as chair of the International Honorary Committee of the Museum Project), saw it this way: 'It was the Jewish Community in Poland that responded to the call of Teodor Herzl, to go back to their homeland ... here was born the man who was ... the greatest Jewish leader we had in the 20th century ... David Ben-Gurion, the founder of the state of Israel ... Poland was pregnant with Jewish life and Jewish independence, but finally it gave birth to a boy: the state of Israel.'[22] Peres saw this museum in Warsaw as showcasing the prehistory of his own state, and he employed a discourse of motherhood and reproduction, often found in nationalist narratives. In this one, Poland is feminized as a mother figure in relation to Israel, which is a 'boy' (Balibar 1991).

Representing the Polish state, Aleksander Kwaśniewski, then president, hoped 'that the future museum will help the cause of Polish-Jewish reconciliation.'[23] A more elaborate Polish message soliciting support for the museum appeared in the daily *Rzeczpospolita* in December 2003. It was written by Maciej Kozłowski, former Polish Ambassador to Israel, in anticipation of the upcoming debate in the Sejm (the Polish Parliament) regarding the allocation of 5 million złotys for the museum (Kozłowski 2003). On the basis of his 'impression that engagement and enthusiasm for this venture are much greater outside of Poland than here,' Kozłowski argued, as Solender did, that Poland needed this museum in order to 'reverse the worrisome intensification – as opposed to diminution – of anti-Semitic attitudes' (ibid.).[24] The museum would also restore the multi-ethnic dimension of Polish history that had been suppressed by the Communist government. Particularly important, it would help counter the widespread view 'that Poland is an anti-Semitic country' (ibid.).[25] Finally, Kozłowski pointed out that by attracting 250,000 tourists to Warsaw every year, the museum would stimulate Poland's economy.

Two issues behind the museum project have been left out of these discourses, though they have been brought to my attention in private. The Museum of the History of Polish Jews is seen by both Polish and Jewish leaders as linked to ongoing negotiations between the Polish government and international Jewish organizations regarding the restitution of formerly Jewish property. The symbolic, quasi-sacred character of museums precludes direct public reference to this quid pro quo; however, newspaper articles have documented how both issues are being discussed in meetings between Polish politicians and American Jewish leaders (Agence France Press 2004). In fact, the land 'donated' to the museum by the city of Warsaw in 1997 had been owned by Jews before the Nazi invasion.[26] Another contemporary Polish problem calling for damage control is the recent revelation of the extent of anti-Semitism in Poland during the Second World War. The publication in 2001 of Jan Gross's case study of a massacre of Jews in the town of Jedwabne in 1941 (Gross 2001) sparked intense debate among Poles regarding Polish responsibility for the Holocaust (Gruber 2002b, 463)[27] and caused outrage among the American and European Jewish publics.

Debates around the Museum in Poland

Despite the often effusive endorsements of public figures on both sides of the Atlantic, the reserve of many Jews in the United States regarding the Museum of the History of Polish Jews is underscored by the elaborateness of Solender's fund-raising strategies and his slow progress. Menachem Rosensaft, a New York lawyer who spent time in Poland in the 1990s, does not believe this museum will receive wide support among American Jews. To him, 'the sanitized storyline appears to gloss over and downplay the deep-rooted anti-Semitism that has shaped the history of Polish Jewry and continues to define Polish-Jewish relations.'[28] Kozłowski's article points to doubts in Poland as well. The project's $63 million budget seems even more formidable to Poles than to North Americans. And there are other issues as well. In Kozłowski's words:

> Public statements – except for those in anti-Semitic periodicals – ... tend to be positive, although critical voices can be heard ... But once one starts to talk about the museum in private, the matter looks much worse ... besides many doubts and reservations ... one can encounter, not only lack of interest, but even some ill disposition. If Jews want to build a museum, let them go ahead, but that is more their business than ours, especially since there are so many other urgent needs, also in the area of preservation and commemoration of the past.[29]

Davies (2003, ch. 7) historicizes this last point, reconstructing the Communist government's 'politics of forgetting.' This included the destruction of Warsaw's Institute of Memory in 1949 and the burning of the British archives. No new museums were built in Warsaw after the war, and most of Warsaw's older museums remain in their prewar condition. The Polish government, then, is being pressured to subsidize a very expensive museum of Jewish history at a time when there are still no adequate museums of Polish history.[30]

And opposition to the museum can be heard, not only among Poland's non-Jewish majority, but also from parts of the Jewish population. Many of Warsaw's Jews would like to see more resources allocated to support the Jewish community's activities, rather than to display Poland's Jews to the world as relics from the past (Green 2003). Some Jews think it might be more appropriate to build a museum of Polish history, with a section on Jewish life. One German journalist working out of Warsaw wondered whether high-tech 'edu-tainment' would be convincing to Polish visitors, who still understand exhibits as displays of original artefacts.[31] And Piotr Paziński, the American-born editor of *Midrasz* magazine, commented: 'Placing a totally virtual museum on this completely sterile plot of land could lead to a museum that has very little to do with reality, a double alienation of the subject matter' (Zadara 2002, 6).[32]

The Team

The Jewish museums of the 'Old Europe' – in cities like Paris, Amsterdam, Berlin, Frankfurt, and Vienna – form a network. Their curators and administrators are in close contact, and exhibits and personnel circulate among them. Cilly Kugelmann, project director of the Jewish Museum Berlin, is a former curator at the Jewish museum in Frankfurt. In the late 1990s, one of the candidates shortlisted for the position of Director of Berlin's Jewish museum was Edward van Voolen, who was then Director of the Jewish museum in Amsterdam. And Joel Cahen, the current director of Amsterdam's Jewish museum, came from the Jewish museum in Paris. The Museum of the History of Polish Jews includes no one from this (West) European Jewish museum community. Rather, the project is being steered by an intercontinental team that includes Polish, American, and Israeli historians, Jewish and non-Jewish Polish administrators, an American Jewish fund-raiser, and a British exhibit design firm. These specialists circulate in a different network, one that extends from the Holocaust Memorial Museum in Washington to Yad Vashem in Jerusalem, Event Communications in London, and the Jewish Historical Institute in Warsaw. The countries from which they come – the United States, Israel, Poland, and the United Kingdom – spearheaded or supported the invasion of Iraq over the objections of France, Germany, and most core countries of the European Union.

Conclusion

The planning team and the circle of friends of the Museum of the History of Polish Jews hope that once built, it will represent a major site of Jewish tourism in Europe. It will certainly constitute a monumental advance in the virtualization of Jewish exhibits – a trend already in progress. In 2001, Vienna's Jewish museum opened a satellite installation underground (a few hundred metres from the main building) that offers a virtual recreation of medieval Jewish Vienna. And Gruber (2002a, 127–30) describes Jewish heritage tours of sites in and around Cracow that are derived from and focus on *Schindler's List*. These tours are another example of postmodern heritage seekers approaching their history through the world of film.

In Poland particularly, the decision to go virtual should also be understood in the context of the increasing difficulty of finding 'authentic' display objects, as more museums compete for a finite number of original artefacts. Because the project in Warsaw is a latecomer to the Jewish museum scene, many choice display objects are already installed in other exhibits. In Washington's Holocaust Memorial Museum, half the original artefacts, including 90 per cent of the important original artefacts, were in fact found in Poland.[33] Some remaining authentic materials are on display in the museum housed in Warsaw's Jewish Historical Institute. This small museum, based on Polish historical research and traditional exhibition concepts, doesn't measure up to the ambitions of the Museum of the History of Polish Jews. Recently, original cobblestones from the Warsaw Ghetto have turned up in Cuba, when they are to be incorporated into a Holocaust memorial now under construction in Havana (Luxner 2004). Since the 1980s, Poland has become an exporter of original Jewish artefacts and an importer of images, sounds, voices, smells, and special effects developed in the West.

Prewar Warsaw had a small Jewish museum based on the donated collection of Mathias Bersohn, a local philanthropist and historian (Gerber 1939). This museum, which opened in 1910, never attracted serious local support, nor did it achieve the sophistication of, for example, the prewar Jewish museums in Vienna, Prague, or Berlin.[34] The Bersohn museum was dismantled by the Nazis in 1941, and large parts of its inventory have been lost (Sieramska 1996). A second museum was opened in 1948 in the Jewish Historical Institute. It was reorganized at several points in the course of the Cold War and is still open to the public. Both museums were small and amateurish, and employed conventional, though occasionally dramatic, display strategies. The Museum of the History of Polish Jews does not build on or even acknowledge these earlier institutions. It is being inspired, rather, by the Holocaust Memorial Museum in Washington. And the political pressure and financial mobilization around this project are being launched from New York, with the design coming from London.

These dynamics in the sphere of Jewish culture mirror broader economic and political patterns. Poznanski (2000) argues that as a major result of the economic and political reforms of the past fifteen years in Eastern Europe, the majority of capital assets in Poland are now in the hands of foreigners.[35] For this reason, Poland's economy today is being driven by outside interests and organized around external needs. In 2003, Poland was purchasing anti-tank missiles from Israel (Gruber 2003, 534) and the United States was announcing plans to move some of its military bases in Germany to Poland.[36] The Museum of the History of Polish Jews, as it is now envisaged and unfolding, may lead some Polish and non-Polish observers to conclude that foreign – especially American – interests are no longer content merely to restructure Poland's formerly Communist political system and economy; but are expanding their activities to include reshaping Poland's culture as well. Solender told me: 'This museum dramatizes the value system that has created the vibrancy of West European culture and the economic success of the West.'[37] It might have been more accurate to say that the team charged with creating this museum derives from – and expresses the values of – the political elites of the United States, Britain, Poland, and Israel, the countries that coalesced around the invasion and occupation of Iraq, against the objections and values of much of Western Europe and large sections of their own populations. The political fault line that has crystallized around the invasion of Iraq extends to the world of Jewish museums.

This kind of externally imposed nation (re)building – and in particular, the use of Jewish history to bring American culture and values to Poland – could misfire and spark a backlash that contains anti-Semitic elements. A precedent for this can already be seen in Dresden, another city in the former East, where the awarding of the contract to renovate the military museum to Daniel Libeskind united the city's right-wing groups against it. Their campaign, called 'Stop the Libeskind Project at the Army Museum,' did not distinguish between the design for the building and the Jewishness of the architect. And it contained pronounced anti-Semitic overtones. In the opposition's literature, Libeskind is described as wanting to use the renovation to 'document his triumph over the historical architecture of the Albertstadt' (Bozic 2004, my translation).[38] This fantasy of Jewish museums as retribution is shared by some people in America's Jewish museum community. Shandler (2004) quotes Yaffa Eliach's comment on the museum she is planning to build in Israel: '"When this museum is complete, I will be able to tell my children and thirteen grandchildren that Hitler lost and we won."' Could a new $63 million Jewish museum built under pressure from American Jewish organizations provoke a similarly aggressive reaction in Warsaw?

And will this museum, originally scheduled for completion in 2007, open its doors in the foreseeable future? In March 2005, the museum's budget had been reduced by half, to $33 million, and the national government and the City of Warsaw had pledged $13 million each. On this basis, in June 2005, an architectural design by a Finnish team led by Rainer Mahlamaki was chosen for the building. Panes of glass covering

6.4 Design of the museum building by Lahdelma & Mahlamaki Architects. (Property of the Museum of the History of Polish Jews, Warsaw and Event Communications, London).

the museum's concrete walls will cause it to glitter against the dull Warsaw city scape behind it, and the Nathan Rapoport Memorial will be left standing in its shadow (fig. 6.4). Poland's president, Lech Kaczynski, noted that the museum's price tag was still high by Polish museum standards, but it was a 'debt' that Poland owed to both the Jewish people and the Polish nation (Lefkovits 2005). Work on the new building began in June 2007. The budget is back up to $58 million, with the opening planned for 2009 or 2010. The announcement states that the museum 'will focus on how Jews lived together with Poles for centuries, but will also confront head-on the subject of anti-Semitism.'[39] But is this new, high-tech museum being conceptualized by Polish politicians in terms of the Jews' traditional social role as money lenders in premodern Europe? And will Poland's new conservative government, which is closely allied with the anti-Semitic right wing of the Catholic Church, honour its commitment?

NOTES

Many thanks to the Social Sciences and Humanities Research Council of Canada for funding the research for this essay, and special thanks to Oliver

Lubrich for his extensive and helpful comments on an earlier draft of this chapter. The author, though, assumes full responsibility for the contents.

1 Both these cities had prewar Jewish museums, which were closed and dismantled by the Nazis. In Vienna, some of the remains of the prewar collection were incorporated into the permanent exhibit of the new museum. In Berlin, the few remains of the prewar collection are housed in a small, locally oriented Jewish museum on the site of the old museum. The large building by Daniel Libeskind that opened as a museum in 2001 has a new collection of display objects and interactive installations.

2 Anderson (1991) discusses how colonial museums and excavated ruins serve to justify the presence of the imperial power. But his analysis would also illustrate how state museums showcase the importance of the state.

3 This formulation was first used by Michael Berenbaum, director of the U.S. Holocaust Memorial Museum's research institute. For him, it meant 'the attempt to link Americans to the story and to highlight professed American values through stark presentation of their antitheses in Nazi Germany.' See Linenthal (1995, 255). In Berenbaum's view, this was the mission of the U.S. Holocaust Memorial Museum.

4 In 1910 a small Jewish museum opened in Warsaw, based on the collection of Jewish art and antiques donated by Mathias Bersohn, a philanthropist and member of the executive board of Warsaw's Jewish community. In 1939, this museum was closed and its contents were appropriated by the Nazis. Very few of the items have been recovered. In 1948 the postwar Jewish Historical Institute Museum opened in the Jewish Historical Institute building at 5 Tłomackie Street. This museum is still open.

5 Warsaw's Jewish Historical Institute was established in 1947 to resume the scholarly work begun by the prewar Institute for Judaic Studies, which was dissolved by the Nazis. Through the late 1990s, it was Poland's only Jewish research institution.

6 Ewa Junczyk-Ziomecka, interview, 14 July 2003.

7 Now semiretired, Solender is former president of United Jewish Communities and former CEO of the 9/11 United Service Group.

8 Stephen Solender, interview, 23 December 2003.

9 Interview, 14 July 2003.

10 Museum of the History of Polish Jews, *Newsletter*, Summer 2003, 5.

11 This firm designed the permanent exhibit for the Talber House Museum in Poperinge, Belgium, which exhibits the Ypres Battle.

12 Museum of the History of Polish Jews, *Newsletter*, Winter 2003, 1.

13 In 2002, between 7,000 and 8,000 people were registered members of Poland's Jewish communities. But up to 40,000 Polish citizens had some

Jewish ancestry and some degree of Jewish identification. See Gruber (2000b, 463–70). Similar local reactions followed the announcement in 1988 of plans to build a Jewish museum in Vienna.

14 István Rév, personal communication, 2 March 2004.

15 Gabriele Lesser, personal communication, 14 July 2003.

16 Ewa Junczyk-Ziomecka, interview, 14 July 2003.

17 Kalina Gawlas, interview, 16 July 2003.

18 Many thanks to Oliver Lubrich for this insight.

19 See her contribution to this volume.

20 Museum of the History of the Polish Jews, *Newsletter*, Winter 2003, 9.

21 Ibid., 8.

22 Ibid., Summer 2002, 8.

23 Ibid., Winter 2003, 6.

24 See Gruber, 2002. She notes that in 2001, Poland's openly anti-Semitic radio station, Radio Maryja, and Warsaw's anti-Semitic bookstore (located in the basement of All Saints Church) were operating unhindered, and that, as every year, there were desecrations of Jewish sites. The European Union Monitoring Center for Xenophobia and Racism reported that in 2002 Poland's right-wing parties gained strength (See www.raxen.eumc.int).

25 See Iwona Irwin-Zarecka, *Neutralizing Memory* (1989). This book documents public discussions in Poland in the early 1980s from which these arguments evolved.

26 Thanks to Menachem Rosensaft for bringing this to my attention.

27 In 'East-Central Europe', Gruber (2002b) notes that these debates took place in the media, in churches, and at conferences and public meetings; and that several websites were devoted to this issue. See also Michlic (2002).

28 Personal communication, October 2005. Rosensaft cites a 2005 survey commissioned by the Anti-Defamation League which found that 52 per cent of Poles believe that Jews are more loyal to Israel than to their own countries, that Jews still talk too much about what happened to them in the Holocaust, and that 43 per cent believe that Jews have too much power in the business world and in international financial markets. More than forty years after Vatican II, 39 per cent of Poles blame Jews for the death of Jesus, as compared with 20 per cent in Hungary, 19 per cent in Switzerland, 18 per cent in Germany, 16 per cent in Austria, 14 per cent in Italy, and 13 per cent in France.

29 Kozłowski 2003, translated by Krystyna Piskorz.

30 There are, though, public discussions about building a museum of Communism in Warsaw's Palace of Culture, and a museum of the Warsaw Uprising opened in the summer of 2005.

31 Gabriela Lesser, personal communication, 13 July 2003.
32 *Midrasz* is a Jewish literary and cultural journal published in Warsaw, subsidized by the Ronald Lauder Foundation in New York.
33 Personal communication, Jerzy Halberstadt, August 1998. See also Linenthal, (1995, 147–66).
34 In the years before the Second World War, Poland had a Jewish population of three million, but most Polish Jews were workers, craftsmen, and owners of small businesses. And most Polish Jews remained faithful to Jewish Orthodoxy. Prewar Poland never developed a large class of wealthy, secular, assimilated Jews corresponding to the Jewish *bildungsburgertum* in New York, Vienna, Prague and Berlin. See Wróbel, (1991) and Wynot (1991). The role of the wealthy and the educated Jewish middle classes in building Jewish museums is described in Cohen (1998).
35 This is true for the Czech Republic and Hungary as well.
36 In 2007, this project is still in progress and is playing a major role in the deterioration of relations between the United States and Russia.
37 Interview, 23 December 2003.
38 See also Lackmann (2000).
39 See 'Polish Jewish Museum to Break Ground.' *Jewish Telegraphic Agency,* 5 June 2007.

BIBLIOGRAPHY

Agence France Presse. 2004. 'Polish Capital Gives Jewish Community Title to Property.' 7 February. http://www.channelnewsasia.com. Accessed 10 February 2004.
Anderson, Benedict. 1991. *Imagined Communities: Reflections on the Orgins and Spread of Nationalism*. Rev. ed. London: Verso.
Balibar, Étienne. 1991. 'The Nation Form.' In *Race, Nation, Class*, edited by É. Balibar and I. Wallerstein. London: Verso.
Bennett, Tony. 1995. *The Birth of the Museum: History, Theory, Politics*. New York: Routledge.
Bozic, Ivo. 2004. '1,2,3, Dresdner Keillerei: Daniel Libeskind baut das sächsische Militärmuseum.' *Jungle World*, 4 February.
Bunzl, Matti. 2004 'Of Holograms and Storage Areas: Modernity and Postmodernity at Vienna's Jewish Museum.' *Cultural Anthropology* 18, no. 4: 435–68.
Cohen, Richard. 1998. *Jewish Icons: Art and Society in Modern Europe*. Berkeley: University of California Press.
Davies, Norman. 2003. *Rising' 44: 'The Battle for Warsaw.'* London: Macmillan.

Event Communions and Museum of the History of Polish Jews . 2003. *Master Plan*. London and Warsaw.

Gebert, Konstanty. 2000. 'Eine unerwartete Wiedergeburt – Judentum in Polen.' In *Jüdische Gemeinde in Europa: Zwischen Aufbruch und Kontinuität*, edited by Brigitte Unger-Klein, Vienna: Picus Verlag.

Gerber, R. ed. 1939. *Muzeum Im. Mathiasa Bersohna*. Warsaw: Gminie Wyznaniowej Żydowskiej.

Gross, Jan T. *Neighbors: The Destruction of the Jewish Community in Jedwabne, Poland*. Princeton, NJ: Princeton University Press, 2001.

Green, Peter S. 2003. 'Jewish Museum in Poland: More Than a Memorial.' *New York Times*, 9 January.

Gruber, Ruth Ellen. 1996. *Filling the Jewish Space in Europe*. New York: American Jewish Committee.

– 2002a. *Virtually Jewish: Reinventing Jewish Culture in Europe*. Berkeley: University of California Press.

– 2002b. 'East-Central Europe'. In *American Jewish Year Book 2002*, edited by David Singer and Lawrence Grossman. 463–70. New York: American Jewish Committee.

– 2003. 'Poland.' In *American Jewish Year Book 2003*, edited by David Singer and Lawrence Grossman, 531–8. New York: American Jewish Committee.

Hobsbawm, Eric, and Terence Ranger. 1983. *The Invention of Tradition*. Cambridge: Cambridge University Press.

Irwin-Zarecka, Iwona. 1989. *Neutralizing Memory: The Jew in Contemporary Poland*. New Brunswick, NJ: Transaction Publishers.

Junczyk-Ziomecka, Ewa, and Agnieszka Rudzińska, eds. n.d. *The Open-Ended Past: 1000 Years of Jewish History in Poland*. Warsaw: Museum of the History of Polish Jews.

Kozłowski, Maciej. 2003. 'Muzeum dla Żydow czy dla Polakow?' *Rzeczpospolita*, 8 December.

Lackmann, Thomas. 2000. *Jewrassic Park: Wie baut man (k)ein jüdisches Museum in Berlin*. Berlin: Philo.

Lefkovits, Etgar. 2005. 'Warsaw Mayor: Museum "Debt" to Jews.' *Jerusalem Post*, 3 March.

Linenthal, Edward T. 1995. *Preserving Memory: The Struggle to Create America's Holocaust Museum*. New York: Penguin.

Luxner, Larry. 2004. 'In Cuban Province, Polish Stone at Center of Holocaust Memorial.' *Jewish Telegraphic Agency*, 3 May. Available at http://www.jta.org, accessed 5 May 2004.

Malkki, Liisa. 1992. 'National Geographic: The Rooting of Peoples and the Territorialization of National Identity among Scholars and Refugees.' In

Culture, Power, Place: Explorations in Critical Anthropology, edited by R. Rouse, J. Ferguson, and A. Gupta. Boulder, CO: Westview Press.

Michlic, Joanna. 2002. *Coming to Terms with the 'Dark Past': The Polish Debate about the Jedwabne Massacre.* Jerusalem: Hebrew University.

Ostow, Robin. 2003. 'Religion as Treasure: Exhibits of Rituals and Ritual Objects in Prague's Jewish Museum.' In *Die Kanon und die Sinne: Religionsästhetik als akademischer Disziplin,* edited by Susanne Lanwerd. Luxembourg: Études Luxembourgeoises d'Histoire et de Sciences des Religions.

Pawlak, Grażyna S. 1996. 'Establishing the Museum of the History of Polish Jews.' In *Jewish Historical Institute: The First Fifty Years, 1947–1997,* edited by Eleonora Bergman, 107–13. Warsaw: Jewish Historical Institute.

Poznanski, Kazimierz. 2000. 'The Morals of Transition: Decline of Public Interest and Runaway Reforms in Eastern Europe.' In *Between Past and Future: The Revolutions of 1989 and Their Aftermath,* edited by S. Antohi and V. Tismaneanu, 216–46. Budapest: Central European University Press.

Shandler, Jeffrey. Forthcoming. 'Staging the Shtetl: Yaffa Eliach's Shtetl Museum.' In *Culture Front: Representing Jews in Eastern Europe,* edited by Benjamin Nathans and Gabriella Safran. Philadelphia: University of Pennsylvania Press.

Sieramska, Magdalena. 1996. 'The Jewish Historical Institute Museum.' In *Jewish Historical Institute: The First Fifty Years 1947–1997,* edited by Eleonora Bergman, 55–61. Warsaw: Jewish Historical Institute.

Slutsky, Carolyn. 2004. 'At New Jewish Museum in Krakow, Past Seen via Lens of Poland's Present.' Jewish Telegraphic Agency, 10 May. Available at *http://www.jta.org,* accessed 12 May 2004.

Weinberg, Jeshajahu, and Rina Elieli. 1995. *The Holocaust Museum in Washington.* New York: Rizzoli Publications.

Wróbel, Piotr. 1991. 'Jewish Warsaw before the First World War.' In *The Jews in Warsaw,* edited by Władysław Bartoszewski and Antony Polonsky, 246–77. Oxford: Basil Blackwell.

Wynot, Edward D., Jr. 1991. 'Jews in the Society and Politics of Inter-War Poland.' In *The Jews in Warsaw,* edited by Władysław Bartoszewski and Antony Polonsky, 291–311. Oxford: Basil Blackwell.

Young, James E. 1993. *The Texture of Memory: Holocaust Memorials and Meanings.* New Haven: Yale University Press.

Zadara, Michal. 2002. 'A World Remembered.' *Jerusalem Report,* 6 May: 42–4.

Zimmerman, Joshua D., ed. 2003. *Contested Memories: Poles and Jews during the Holocaust and Its Aftermath.* New Brunswick, NJ: Rutgers University Press.

Zolberg, Vera. 1995. 'Culture and the Threat to National Identity in the Age of the GATT.' *Journal of Arts Management, Law and Society* 25, no. 1: 5–16.

PART FOUR

Displaying War, Genocide, and the Nation:
From Ottawa to Berlin, 2005

7 Constructing the Canadian War Museum/Constructing the Landscape of a Canadian Identity

REESA GREENBERG

Opened in May 2005, Canada's new war museum is the most important element in the recent institutionalization of a Canadian identity that is inseparable from the nation's military history. The scale and location of the new museum, so close to the Parliament Buildings, serve as advocates for the importance of Canada's military in the national psyche, as do the processes of identification built into the project's design and the museum's role in a new ceremonial landscape at the architectural heart of the nation's capital.

As a genre, national war museums are predicated on paradoxical premises. War museums are built to glorify victory but must also acknowledge the human cost. In countries like Canada, which have large immigrant populations from all over the globe, the detailed histories recounted in the exhibitions of national war museums are alien to growing segments of the population. And in countries divided by different responses to war, the histories represented in war museums are often presented as partisan. National war museums invariably are conservative and comforting, even though the experiences they present are radical and disruptive.

I want to look at how some of these paradoxes play out in the new Canadian War Museum in terms of the familiar trope of landscape and its relationships to Canadian identity. Assessing how the building works from the *outside* parallels my position as a War Museum outsider, as well as the architect's creation of an identity for the museum, which is related to but independent of its contents.

My argument is that the expanded fields of landscape in which the new Canadian War Museum operates – specifically, the newly created urban, ceremonial route that passes in front of the Parliament Buildings

7.1 The Canadian War Museum, with the Ottawa skyline in the background, 2005. Architect: Raymond Moriyama. (Photo: Harry Foster, CMC.)

linking the National War Memorial and the War Museum, and the war/peace landscape walking experience designed by the architect on site – construct two distinct identification processes: the processional and the private, neither of which entails entering the museum. As such, the new Canadian War Museum building and its site function as a potent, symbolic entity in the national imaginary, one that makes its own commentary on Canada's military history and the Canadian identity, regardless of programs *inside* the building. The generic symbolism of the war museum, with its surrounding and embodied landscapes of trauma and regeneration, allows the complex to work as a symbol for all Canadians regardless of origin, personal history, or direct involvement in Canada's wars, and serves as a bridge between a national past and a national future.[1]

Background

Talk of building a new Canadian War Museum became public in 1997, when then director Daniel Glenny suggested that one-third of a proposed $12 million addition to the Sussex Street branch be used for a Holocaust exhibit. At the time, the existing Canadian War Museum was housed in two locations. The Sussex Street building, a quasi-English, castle-like structure, originally built as Canada's Public Archives, located between the National Gallery of Canada and the Canadian Mint (see fig. 7.2), housed a three-floor chronological narrative of Canada's military history, which was told through tableaux, documents, and artefacts as well as a selection of the War Art Collection on the third floor. Vimy House on Champagne Street North, a ten-minute car ride away, was a warehouse display area and storehouse for military equipment such as airplanes, tanks, guns, and other war-related artefacts, numbering half a million items. The physical plant in both locations was undeniably outdated.

The idea for a permanent Holocaust display grew out of a well-attended May 1992 exhibition – Anne Frank in the World, 1929–1945 – at the War Museum and strong support in a visitor poll taken during that exhibition for a permanent Holocaust gallery. The plan was bolstered by recent interest in Holocaust history in the United States, which led in 1993 to the opening of the United States Holocaust Memorial Museum in Washington, DC,[2] a national and very successful museum based on the experiential forms of chronological display favoured by George MacDonald, the first director of the Canadian

Museum of Civilization (opened in 1989), under whose aegis the Canadian War Museum falls.[3] Simultaneous with discussions about expansion at the Canadian War Museum, plans for a six-storey addition to the Imperial War Museum in London – to include a two-floor, 1400 square metre Holocaust exhibit – had been accepted. (That addition opened in May 2000.) Based on the experiences of other museums, the proposed Holocaust Gallery seemed the answer to making the Canadian War Museum relevant to a wider audience, thereby increasing its visitor numbers and funding.[4]

Unlike the planning processes in the United States and in Britain, the scheme for a permanent Holocaust exhibit at the Canadian War Museum became public knowledge *before* it received a government mandate or broad endorsement from Canadian Jewish communities and, most importantly, from Canadian war veterans, who believed that all of the War Museum should be devoted to Canadian military history. The proposal became extraordinarily controversial, so much so that after Senate subcommittee hearings were held in February 1998, the concept was vetoed in favour of devoting all of the space of the proposed addition to Canada's war history. The idea that the existing museum was inadequate and the desire to build a memorial museum to the war dead had been planted in the museal and public imaginary, even if the landscape literally shifted when plans were made to erect a new building on a new site.

In the first stages of selecting a site for the new War Museum, land with military associations was chosen. On 4 November 1998, approximately one year after the controversy began, the federal government allocated 28 acres (8 hectares) of land at a decommissioned airbase in eastern Ottawa for a new, purpose-built war museum. Subsequently, that site was abandoned in favour of a more central location, adjacent to the Western Parkway and LeBreton Flats, in view and within walking distance of the Parliament Buildings (see fig. 7.2). On 23 October 2001 it was announced that the Toronto architectural firm Moriyama and Teshima, in a joint venture with the Ottawa firm Griffin Rank Cook Architects, had won the competition to design the new museum, with Raymond Moriyama as prinicipal in charge of design. To review: the proposed new Canadian War Museum morphed from an addition to an existing building, to the merging of two facilities on a former military site, to an entirely new museum as a prominent addition to the capital's museal, ceremonial, and war memorial landscape.

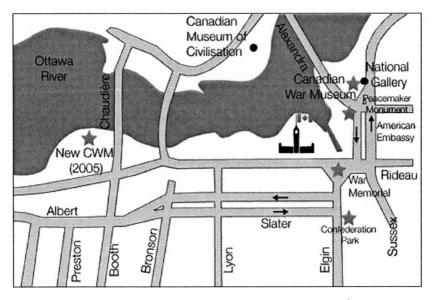

7.2 Map showing Ottawa monuments and museums.

The Site

The Canadian War Museum joins four recent memorializing projects associated with Canada's military history near the Parliament Buildings. The first was the 1997–9 reconstruction of Confederation Square to provide safer (summer) pedestrian access to the 1939 National War Memorial.[5] The rehabilitation of the square was a precondition for the construction of the Tomb of the Unknown Soldier, installed in front of the War Memorial in 2000.[6] The new addition consists of a three-tiered granite sarcophagus containing the remains of a soldier previously buried in the Canadian war cemetery at Vimy, France. The sarcophagus was designed to become the focus of future memorial events at the War Memorial site.[7]

Also in 2000, the Peacekeeping Monument, The Reconciliation, was dedicated. It is located in a traffic island between the National Gallery and the new American Embassy, within sight of the Sussex Drive War Museum building and the Parliament Buildings. The monument's vertical lines, realist portrayals of soldiers, and lists of names of those killed in action follow the model of traditional war memorials, but have been recast here to visualize Canadian peacemakers engaged in observation rather than in conflict.[8]

The Aboriginal War Veterans Monument in nearby Confederation Park, dedicated on 21 June 2001, Aboriginal Day, was *not* commissioned by the federal government; rather, it was designed and paid for by the Aboriginal community. Lloyd Pinay's stone-and-bronze twenty-seven-foot monument is prominently positioned on Elgin Street within sight of the War Memorial and the Parliament Buildings. On the day of its inauguration, Aboriginal people demonstrated in support of their land claims in front of the nearby Supreme Court of Canada suggesting that the monument is part of a broader Aboriginal strategy for full recognition of Aboriginal rights. Their argument can be summarized this way: If we fought to safeguard the land (Canada), why are our land claims not honoured?[9]

The Aboriginal War Veterans Memorial is the largest of a number of monuments that have been either designed for or moved to Confederation Park, located two blocks southeast of the War Memorial and within sight of it. These include monuments to the Boer War, monuments to Ottawans who died in wars, and most recently, the Korean War Memorial, dedicated on 23 May 2003.[10] The placement of war memorials rather than statues of politicians or monuments commemorating events that took place *in Canada* in a public space named Confederation Park seems strange, unless it is interpreted as a consolidating discourse that intertwines Canadian identity with war trauma that occurs *elsewhere*. Exemplary commitment and valiant sacrifice have long been deemed catalytic in establishing Canada's confidence as an independent nation. Today, these traits are used as a means to differentiate Canada from the United States.

The increased visibility of the military in the downtown core of the national capital parallels the increased visibility of the political profile of the military in recent years. Then Governor General Adrienne Clarkson, past chair of the Canadian Museum of Civilization (under whose aegis the Canadian War Museum falls) at the time of the War Museum expansion controversy, chose to highlight her role as commander-in-chief of the Canadian armed forces, regularly visiting troops and participating in military ceremonies, as well as taking every opportunity to support Canada's armed forces in the media. News coverage of Canada's military has grown so that almost everyday there is discussion of either the inadequacy of the armed forces' budget, or Canadian forces in peacekeeping operations, or both. In the 2006 federal election, for the first time in decades, increased funding for Canada's military was a prominent part of the platform for both leading national political parties.

Paradoxically, a new War Museum was planned and built at a time when the strength, efficacy, and reputation of Canada's armed forces were at their lowest. Proponents of Canadian military history – including Jack Granatstein, former director of the Canadian War Museum, author of the popular 2004 book *Who Killed the Canadian Military?* and a major figure in obtaining support for the final vision of the new building – berate Canadians for their ignorance of Canadian military history. The subtext is that one cannot be a Canadian without understanding that history and the importance of giving the military a prominent place in Canada's future.

In the 1970s, under Prime Minister Pierre Elliott Trudeau, the modernist concept of Canada as a colonial country gave way to the postmodern identity of Canada as a compassionate, post-colonial, multicultural nation dedicated to social justice. Canada's military history was downplayed. By the beginning of the twenty-first century, the postmodern image of Canada was set beside an increasingly visible image of Canada's role in wars fought in foreign countries. In this revived national narrative, Canada's exemplary participation in the First World War was instrumental in changing the status of Canada from colony to country; then, after the Second World War, Canada, a new nation, redefined the role of peacekeeping and won international acclaim for its exemplary leadership and ongoing service. Those who advocate increased support for Canada's military point out that without adequate funding, equipment, training, and personnel, the Canadian Armed Forces cannot fulfil their intertwined war and peacekeeping roles.[11]

The erecting of new war memorials in the nation's capital and the prominence given to the new War Museum are key elements in the institutionalization of a post-Trudeau national identity, one that links the military with social justice. When we plot it on a map, we find that the new Canadian War Museum is the western node of a cluster of military monuments near the Parliament Buildings on the Ontario side of the Ottawa River. Individually, these memorials are dedicated to the many Canadians who served and died in war – the 600,000 who served in the First World War and the 1.1 million (10 per cent of Canada's population) who served in the Second. Together, these memorials – including the new War Museum – construct a landscape of war trauma in the centre of the nation's capital. At the centre of this landscape, however, is the Peace Tower.

On Remembrance Day, the ceremony now moves from Canada's War Memorial, past the Parliament Buildings and their central Peace

Tower, to the War Museum in a ritual that links the three sites. Those participating in the procession – politicians, government officials, and, above all, veterans – enact a public, televised rite that embodies the national narrative of wars fought for peace. The collective manifestation of a nation sacrificing its citizens for world peace moves from the figurative, traditional style of the War Memorial (fig. 7.3), associated with the past, to the abstract, contemporary forms of the War Museum in a move that parallels Canada's shift from a colony to a country with worldly and worldwide aspirations. The shift from a specific to a generic national symbolic vocabulary grounded in and around the national icon of the Peace Tower also responds to a nation whose demographic composition increasingly consists of a populace with no direct links to Canada's military history. By reformulating the iconography of the national narrative, newer Canadian citizens can identify with Canada's aspirations for a peaceful country and world.

The Museal Landscape

The distinguishing feature of Raymond Moriyama's new Canadian War Museum is its emphasis on landscape. Moriyama's design retains the existing park fields of grass on the site, but as reconfigured – especially outside the museum's Military History Research Centre – the landscape is intended to allude to the undulating terrain and trenches of Beaumont Hamel in France, the site of an early First World War battle which Canadian troops won at the cost of many lives. Except for a tower that rises slowly 24.5 meters to the east, angled 'in a salute' towards the Peace Tower, the 40,860 square metre building is modest, low-lying, horizontal, and as hidden as possible. For Moriyama, its sloping grass roof symbolizes regeneration,[12] and the rooftop Memorial Garden is a 'landscape of inspiration, a quiet garden of Canadian achievements.'[13] The emptiness of the expanse of groomed land in the drawings, however, is striking, suggesting lawn cemeteries without individual graves, and the building can be likened to a burial mound (see fig. 7.4). Despite Moriyama's insistence on the regenerative qualities of the landscape, the museum can be interpreted as set in and under a landscape of loss.

The restraint of Moriyama's design contrasts with Daniel Libeskind's 2002 Imperial War Museum North in Manchester, England, the sole other recent purpose-built war museum. Libeskind's building comprises sprawling, horizontal forms and a tower – the two primary elements of

7.3 War Memorial with a view of the Parliament Buildings and Peace Tower at the left. (Photo by Reesa Greenberg.)

Moriyama's design – but Libeskind's shiny aluminium covering acts as a magnet, attracting and reflecting light and drawing attention to the building. Moriyama's self-effacing, light-absorbant surfaces and extended lines merge with the landscape of the site; by contrast, Libeskind's twisting, dynamic forms evoke the energies and transformative powers of war and fit with other postmodern buildings near its decidedly urban/industrial site. The more sober ethos of the Canadian War Museum – a building that attempts to disappear – is reminiscent of Maya Lin's 1982 Vietnam Veterans Memorial in Washington, DC, as is its more horizontal orientation and its reiteration of the earth as burial ground.[14]

Moriyama's design also echoes two other new Canadian national museums near the Parliament Buildings: it combines the triumphalist tower structure of Moishe Safdie's 1988 National Gallery of Canada to the east of the Parliament Buildings with the literal and symbolic uses of landscape in Douglas Cardinal's 1990 Museum of Civilization, directly across the river from the Parliament Buildings.[15] The three museums form a semicircle around the back of the Houses of Parliament, thus articulating Canada's varying relationships with nature and the country's proclivity for using landscape elements as symbols of national identity. Safdie's National Gallery, perched on the cliffs above the Ottawa River, is a vision of culture *dominating* nature; Cardinal's curvilinear, landscape-inspired forms for the Museum of Civilization embody an *integration* of civilization with nature which speaks to (and from) his Aboriginal status; Moriyama's war museum is designed to become *one* with nature, to be *subsumed* within nature, to *prefigure* its future as ruin in nature.[16] In Moriyama's words: 'Nature may be ravished by human acts of war, but inevitably it hybridizes, regenerates and prevails.'[17] Coincidentally, the earth on the museum's site was so contaminated that it was necessary to dig down to bedrock to remove it.

Other sights and sounds of Canada's landscapes permeate the design. Moriyama positioned the museum so that from it, in winter, the sun is seen to set in Ontario and, in summer, in Quebec. He has designed the Memorial Hall to ensure that on a sunny Remembrance Day a ray of sun will fall on the First World War soldier's tomb at its centre and, every twenty seconds or the breath cycle, a drop of water falls from the skylight into the pool below. By contrast, what Moriyama calls 'the whisper' of the Ottawa River can be heard outside the building. Moriyama speaks of the Regeneration Hall as a mountain form and describes the exterior tower as 'a symbol of our Rockies, a mountain rising out of the Prairies.'[18] For Moriyama, landscape symbolizes Canada.

7.4 Architectural sketch looking northeast along the new Canadian War Museum proposed by Raymond Moriyama. (Peter Roper).

Aside from the Canadian flag with its Maple Leaf and abstract allusion to the Atlantic and Pacific oceans, the most notable instance of visually conflating Canada with nature is the promotion of the Group of Seven's Northern Ontario landscapes as emblematic of the country's power by Eric Brown, director of the National Gallery of Canada in the 1920s and 1930s. The use of *painted* landscape as a national symbol has also played a key role with regard to building the new War Museum. In Canvas of War: Masterpieces from the Canadian War Museum (2000), a coast-to-coast travelling exhibition of sixty-eight works portraying a history of the two world wars, wall panels and the catalogue-book connect paintings of ravaged landscapes by Canadian war artists in the First World War – some of whom became members of the Group of Seven – with the development of that group's rugged landscape iconography.[19] Over the years, art historians – notably François-Marc Gagnon – have demonstrated the mythic nature of constructing an image of a national Canadian landscape based on the forests and scrub lands of Northern Ontario;[20] but in Canvas of War, an exhibition designed to garner support for the new War Museum based on the importance for Canadian heritage of the war art collection in its possession, there was no deconstruction of the myth.

Conflating the preservation of art with a desire 'to remember those who served valiantly in war and peacekeeping,' – to quote the exhibition's promotional brochure – allowed the museum to construct an acceptable rationale for its new building, thus deflecting criticism that might arise if the focus was on the $135.75 million spent for a 45,000-square-foot exhibition space devoted primarily to war histories and machinery.

Entering the Landscape

The use of travelling exhibitions designed to unite the land is a traditional device in Canada for constructing identity and identification. With the advent of the Internet, other technologies can be used to bind the country. The Canadian War Museum's website provided a live web cam of the construction site and still offers numerous web pages with information about the building, almost all of them with drawings, diagrams, maps, or photographs. The website collapses real and virtual landscape and, with its careful messaging, since its launch has been building consensus for the new museum. At one point in the design process, three sketches were posted and feedback requested. Twelve hundred responses were received.

During the time of the museum's construction, at the top of each new section of the website there was a greyscale detail of a treated photograph of soldiers moving across an empty First World War landscape.[21] The same device was used on the cover page of the museum's conceptual brochure, downloadable from the website. In both, the gentle rise of open land gestured towards the actual site of the War Museum while the walking soldiers prefigured the walk Moriyama wanted visitors to make along the museum's sloped, landscaped roof towards the Peace Tower. Originally, Moriyama's design for the War Museum was much more horizontal, but during the design process, he was asked to include an ascending feature that would function as a symbol of hope.[22] Moriyama integrated the addition with a narrative of peace, to be enacted by visitors as they walked the roof.

Moriyama's walkway rises towards what he refers to as the 'mast' of the building, which emerges from the Memorial Hall below, and framed views of the Peace Tower.[23] There are two points of access. The main route, beginning to the east of the museum entrance and placed between 9 metre walls, recreates the sense of being in a trench. A sharp turn over the entrance to the museum provides a sudden view of the Parliament Buildings. From the west, walkers re-enact the movement from war to peace, literally ascending to higher ground as they perform a transcendent ritual.

Moriyama's walk uses personal experience and participatory knowledge rather than the historical knowledge contained in the galleries below to construct embodied sensations of the route to peace. Accessible to all regardless of origin, background, or physical state, the roofscape walk is an example of what William Connolly identifies as neuropolitics, in which formal devices in mass culture mobilize thought processes subconsciously and lead to a dissection of the organization of perception. For Connolly, ideally, shifts at the individual and micropolitical level become changes in cultural values on a mass scale.[24] Moriyama's roof walk and its somaesthetics can be interpreted as a spatial device for literally rising above war. Depending on the season, the walk is pastoral or perilous.[25]

Seen in an aerial view from the riverside, the roofscape resembles an enormous, sophisticated military runway/launch pad system. From the ground, on the city sides, the building looks like a billowing ship. Morse code cut-outs for the museum's name on the facades speak to the languages of war (CWM for Canadian War Museum and MCG for Musée Canadienne de la Guerre) and the need to remember ('Lest we forget'). Moriyama describes the angled walls (7 to 31 degrees) as evoking the tumult of an urban landscape during war. Though neither the museum literature nor Moriyama address the possibility of multiple military meanings in the architectural-landscape forms, their existence complicates what might become a simplistic reading of the design.

Moriyama does speak of the dual personality of the building at street level – it is open to the city but closed to the river, the Quebec side[26] – but he does not state that these elements and the less coded river facade can be interpreted in relation to different responses to war in English- and French-Canadian communities: historically, French Canadians have been reluctant to join what they have perceived as 'England's wars.' Nor does Moriyama cite his own culture as a possible source for his use of 'borrowed scenery' – a device used in Japanese landscape architecture – to expand the actual and symbolic vista of the War Museum, most notably by incorporating the distant Peace Tower.[27] As a Japanese Canadian, Moriyama was interned in Canada during the war; yet at the beginning of his architect's statement about the Canadian War Museum, he articulates only his awareness of the 'irony and appropriateness' of being chosen as the War Museum's architect.

It is very tempting to read Moriyama's buried building in psychoanalytic terms. I know of only one other modern gallery space that has been buried intentionally: Philip Johnson's 1965 Painting Gallery on his Connecticut estate. Johnson contends that he buried the Painting Gallery because he did not wish to see it from his Glass House. In an earlier study of Johnson's gesture, I suggested that burying what he referred to as 'the bunker' may be a symbolic burying of his identity as a Nazi sympathizer in the 1930s.[28]

At the new Canadian War Museum, the building is only slightly buried, suggesting that retrieval – regeneration – of the repressed in an individual or national psyche is both preferable and possible. Moriyama's consoling, ahistoric, universalist, symbolic superstructure for the more detailed, specific, and more controversial exhibitions it covers does not preclude embedding individual identities in a national institution but it does not enshrine them. As such, Moriyama constructs a representation of nationhood that allows for diversity and various paths of identification with the national emblem of peace.

By reworking Canadian landscape tropes at the Canadian War Museum, Moriyama has done more than rework the notion of an architectural facade; he has created a model of a political landscape in which people may move as they wish but are encouraged to aspire towards peace. Moriyama's personal, private, pastoral rooftop walking experience combines with the public, processional, political, ceremonial march past the Peace Tower to inscribe rituals of Canadian citizenship onto a new national landscape, a landscape that requires collective will as well as individual participation. Both landscape experiences are 'civilized,' far removed from the untamed, unpeopled landscapes of the Group of Seven. The new icons of Canadian landscape respond to Canada's twenty-first-century national identity as a settled country that privileges peace in its national narratives.

NOTES

1 The website of the Canadian War Museum contains extensive information on the building and its exhibitions. See www.warmuseum.ca.
2 See Peter Novick, *The Holocaust in American Life* (Boston and New York: Houghton, Mifflin, 1999).
3 See George F. MacDonald and Stephen Alsford, *A Museum for the Global Village: The Canadian Museum of Civilization* (Hull: Canadian Museum of Civilization, 1989).
4 Despite different contexts, the issues posed by a memorial museum defining ethnic or national identity primarily in terms of past trauma are similarly restrictive, as is the narrative of building a nation from the ashes of war.
5 The square was 'rehabilitated' by Phillips, Farevaag, Smallenberg, Inc., of Vancouver and Ottawa to improve pedestrian access to the War Memorial and to restore the Plaza Bridge. For further information and a colour image, see http://www.cement.ca/cement.nsf/0/ 996810B2565AA9AE05256CF5006F81FA?OpenDocument
6 Illustrations, virtual tours, and additional information for the main monuments discussed in this section can be found at the following websites: National War Memorial: http://www.ottawakiosk.com/ national_war_memorial.html; Tomb of the Unknown Soldier: http://www.ottawakiosk.com/ unknown_soldier.html; Peacekeeping Monument: http://www.ottawakiosk.com/ peacekeeping_monument.html; Aboriginal War Veterans Monument: http://www.turtleisland.org/news/ news-veterans3.html.

7 A 1982 update to the War Memorial was more modest: the addition of the dates of the Second World War (1939–45) and the Korean War (1950–3).

8 The Peacekeeper Monument was designed by sculptor Jack Harman, urban designer Richard Henriquez, and landscape architect Cornelia Oberlander.

9 Stephen Thorne, 'National Aboriginal Day Celebrates Triumphs, Laments Failures,' 21 June 2001, available at http://cnews.canoe.ca/CNEWSFeatures0106/21_aboriginal-cp.html, accessed 3 February 2004. Volunteerism in the two world wars was highest among Aboriginals.

10 The design, a soldier without weapons or helmet carrying a Korean child with a second child at his side, duplicates the one at the UN War Memorial Cemetery in Korea. Prime Minister Jean Chrétien dedicated the memorial.

11 See J.L. Granatstein, *Who Killed the Canadian Military?* (Toronto: Harper-Flamingo, 2004); and Sean M. Maloney, *Canada and UN Peacekeeping: Cold War by Other Means, 1945–1970* (St Catharines, ON: Vanwell Publishing, 2002). Similar thoughts are expressed by Andrew Cohen in *While Canada Slept: How We Lost Our Place in the World* (Toronto: McClelland and Stewart, 2003).

12 Moriyama describes his ideas for the museum in the architect's statement section of the 'Building the New Museum' pages of the Canadian War Museum website. See http://warmuseum.ca/cwm/new/ca_arche.html Drawings for the museum can be found at http://warmuseum.ca/cwm/new/ca_imagese.html. Moriyama provided additional information to the author in an interview on 24 June 2004.

13 E-mail to the author, 29 June 2004.

14 Images of Libeskind's Imperial War Museum North are available at http://www.daniel-libeskind.com/projects/pro.html?ID=34. Images of Maya Lin's Vietnam War Memorial are available at http://www.bluffton.edu/~sullivanm/vietnam/vietnamlin.html.

15 Images and virtual tours of each museum are available at http://www.ottawakiosk.com/national_gallery.html and http://www.ottawakiosk.com/civilization.html.

16 See my 'Defining Canada,' *Collapse* 3 (1997): 99–102, for additional interpretive commentary on the meaning of the designs of the National Gallery and the Canadian Museum of Civilization and the importance of landscape in Canadian iconography.

17 Quoted in Director's Message on the museum's website, http://www.civilization.ca/cwm/new/ca_indexw.html.

18 E-mail to the author, 29 June 2004.

19 Dean F. Oliver and Laura Brandon, *Canvas of War: Painting the Canadian Experience, 1914–1945* (Vancouver: Douglas and McIntyre, 2000). See also http://

www.civilization.ca/cwm/canvas/cwint01e.html. Canvas of War was produced at the Canadian War Museum in Ottawa and created by the curator of the War Art Collections, Laura Brandon, who chose works drawn exclusively from the War Museum's almost 1,300 item holdings.

20 François-Marc Gagnon, 'La Peinture dans les années trente au Québec,' *Journal of Canadian Art History* 111, nos. 1 and 2 (1976): 2–20.

21 The website has been redesigned since the opening of the museum. The museum logo now consists of three abstracted ascending soldiers coloured blue on a stylized landscape of three wavy red lines. The move from specific to abstract imagery parallels the shift from the realistic imagery of the War Memorial, with its soldiers struggling in battle, to the abstract imagery of the museum.

22 The lengthy design process is discussed in Katherine Jeans's DVD documentary *In Search of a Soul: Building the Canadian War Museum* (Ottawa: Sound Venture Productions, 2005).

23 The rest of the roof is pitched and covered in copper, echoing the Parliament Buildings.

24 William E. Connolly, *Neuropolitics: Thinking, Culture, Speed* (Minneapolis: University of Minnesota Press, 2002).

25 Access to the walkway at all times is dependent on Canadian War Museum policy.

26 Moriyama cites the copper roofing on the city side of the museum as a reference to Ottawa's vernacular architectural vocabulary.

27 See Teili Itoh, *Space and Illusion in the Japanese Garden* (New York and Tokyo: Weatherhill/Tankosha, 1973) for more on borrowed scenery.

28 See my 'Private Collectors, Museums and Display: A post-Holocaust Perspective,' *Jong Holland* 1 (2000): 29–41, also available at www.reesagreenberg.net.

8 Peter Eisenman's Design for Berlin's Memorial for the Murdered Jews of Europe: A Juror's Report in Three Parts

JAMES E. YOUNG

In this three-part essay, I begin by reprinting the report I wrote on behalf of the Findungskommission* commissioned by the Berlin Senate to choose a design for Germany's national Memorial to the Murdered Jews of Europe. In the second part of this report, I tell the story of the Bundestag's debate and vote on the memorial, its role in the 1998 elections, and its eventual mandate for realization. In the final section, I reflect on the visitor's actual experience in the memorial field of stelae, after its May 2005 dedication. In this way, I hope to make it clear that Berlin's Memorial to the Murdered Jews of Europe remains a process, a public memorial in stages that continue to unfold from year to year, generation to generation.

Findungskommission Report Recommending the Eisenman/Serra Design to the Memorial Commissioners (1998)

In its original conception, the proposal by Peter Eisenman and Richard Serra suggests a startling alternative to the very idea of the Holocaust memorial. Like others in a postwar generation skeptical of a memorial's consoling function, theirs is a pointedly anti-redemptory design: it finds no compensation for the Holocaust in art or architecture. In its waving field of 4,200 pillars, it at once

---

* The *Findungskommission* was a five-member panel convened in 1997 by the City of Berlin to judge the competition to select a design for the planned Memorial to the Murdered Jews of Europe. The author of this article was the only American citizen to serve on this panel.

echoes a cemetery, even as it implies that such emblems of individual mourning are inadequate to the task of remembering mass murder. Toward this end, it takes the vertical forms of its pillars – sized from ground level to seven meters high, spaced 92 cm. apart – and turns their collected mass into a horizontal plane. Rather than pretending to answer Germany's memorial problem in a single, reassuring form, this design proposes multiple, collected forms arranged so that visitors have to find their own paths to the memory of Europe's murdered Jews. As such, this memorial provides not an answer to memory, but an ongoing process, a continuing question without a certain solution.

Part of what Peter Eisenman calls its *Unheimlichkeit*, or uncanniness, derives precisely from the sense of danger generated in such a field, the demand that we now find our own way into and out of such memory, alone and together. And because the scale of this installation would be almost irreproducible on film shot from the ground, it also demands that visitors actually enter and experience the memorial space and not try to know it vicariously through their snapshots. If the designers have their way, what will be remembered here are not photographic images but the visitors' actual experiences *in situ*. And, as might be expected in a piece partly designed by Richard Serra, with the imposing sizes of the largest stelae, the danger implied in this installation feels like something closer to an actual, rather than only metaphorical, threat.

With these thoughts in mind, we enthusiastically recommend the design by Peter Eisenman and Richard Serra to the Chancellor, the Berlin Senate, and the Citizens' Initiative Committee, but with this caveat: we ask that the designers reduce both the scale and number of stelae. For in the sheer number of its pillars and its overall scale in proportion to the allotted space, the original design leaves less room for visitors and commemorative activities than we had wanted. Some of us also find a potential for more than figurative danger in the memorial site: at seven meters high, the tallest pillars will hide many visitors from view, thereby creating the sense of a labyrinthine maze, an effect desired neither by designers nor commissioners. The potential for a purely visceral experience that might occlude a more contemplative memorial visit is also greater than some of us would have preferred. We recommend, therefore, that designers reduce both the scale and number of stelae toward these three ends: to reduce their literal, physical danger; to bring them into more human, less monumental proportion; and to open up further commemorative space along the memorial's perimeter.*

In Eisenman's revised design, I find that he has reduced both the number of pillars (from 4200 to about 3000) and their height, so that they would now range from half a meter tall to about 3 meters or so in one section of the field. Where the 'monumental' has traditionally used its size to humiliate or cow viewers into submission, this memorial in its humanly-proportioned forms should put people on an even-footing with memory. Visitors and the role they play as they wade knee-, or chest-, or shoulder-deep into this waving field of stones will not be diminished by the monumental but will be made integral parts of the memorial itself, now invited into a memorial dialogue of equals. Visitors will not be defeated by their memorial obligation here, nor dwarfed by the memory-forms themselves, but rather enjoined by them to come face to face with memory.

Able to see over and around these pillars, visitors will have to find their way through this field of stones, on the one hand, even as they are never actually lost in or overcome by the memorial act. In effect, they will make and choose their own individual spaces for memory, even as they do so collectively. The implied sense of motion in the gently undulating field also formalizes a kind of memory that is neither frozen in time, nor static in space. The sense of such instability will help visitors resist an impulse toward clo-

---

* Author's note: Before long, public consensus gathered around the design by Eisenman and Serra. It was reported that Chancellor Kohl also strongly favoured their design, and so invited the team to Bonn to hear them personally explain their proposal. During their January 1998 visit with the chancellor, Eisenman and Serra were asked to consider a handful of design changes that would make the memorial acceptable to organizers. As an architect who saw accommodation to his clients' wishes as part of his job, Eisenman agreed to adapt the design to the needs of the project. As an artist, however, Richard Serra steadfastly refused to contemplate any changes in the design whatsoever. Unlike the architect, the artist saw these suggested changes, not as modifications, but as fundamental changes to what he regarded as the work's internal logical and integrity. As a result, Serra withdrew from the project, suggesting that once changed, the project would in effect no longer be the work of art he had proposed.

In June 1998 I spent a day in Eisenman's New York City studio to hear his rationale, and to see the changes he had made, a day before he sent his newly designed model off to Berlin for safe keeping. Shortly after, I could report to the other commissioners that our suggestions had not only been expertly incorporated into Eisenman's design, but also that they worked in unexpected ways to strengthen the entire formalization of the concept itself.

sure in the memorial act and heighten one's own role in anchoring memory in oneself.

In their multiple and variegated sizes, the pillars are both individuated and collected: the very idea of 'collective memory' is broken down here and replaced with the collected memories of individuals murdered, the terrible meanings of their deaths now multiplied and not merely unified. The land sways and moves beneath these pillars so that each one is some 3 degrees off vertical: we are not reassured by such memory, not reconciled to the mass murder of millions, but now disoriented by it.

In practical terms, the removal of some 1200 pillars out of an originally proposed 4200 or so has dramatically opened up the plaza for public commemorative activities. It has also made room for tourist buses to discharge visitors without threatening the sanctity of the pillars on the outer edges of the field. By raising the height of the lowest pillar-tops from nearly flush with the ground to approximately a half-meter tall, the new design also ensures that visitors will not step on the pillars or walk out over the tops of pillars. Since the pillars will tilt at the same degree and angle as the roll of the ground-level topography into which the pillars are set, this too will discourage climbing or clambering-over. In fact, since these pillars are neither intended nor consecrated as tombstones, there would be no actual desecration of them were someone to step or sit on one of these pillars. But in Jewish tradition, it is also important to avoid the appearance of a desecration, so the minor change in the smallest pillars was still welcome.

In their neutral tone, the concrete-form pillars will reflect the colors of the sun and sky on the one hand and remain suggestive of stone, even sandstone, on the other. The concrete will not have the rough lines of their pour forms but will be smooth, close to the texture of sidewalk. They can also be impregnated with an anti-graffiti solution to make them easy to clean. Over time, it will be important to remove graffiti as it appears, in order not to allow it to accumulate.

The architect prefers that the pillars, though stone-like, remain under-determined and open to many readings: they are alternately stones, pillars, blank tablets, walls and segments. This said, in their abstract forms, they will nevertheless accommodate the references projected onto them by visitors, the most likely being the tombstone. This is not a bad thing, and suggests the need to keep these pillars blank-faced. With written text, they would look too much like tombstones, in fact, and could begin to generate a dynamic demanding some sort of formal treatment as tombstones, even symbolic ones.

For this reason, I suggest that a permanent, written historical text be inscribed on a large tablet or tablets set either into the ground or onto the ground, tilted at a readable angle. This position will bring visitors into respectful, even prayerful repose as they read the text, with heads slightly bowed in memory. These could be placed at the entrance or on the sides, under the trees lining the perimeter of the field, leaving the integrity of the field itself formally intact, while still denoting exactly what is to be remembered here. Thus placed, the memorial texts will not create a sense of beginning or end of the memorial field, leaving the site open to the multiple paths visitors take in their memorial quest. This, too, will respect the architect's attempt to foster a sense of incompleteness; it will not be a memorial with a narrative beginning, middle and end built into it.

The introduction of rows of evergreen trees and Linden trees is also welcome, insofar as they simultaneously demarcate this space, even buffering it from the rest of the city, while integrating it into the cityscape by connecting the memorial site visually to the trees of the Tiergarten on the west side of the street. Because the lower branches of the trees will be trimmed upward to a height of three meters or so, the memorial site itself will be fully visible from the street, sidewalk, and adjacent build-ings. When visitors enter the area, their line of sight will take in the sur-rounding skyline, but as they come further into the center of the field of pillars, the horizon of tree tops will gradually rise to screen out all but the tops of surrounding buildings, thereby removing visitors from the urban landscape and immersing them gently into the memorial space.

For these reasons, the *Findungskommission* unanimously approves Eisenman's revised design (Eisenman-II) and recommends it to the Chancellor and memorial commissioners. We had hoped for a memo-rial that would evolve over time to reflect every generation's preoccu-pations, the kinds of significance every generation will find in the memory of Europe's murdered Jews. In this design, which insists on its own incompleteness, its own working through of an intractable prob-lem over any solution, we find a memorial that is as suggestive in its complex conception as it is eloquent in its formal execution. As such, it comes as close to being adequate to Germany's impossible task as is humanly possible. This is finally all we can ask of Germany's national attempt to commemorate the Nazis' murder of European Jewry.

Memory Meets Politics

By the late summer of 1998, national elections were looming. Helmut Kohl's Christian Democratic Union (CDU) had suffered several losses in preliminary regional elections earlier in the spring. All watched and waited as deadlines for the chancellor's announced decision regarding the memorial passed without comment. Into this void, other politicians occasionally leaped. Berlin's CDU mayor, Eberhard Diepgen, declared that he did not want Berlin turned into a 'capital of remorse' and that it would be best to suspend the entire process indefinitely.[1] And then, with national elections only weeks away, Social Democratic Party (SPD) leader Gerhard Schroeder's culture minister-designate, Michael Naumann, was asked whether an SPD government led by Schroeder would support the building of Eisenman's Holocaust memorial. No, he answered, and he gave two reasons: first, he was sceptical of any monument's adequacy to remember the Holocaust, believing that any such monument would serve merely as a 'suspension of guilt in art': and second, though he had not yet seen a model of Eisenman's design, photographs of it suggested a certain 'Speer-like monumentality' that he found inappropriate in such a memorial.[2] Naumann's response to this question on his first day as culture minister-designate was as refreshingly honest as it may have been impolitic. For whether he had intended it or not, the memorial had now become an electoral issue dividing the two candidates and their party agendas. Many in the SPD seemed to hold an underlying belief that this memorial and its design had become so closely associated with Chancellor Kohl that it would have to be defeated with him. In German interviews, Schroeder publicly backed his minister-designate on this issue; but in America, he diplomatically side-stepped the question altogether. By the time of the elections, in September 1998, the fate of the memorial seemed to be hanging solely on the voting results.

As it turned out, once it became clear that as an electoral issue, the memorial would only burn those politicians who came too close to it, a truce of sorts was called. On the eve of a vote in the Berlin Senate on 26 August to determine whether the city of Berlin would continue to support a central 'memorial for the murdered Jews of Europe,' Mayor Diepgen announced that he had enough votes to block the memorial. In response, the memorial's organizers asked me to publish my assessment of Eisenman's revised design (printed above). This would be the first public presentation of the new design itself, and the organizers hoped it would sway the vote towards the memorial.[3] Whether it was as a result of my article or not, two days after the assessment appeared, Chancellor Kohl and Mayor Diepgen agreed to defer all further discussion on the memorial until after the elections of 27 September.

After handily defeating Helmut Kohl and his CDU by a solid 6 percent margin, Gerhard Schroeder and his SPD entered into a 'red-green' governing coalition with Joshka Fischer's Green Party. The Greens had supported the memorial for Europe's murdered Jews; consequently, the coalition agreement stipulated that the memorial be put to a vote in the Bundestag (the lower house of the German Parliament) sometime in the new year. At about the same time, editorial writers began to ask whether the memorial procedure already in place had been abandoned, or whether the previous memorial procedure itself had been secretly abrogated.[4] Government lawyers launched an inquiry to determine just what the legal status of the memorial procedure actually was.

They found that despite the *Findungskommission's* explicit recommendation that Peter Eisenman's revised design for the memorial (now called Eisenman-II) be accepted, as well as the support of two out of the three groups of organizers (the Citizens' Committee headed by Lea Rosh and the federal government itself), the coalition agreement's stipulated vote in the Bundestag on whether or not to accept the winning design had yet to be taken. But even here, the issue as to what constituted the 'winning design' had become muddled. For even though it was becoming clear to all that the original procedure was still in place, and that there were enough votes on both sides of the aisle in the Bundestag to approve Eisenman's design, the new culture minister, Michael Naumann, still hoped to reach a compromise whereby both Eisenman's memorial and Naumann's own plan for an accompanying interpretive centre would be adopted together in the same space.

With this in mind, and with the tacit approval of members of Parliament, the *Findungskommission*, and the *Auslober* (commissioners), Eisenman and Naumann began unofficial discussions on how a synthesis might be achieved between Eisenman-II (now supported by Naumann) and the culture minister's own desire for an added 'interpretive center, library, and research center.' These discussions were moderated by Michael Blumenthal, director of Berlin's Jewish Museum, amid consultations with members of the *Findungskommission* and the *Auslober*. Having appeared to reach a synthesis in which both the memorial and an added interpretive centre would be acceptable to the minister and the architect, all parties hoped that the process itself could go forward. Naumann would now support Eisenman-II, and the architect would agree to consider ways to integrate into the site a possible 'Orte der Information' (place of information).

In what seemed to be a last-ditch effort to save the memorial from itself, Elke Leonhard, an SPD MP and chair of the Bundestag Committee on Cultural and Media Affairs, convened a public hearing in the Bundeshaus (federal Houses of Parliament) on 3 March 1999, the intent of which was to address the 'state of deliberations' surrounding Berlin's Memorial for the Murdered Jews of Europe. If the Bundestag was going to vote on the memorial, as mandated by the coalition agreement, it now needed to know exactly what it would be voting for or against. As the so-called speaker for the *Findungskommission*, I was invited to open the hearing with a short history of the project and with answers to four pointed questions: (1) *Why* should a monument be erected? (2) *Where* should a monument be erected? (3) *How* should a monument to the murdered Jews of Europe be designed? (4) *What* conclusions can be drawn from the current state of deliberations for the further discussions and decision-making processes of the German Bundestag? The session lasted six hours. My presentation was followed by statements from two other members of the *Findungskommission* (Josef Paul Kleihues and Dieter Ronte), as well as from representatives of the memorial's organizing team, including Lea Rosh for the Citizens' Committee, Peter Radunsky for the Berlin Senate, and Michael Naumann for the federal government. In addition, two of the memorial's leading opponents – Gyorgy Konrad, president of Berlin's Academy of Art, and cultural critic Solomon Korn – were also invited to make presentations against the memorial.

After each presentation, members of the parliamentary committee asked questions of the speakers. In my presentation, I described both my initial opposition to the memorial and my eventual active role in trying to accomplish it. Shortly after, Naumann eloquently detailed his own initial opposition to the memorial and his qualified support for it now. Konrad and Korn both questioned the premises of such a memorial, suggesting that by definition it would have to result in bad and bombastic art and that, in fact, Eisenman's design only proved their point. And in a somewhat startling formulation, the Speaker of the Berlin Senate, Peter Radunsky, confounded all by suggesting that the Berlin Senate could not vote on whether to support the memorial until the Bundestag itself had voted on it. This, even though the procedure seemed to demand precisely the opposite sequence.

At the end of the session, which had proceeded without a break, Elke Leonhard asked me to make a concluding statement. In it, I suggested that it was now time for the Bundestag to vote on Eisenman-II only, to approve it or reject it on the basis of the arguments we had made that day. Once the memorial has been voted into existence, the organizers could then consider whether a library and research centre should be added to it and what those might consist of. I cautioned that attaching an addition to the memorial before a vote could introduce a number of complicating dimensions, some of them possibly fatal to the entire project. I was thinking in particular of questions of institutional redundancy, and of archival materials already housed elsewhere. Such an addition would demand its own debate and process, I said, separate from and subsequent to the Bundestag's approval of Eisenman-II. Proponents of such an addition might well make a persuasive case for it, but unless they consulted and collaborated closely with the directors of other well-established pedagogical centres (such as those at the Wannsee Villa, Topographie des Terrors, Sachsenhausen, and Buchenwald), such a project might not find the support it needed among existing memorials and research centres.

'Should the memorial go forward?' I asked aloud. 'Yes.' And I continued that the Schroeder government should build the memorial and thereby give the German public a choice, even if an imperfect one: let them choose to remember what Germany once did to the Jews of Europe by coming to the memorial, by staying at home, by remembering alone or in the company of others. Let the people decide whether to animate such a site with their visits, with their shame, their sorrow, or their contempt. Or let the people abandon this memorial altogether, if that is what they choose, and let the memorial itself become the locus for further debate. Then let the public decide just how hollow or how substantial a gesture this memorial is, and whether any memorial can ever be more than a ritual gesture to an unredeemable past. With these words, I sat down.

The committee chair, Leonhard, thanked me and adjourned the hearing. Having beaten us all into exhaustion on that day in March, the question of Germany's national Memorial for the Murdered Jews of Europe was returned to parliamentary committee, where it was drafted for a vote in the Bundestag on 25 June 1999. There it became enmeshed yet again in parliamentary politics, but it was also back in German hands, where it belonged. Naumann continued to lobby for as large an interpretive centre as possible – something approaching a national museum to share Eisenman's field of waving pillars. Other proposals included theologian Richard Schroeder's suggestion that a single tablet be installed, inscribed in both the Hebrew original and several other languages: 'Thou shalt not kill.'

Beginning at 9 a.m. and running until after 2 p.m. on 25 June 1999, a full session of the German Bundestag met in public view to debate and finally vote on Berlin's Memorial for the Murdered Jews of Europe. Both opponents and proponents were given time to make their cases, with each presentation followed by noisy but civil debate. By this time, the positions of all the MPs were well known and their votes had already in effect been counted. A number of alternative measures to the memorial were duly proposed and defeated, including a memorial for all of the Nazis' victims and the above-mentioned tablet. Finally, by a vote of 314 to 209, with 14 abstentions, the Bundestag approved the memorial in four separate parts. (1) The Federal Republic of Germany would erect in Berlin a memorial for the murdered Jews of Europe on the site of the former Ministerial Gardens in the centre of Berlin. (2) Eisenman's field of pillars (Eisenman-II) would be realized. (3) An information centre would be added to the memorial site. And (4) a public foundation comprising representatives from the Bundestag, the City of Berlin, and the citizens' initiative for the establishment of the memorial, as well as the directors of other memorial museums, members of the Central Council of Jews in Germany, and other victim groups, would be established by the Bundestag to oversee the building of the memorial and its information centre in the year 2000.[5]

The Memorial's Return to History

Now that Germany's Memorial for the Murdered Jews of Europe has been dedicated, is this the end of Germany's Holocaust memory work? I had initially feared so, but no, debate and controversy continue unabated. Moreover, once the Parliament decided to give Holocaust memory a central place in Berlin, an even more difficult task awaited the organizers: to define exactly what was to be remembered in Eisenman's waving field of pillars. What would Germany's national Holocaust narrative be? The question of the memorial's historical content began at precisely the moment that the question of the memorial's design ended. Memory, which had followed history, would now be followed by further historical debate.

Indeed, as so brilliantly conceived by the architect and by Dagmar von Wilcken, the exhibition designer for the Orte der Information, this site's commemorative and historical dimensions interpenetrate to suggest an interdependent whole in which neither history nor memory can stand without the other. As one descends the stairs from the midst

8.1 Field of Pillars, Memorial to the murdered Jews of Europe, Berlin. (Stiftung Denkmal für die ermordeten Juden Europas)

of the field into the Orte der Information, it becomes clear just how crucial a complement the underground information center is to the field of pillars above. It does not duplicate the field's commemorative function, but neither is it arbitrarily tacked onto the memorial site as a historical afterthought. Rather, in tandem with the field of stelae above it, the information centre reminds us of the memorial's dual mandate as both commemorative and informational, as a site of both memory and history, each as shaped by the other. Yet while remaining distinct in their respective functions, these two sides of the memorial are formally linked and interpenetrating.

By seeming to allow the aboveground stelae to sink into and thereby impose themselves physically onto the underground space of information, the underground information centre audaciously illustrates both that commemoration is 'rooted' in historical information and that the historical presentation is necessarily 'shaped' formally by the commemorative space above it. Here we have a 'place of memory' that is literally undergirded by a 'place of history,' which is, in turn, inversely shaped by commemoration, and we are asked to navigate the spaces in between memory and history for our knowledge of events. Such a design makes palpable the yin and yang of history and memory, their mutual interdependence and their distinct virtues.

Like the mass murder of European Jewry that it commemorates, Eisenman's memorial design provides no single vantage point from which to view it. From above, its five-acre expanse stretches like an Escherian grid in all directions, and even echoes the rolling, horizontal plane of crypts covering Jerusalem's Mount of Olives. From its edges, the memorial is a somewhat forbidding forest of stelae, most of them between one and three metres in height, high enough to close us in, but not so high as to block out sunlight or the surrounding skyline, which includes the Brandenburger Tor (Brandenburg Gate) and the Reichstag (Parliament building) to the north, the renovated and bustling Potsdamer Platz to the south, and the Tiergarten across Ebertstrasse to the west. The colour and texture of the stelae change with the cast of the sky, from steely-grey on dark, cloudy days, to sharp-edged black and white squares on sunny days, to a softly rolling field of wheat-coloured stelae, glowing almost pink in the sunset.

As one enters the waving field of stelae, one is accompanied by light and sky, but the city's other sights and sounds are gradually occluded, blocked out. From deep in the midst of the pillars, the thrum of traffic is muffled and all but disappears. Looking up and down the pitching rows of stelae, one catches glimpses of other mourners, and beyond them one can even see to the edges of the memorial itself. At the same time, however, one feels very much alone, almost desolate, even in the company of hundreds of other mourners nearby. Depending on where one stands, along the edges or deep inside the field, the experience of the memorial varies – from feelings of reassurance one encounters on the sidewalk by remembering in the company of others, invigorated by the life of the city hurtling by; to feelings of existential aloneness from deep within this dark forest, oppressed and depleted by the memory of mass murder and not reconciled to it.

Only when one moves back out towards the edges, towards the streets, buildings, sidewalks, and life, does hope come back into view. Neither memory nor one's experience of the memorial is static here; each depends on one's own movement into, through, and out of this site. One does not need to be uplifted by such an experience in order to remember and even be deeply affected by it. The result is that the memory of what Germany once did to Europe's Jews is now forever inflected by the memory of having mourned Europe's murdered Jews here, of having mourned the Holocaust both together with others and alone by oneself.

The year the Bundestag voted the memorial into existence, 1999, was a watershed for German memory and identity. No longer paralyzed by the memory of crimes perpetrated in its name, Germany was now acting on the basis of such memory: it participated boldly in NATO's 1999 intervention against a new genocide perpetrated by Milosevic's Serbia; it began to change citizenship laws from blood- to residency-based; and it dedicated a permanent place in Berlin's cityscape to commemorate what happened the last time Germany was governed from Berlin. Endless debate and memorialization were no longer mere substitutes for actions against contemporary genocide but reasons for action. This is something new, not just for Germany but for the rest of us as well.

For whether Germans like it or not, in addition to their nation's great accomplishments over the past several centuries, they will also always be identified as the nation that launched the deadliest genocide in human history, that started a world war which eventually killed some fifty million human beings, and that used this war to screen its deliberate mass murder of some six million European Jews. It is not a proud memory. But neither has any other nation attempted to make such a crime perpetrated in its name part of its national identity. This space will always remind Germany and the world at large of the self-inflicted void at the heart of German culture and consciousness – a void that defines national identity even as it threatens such identity with its own implosion.

NOTES

1 For further details and an insightful summary of the entire process up to September 1998, see Michael Wise, 'Totem and Taboo: The New Berlin Struggles to Build a Holocaust Memorial,' *Lingua Franca* (1999): 38–46. For a full-length version of the entire process, also see James E. Young, *At Memory's Edge: After-Images of the Holocaust in Contemporary Art and Architecture* (New Haven, CT: Yale University Press, 2000), from which parts of this essay have been adapted.

2 As recalled by Michael Naumann to the author in April 1999; also cited in Alan Cowell, 'An Opponent of Kohl Puts Taboo Topic into Election,' *New York Times*, 26 July 1998, 13.

3 I published this as 'Die menschenmögliche Lösung des Unlösbaren,' *Der Tagesspiegel,* 22 August 1998, 25.

4 On the eve of a planned visit by Peter Eisenman and Michael Naumann, I was invited to write an op-ed piece for the *Berliner Zeitung*, in which I asked just these questions, among others. See Young, 'Was keine andere Nation je versucht hat,' *Berliner Zeitung* 18 December 1998, 13–14.

5 For sending me the actual wording of the measure, I thank Dagmar Schwermer of Bayerischer Rundfunk (Bavarian Radio). I also thank Guenter Schlusche at the Stiftung Denkmal für die ermordeten Juden Europas for providing me with further details surrounding the parliamentary process and for access to the site during construction.

Contributors

Mieke Bal is Royal Netherlands Academy of Arts and Sciences (KNAW) Professor. She has received numerous honours and awards and served as Getty Visiting Scholar at the Getty Research Institute for the History of Art and the Humanities, Los Angeles (2001–2); Clark Visiting Fellow at the Sterling and Francine Clark Art Institute, Williamstown, Massachusetts (2001); and Visiting Professor of Cultural Analysis at the AHRB Centre for Cultural Analysis, Theory and History in the School of Fine Art, Art History and Cultural Analysis, Leeds University. (2000–3). She is the author, most recently, of *A Mieke Bal Reader* (Chicago: University of Chicago Press, 2006) and of *Traveling Concepts in the Humanities: A Rough Guide* (Toronto: University of Toronto Press, 2002); *Mieke Bal Kulturanalyse* (ed. Thomas Fechner-Smarsly and Sonja Neef; (Frankfurt a/m: Suhrkamp, 2002); *Louise Bourgeois' Spider: The Architecture of Art-writing* (Chicago: University of Chicago Press, 2001); and *Quoting Caravaggio: Contemporary Art, Preposterous History* (Chicago: University of Chicago Press, 1999). She is also a video artist and an independent curator.

Elizabeth Crooke is Senior Lecturer in Museum and Heritage Studies at the University of Ulster. She obtained her PhD in 1999 from Cambridge University and her BA from Trinity College, Dublin. Her research considers the social, cultural, and political roles of museums in the historical and contemporary contexts. She is shortly to publish a book on museums and community as part of the Museum Meanings series with Routledge. She is author of *Politics, Archaeology, and the Creation of a National Museum of Ireland* (Dublin: Irish Academic Press, 2000); 'Museums and Community' in Sharon MacDonald (ed.), *A*

Companion to Museum Studies (Oxford: Blackwell, 2006); 'Exploring History, and the Politics of Museums in Northern Ireland and South Africa,' *International Journal of Heritage Studies* (2005); and 'Museums, Communities, and the Politics of Heritage in Northern Ireland,' in J. Littler and R. Naidoo, eds., *The Politics of Heritage: Race, Identity and National Stories* (New York: Routledge, 2004).

Reesa Greenberg is an adjunct professor at Concordia University and York University. She has consulted on exhibitions and installations for the Art Gallery of Ontario, the Edmonton Art Gallery, the Jewish Museum in New York, and the Jewish Museum in Amsterdam. Her publications include 'La représentation muséale des génocides: Guérison ou traumatisme réactualisé?' *Gradius* (2007); 'Jews, Museums, and National Identities,' *Ethnologies* (2003); 'Playing It Safe: The Display of Transgressive Art in the Museum,' in *Mirroring Evil: Nazi Imagery, Recent Art* (Camden: Rutgers University Press, 2001); *and Thinking about Exhibitions* (co-edited with Bruce Ferguson and Sandy Nairne; New York: Routledge, 1996). See reesagreenberg.net.

Edin Hajdarpašić is a PhD candidate in the Department of History at the University of Michigan. His primary fields are modern Balkan and East European history, with general interests in nationalism, political violence, and representations of culture and identity. He is currently finishing his doctoral dissertation on political reform and the emergence of national movements in late Ottoman Bosnia (ca. 1800–78). The research for his contribution to this volume was made possible by a German Marshall Fund Fellowship and an Andrew W. Mellon Fellowship in the Humanistic Studies.

Robin Ostow is a Fellow at the Centre for Russian, European, and Eurasian Studies, University of Toronto. She has written extensively on Jews and Jewish culture in both Cold War Germanys and in post-unification Germany. Her publications include 'Imagined Families and "Rassenschande": Germans and Russians, Nation and Gender at the Ravensbruck Memorial,' *Journal of European Area Studies* (2001); *Die Ostdeutsche Juden und die deutsche Wiedervereinigung* (Berlin: Wichern Verlag, 1996); and *Jews in Contemporary East Germany: The Children of Moses in the Land of Marx* (London: Macmillan, 1988). She recently guest-edited a special issue of *Journal of East European*

Jewish Affairs on post-Soviet Jewish immigration to Germany (Winter 2003) and is currently completing an ethnographic study of Jewish museums in Europe.

Bernhard Purin has been the director of the Jewish Museum in Munich since 2003. He served previously as director of the Jewish Museum of Franconia Fürth & Schnaittach (1995–2002); and as Curator of the Jewish Museum in Vienna (1993–5). He is a lecturer at the University of Tübingen (Empirische Kulturwissenschaft) and the University of Potsdam (Jewish Studies), and the author, most recently, of *Jewish Museum Munich* (with Jutta Fleckenstein) (Munich: Prestel, 2007); *Die Sammlung des Jüdischen Museums Franken in Schnaittach* (Fürth, 2003); and 'Gerettet oder geraubt? Zur Aneignung von Judaica im Nationalsozialismus und heute' in *Museen im Zwielicht. Ankaufspolitik 1933–1945* (Kolloquium vom 11. und 12. Dezember 2001 in Köln – die eigene Geschichte. Provenienzforschung an deutschen Museen im internationalen Vergleich. Tagung vom 20. bis 22. Februar 2002 in Hamburg, hrsg. von der Koordinierungsstelle für Kulturgutverluste, Magdeburg 2002, pp. 403–18).

István Rév is Professor of History and Political Science, Central European University, and Director of the Open Society Archives. His research interests are the display of history, death and mourning, and archival, classification and retrieval techniques. He is the author of 'Covering History' in M. Roth and C. Salas, eds., *Disturbing Remains: Memory, History and Crisis in the Twentieth Century* (Los Angeles: Getty Research Institute, 2001). He is currently completing a book for Stanford University Press on retroactive justice.

James E. Young is Professor of English and Judaic Studies at the University of Massachusetts, Amherst, where he has taught since 1988, and currently chair of the Department of Judaic and Near Eastern Studies. He has also taught at New York University as a Dorot Professor of English and Hebrew/Judaic Studies (1984–8), at Bryn Mawr College on the History of Religion, and at the University of Washington, Harvard University, and Princeton University as a visiting professor. He received his PhD from the University of California in 1983. He is the author of *At Memory's Edge: After-Images of the Holocaust in Contemporary Art and Architecture* (New Haven: Yale University Press,

2000); *The Texture of Memory* (New Haven: Yale University Press, 1993); and *Writing and Rewriting the Holocaust* (Bloomington: Indiana University Press, 1988); a well as numerous articles and reviews. He was guest curator of an exhibition at the Jewish Museum in New York City titled The Art of Memory: Holocaust Memorials in History (March – August 1994) and was editor of *The Art of Memory* (Munich: Prestel Verlag, 1994), the exhibition catalogue for the show. In 1997, he was appointed by the Berlin Senate to the five-member *Findungs-skommission* for Germany's national 'Memorial to the Murdered Jews of Europe,' which was inaugurated in the spring of 2005. He has received numerous awards and fellowships, including a Guggenheim Fellowship, an ACLS Fellowship, NEH exhibition planning, implementation, and research grants, Memorial Foundation and Jewish Culture grants, an American Philosophical Society grant, and a Yad Hanadiv Fellowship at the Hebrew University in Jerusalem.

Index

Aboriginal War Veterans Monument, 188

Adams, Eddie, *Murder of a Vietcong Suspect* (photograph), 21, 34, 38, 39

Adler, Jankel, 142

aesthetics, and politics, 39

affect, and display, 16–17, 20, 26, 34, 35; and film, 26, 35

affect-images, 35–7, 39

Alphen, Ernst van, 20–1, 22, 40n9, 41n16

Altieri, Charles, 35

Anderson, Benedict, *Imagined Communities*, 4, 139, 157, 176n2

Anne Frank in the World 1929–1945 (exhibit), 185

anti-Judaism, 142. *See also* anti-Semitism

anti-Semitism, 70; and the Catholic Church, 175; in Germany, 139, 141, 142, 146; in Poland, 165, 169–71, 174, 175, 177n24 and 28. *See also* Holocaust; Jews

Arbus, Diane, 17, 27, 30

Ars Aevi Museum of Contemporary Art (Sarajevo), 7, 109–10, 120–38

art, looted. *See* looted art

Ash, Timothy Garton, 5

Ashdown, Paddy, 138n60

Auschwitz, 58, 59; Auschwitz Trials, 139

Austria: Jewish museums in, 142–3, 145–6, 149, 151

Bajavić, Maja, 123: *Double Bubble*, 127–8

Bakaršić, Kemal, 116, 132n12

Baudrillard, Jean, 4, 9

Beauvoir, Simone de, 76

Bennett, Tony, *Birth of the Museum*, 4

Berenbaum, Michael, 176n3

Berger, Max, 145

Bergson, Henri, 35

Bersohn, Mathias, 176n4

Bersohn Museum (Warsaw), 173, 176n4

Between (exhibit, Sarajevo), 124, 127

Blumenthal, Michael, 206

Boltanski, Christian, *Inhabitants of the Hotel de Saint-Aignan in 1939* (installation), 165

Boniface VIII (pope), 78

Boraine Alex, 102

Bosnia (and Herzegovina), 109–38:
ethnic cleansing, 11; ethnicity in,
109–10; ethnoconfessionalism, 109–
10, 112, 114, 117; and globalization,
110; Holocaust in, 111, 119, 131n11;
international organizations'
involvement in, 114–16, 118, 120,
122–7; invented tradition in, 109;
Ministry for Education, Culture,
and Sport, 113, 122; multicultural-
ism/multiethnicity in, 109–10, 113–
19, 125–7, 129; Muslim Party of
Democratic Action (SDA), 113, 114,
133–4n21; national identity, 117;
nationalism, 110, 116, 118–19, 123,
129, 131n; peacekeeping in, 118–19;
religion, 116–19, 129; religious tolerance in, 109–15; understanding of
culture, 116–19, 129
Bourgeois, Louise, *Geometry of Desire*,
40n1
Brandon, Laura, 199n19
Breuer, Marcell, 64
British Archives (Warsaw), 171
Brooks, Peter, 21
Brown, Eric, 194
Browne, Malcolm, *Sacrificial Protest
of Thich Quang Duc* (photograph),
21, 34, 38, 39
Buck-Morse, Susan, 40n8
Bunzl, Matti, 157
Buren, Daniel, 120

Calle, Sophie, 120
Canada: identity, 183–97; and peacekeeping, 189–90; Remembrance
Day, 189–90, 192; role of military,
188–9
Canadian Museum of Civilization,
185–6, 188, 192

Canadian War Museum, 7, 8, 10,
183–99; visitors' experiences, 195
*Canvas of War: Masterpieces from the
Canadian War Museum* (exhibit),
194
Capa, Robert, *Falling Soldier*, 47, 81–
2n1, 86n40
Cardinal, Douglas, 192
Cattelan, Maurizio, *Him* (installa-
tion), 23–6, 27, 33, 40n9
Chakrabarty, Dipesh, 3, 8, 11, 120
Clarkson, Adrienne, 188
Cohen, Joel, 172
Cold War, 62
Coleman, James, *Box (Ahhareturn-
about)* (installation), 21
collecting, 4, 9
collective memory, 203. *See also*
world memory
Collegium Artisticum (Sarajevo), 121
community curation, 100
*Confiscated: The Collection of the
Vienna Jewish Museum after 1938*
(exhibit), 149
Connolly, William, 8, 195
Council of Europe, 126
Crane, Susan, 4
Cuchulainn, 93–4

D'Appollonia, Ariane Chebel, 5
Darboven, Hanne, *Ansichten >82<*,
21, 33–4, 36
Davies, Norman, 171
Dayton Peace Agreement, 113–16,
124, 126
Delacroix, Ferdinand, 165
Deleuze, Gilles, 30, 31, 35, 36, 37,
41n11
Derrida, Jacques, 4
Diary of Anne Frank, 139

Diaspora Museum (Tel Aviv), 160
display. *See* exhibition
display objects: uses of, 7. *See also*
    looted art

Eichmann, Adolf, 66, 149; trial of, 139
Eisenman, Peter, Memorial for the
    Murdered Jews of Europe, 10–11,
    200–13
Eliach, Yaffa, 174
emotions. *See* affect
European Commission, 126
EU (European Union), 118
Event Communications (London),
    160, 164, 166, 172, 175
Every Picture Tells a Story (exhibit),
    100–1
exhibition, 95; as commemoration,
    90–105; and film, 14–41, 162–5,
    167; of history, 103–4, 120; and the
    Holocaust, 15–41 (*see also* Holo-
    caust); *mise-en-scène*, 19–20; narra-
    tive (*see* narrative); nations, 27, 29;
    and nationalism (*see* Bosnia,
    nationalism; Hungary, national-
    ism); and poetry, 22; and preposte-
    riority, 38; and redemption, 10;
    and theatre, 17, 19–20, 22; and
    time, 15–43
Exhibition of the Fascist Revolution
    (Rome), 74–6
exhibits: travelling, 194

Federal Army Museum of Military
    History (Dresden), 174
Federal Republic of Germany: anti-
    Semitic past, 139, 141, 142, 146;
    Berlin Senate, 200–13; Bundestag
    (lower house of Parliament) 206,
    207; Central Council of Jews in

Germany, 153, 209; Christian
    Democratic Union (CDU), 204–6;
    Christian Social Movement, 142;
    Citizens Initiative for the
    Establishment of a Memorial to
    the Murdered Jews of Europe,
    201, 206, 207, 209; Dresden, 174;
    Green Party, 206; Jewish commu-
    nities in, 152–3; Jewish museums
    in, 139–54; Munich, 148, 152;
    Social Democratic Party (SPD),
    205, 206, 207
Felix the Cat, 17, 22
Feszty, Adolf, 60
film: in museums and exhibits, 7, 8,
    16, 22–3, 163–7; and the nation, 16;
    and photography, 22–3, 26, 27, 30,
    37–40 (*see* also photography); and
    politics, 22–3, 35
Fischer, Joshka, 206
Fuchs, Rudi, 22, 40n5

Gagnon, François-Marc, 194
Gehry, Frank, 160
Genet, Jean, 87n47
genocide. *See* Holocaust
Glenny, Daniel, 185
Goebbels, Joseph, 76
Goering, Hermann, 76
Gorée Island, 59, 84–5n25
Granatstein, Jack, 189
Greenberg, Reesa, 145
Griffin, Roger, 73, 87n46
Griffin Rank Cook Architects, 186
Griffith, D.W., 22
Group of Seven (Canada), 194, 197
Gruber, Ruth, 172
Guattari, Félix, 36
Gulag (Siberia), 56, 58, 65
Gyöngyössy, István, 86n38

Habermas, Jürgen, 4
Hacking, Ian, 60
Hadžifejzović, Jusuf, 123, 127–9;
  *From Kitsch to Blood Is Just One
  Step*, 128
Hadžiomerspahić, Enver, 121, 123,
  126
Halberstadt, Jerzy, 158–9
Halbwachs, Maurice, 4, 79, 80
Hardt, Michael, 40n7
Harman, Jack, 198n8
Haus der Kunst. *See* Ydessa Hendeles,
  Partners (The Teddy Bear Project)
healing: and history, 100; and mem-
  ory, 100, 102; and museums, 9, 10,
  142, 151. *See also* museums and
  regeneration
Heimann-Jelinek, Felicitas, 145
Hendeles, Ydessa, *Partners (The
  Teddy Bear Project)*. *See* Partners
  (The Teddy Bear Project)
Henriquez, Richard, 198n8
heritage: and community capacity
  building, 99–100; cultural, 125; and
  legitimization, 96–9; uses of, 90–
  105
Historical Museum (Sarajevo), 122–
  3. *See also* Museum of Revolution
Hitler, Adolf, 70
Holocaust, 56, 58, 61, 67, 71, 75, 157:
  Americanization of, 158; in Bosnia
  and Herzegovina, 111, 119, 131n11;
  and European identities, 5, 9;
  exhibits of, 163–5, 185, 186; in Germany, 139–40, 142–3; memorials,
  159, 165–6, 200–13; in museum
  exhibits, 8, 10, 56, 139–54, 159, 165–
  6, 173; Polish role in, 167–70; Son-
  dereinsatzkommando Eichmann,
  66. *See also* Auschwitz; looted art

Holocaust (American television
  series), 140
Holocaust Memorial Day, 78
Hollós, Ervin, 48
Horthy, Miklós, 67, 72
host desecration, 78–80
House of Terror (Budapest), 6, 7, 8, 9,
  60–89; visitors' experiences, 68–9,
  73, 74, 75, 79
Hungary: Arrow Cross Party, 61, 64–
  5, 67–72, 73, 77, 86n46 and 47;
  Budapest Sewage Company, 50,
  51; CP headquarters, 47–58; Communist ideology, 73; Communist
  historiography, 62–3; Communist
  Party, 47–89; cross-dressing, 69–70;
  Hungarian Democratic Forum, 56,
  58; Hungarian Socialist Party, 56,
  58, 85n27; Hungarian Socialist
  Worker's Party, 56; Hungarian-
  Soviet Oil Exploration Company,
  50; Jewish population, 60–1, 65–8,
  70–2, 75; Memorial Day Dedicated
  to the Victims of Communism, 71,
  78; National Geophysics Institute,
  50, 58; National Guard, 50–1;
  National Penal Authority, 77;
  National Radio, 50; National Television (Hungary), 56; Nazi occupation, 60–1, 64–8, 71–2; Republic
  Square massacre, 47–58, 78; Revolution (1956, reports of), 47–58, 66;
  Second World War, 60–1, 64, 66–9;
  Secret Police (AVH), 47–51, 53–4,
  56, 62–3, 65–6, 70, 80; show trials,
  2–3; Truth and Life Party, 78;
  underground prisons (Budapest),
  50–62, 66–7, 77, 79–80; underground railway (Budapest), 53;
  White Book, 49–50, 52, 55; White

House Budapest), 55, 56, 57; White Terror, 60; Young Liberal Party, 78
Huntington, Samuel, clash of civilizations, 119
hyperfacts, 49; in museum exhibits, 8, 167

Icons of Identity (exhibit), 92–4
identities: Bosnian, 117; European, 4, 5, 9; national, 3, 4; Canadian (*see* Canada); in Northern Ireland, 92–4
Imperial War Museum (London), 186
Imperial War Museum North (Manchester) 190–2
Institute of Memory (Warsaw), 171
Izetbegović, Alija, 113, 131n11, 133n15

James, (king), 97
Jewish Historical Museum (Amsterdam), 162, 172
Jewish Historical Institute (Warsaw), 158, 163, 172–3, 176n4 and 5
Jewish Historical Institute Museum (Warsaw), 163, 173, 176n4
Jewish Museum (New York), 146
Jewish Museum (Vienna), 145–6, 149, 157, 161–2, 165, 167, 172–3
Jewish Museum Berlin, 73, 75–6, 141, 143, 146, 153, 172–3
Jewish Museum of Franconia, 141, 145–7, 150, 152
Jewish Museum Frankfurt, 141, 143, 172
Jewish Museum Hohenems, 142–3, 151
Jewish Museum Munich, 7, 9, 141, 147–9, 150–2
Jewish Museum of Prague, 158, 161–2, 165, 173

Jewish Museum of Westphalia, 143–4
Jewish museums: class structure of Jewish population, 178n34; displays of Holocaust, 146, 163–5; in Europe, 157–78; in Germany, 139–54; and healing, 142, 151; Holocaust memorials in, 165–6; library installations, 162; and reconciliation, 152; and redemption, 142; and remembrance, 139–54; and restitution, 9, 150, 170; tombstones in, 161
Jews: in France, 79; in Germany, 152–3, 209; in Hungary, 60–1, 65–8, 70–2, 75; in Poland, 158. *See also* Holocaust
Johnson, Philip, 196
Judt, Tony, 5, 9, 11
Junczyk-Ziomecka, Ewa, 159

Kabakov, Ilya, 120
Kaczynski, Lech, 175
Kádár, János, 62, 63
Kavanagh, Gaynor, 93
Kawara, On, *I Am Still Alive* series, 21, 37; *Today* series, 21
Kertész, Imre, 59
Király, Béla, 50
Kleihues, Josef Paul, 207
Klein, Jacques Paul, 114, 115, 118, 132n13, 135n33, 138n60
Koestler, Arthur, *Darkness at Noon*, 64, 85n33
Kohl, Helmut, 202n, 204–6
Kohlbauer, Martin, 146
Komintern, 63
Konrad, Gyorgy, 207
Korn, Solomon, 207
Kovács, Attila Ferenczfy, 8
Kozłowski, Maciej, 170–1

Kristallnacht (Night of Broken Glass): commemoration of in Germany, 141–2
Kugelmann, Cilly, 172
Kymlicka, Will, 5
Kwaśniewski, Aleksander, 169–70

Le Corbusier, 76
Lehmann, Hans-Thiess, 19, 40n3
Leonhard, Elke, 207–8
Libeskind, Daniel, 174, 190, 192
Library of the University of Vienna, 149
Liebermann, Max, 142
Life Magazine: photos of Hungarian Revolution, 47–8
Lin, Maya, 192
Lissitzky, El, 76
Local Identities (exhibit) (Northern Ireland), 92
looted art, 6, 9, 143, 149–51

MacArthur, Douglas, 84n24
MacDonald, George, 185–6
Mahlamaki, Rainer, 174–5
Mahmutčcehajić, Rusmir, 119
Maison des Esclaves. *See* Gorée Island
Malkki, Liisa, 162
Mandić, Asja, 123, 124
March on Rome, 74
Markowitz, Wiktor, 169
Mattifort de Bucy, Simon, 78
May, Karl, 29
Maze Prison (Northern Ireland), 96, 97
McCarthy, Paul, *Saloon* (installation), 21, 30, 38
Melnikov, Konstantin, 76
Memorial for the Murdered Jews of Europe (Berlin), 10–11, 200–13; visitors' experiences, 201, 202–3, 204, 211
memorials, 6; national, 5, 9, 11; and healing (*see* healing); Holocaust, 200–13; Jewish sites in Germany, 141
memory, 36, 37, 93, 95, 102; collective, 203; and healing (*see* healing); and history, 209–11; and photography (*see* photography). *See also* world memory
Mephisto (film), 80
Mikes, George, 51
Minnie Mouse, 17, 21; *Minnie Mouse Carrying Felix in Cages*, 22, 36
Mirroring Evil: Nazi Imagery/Recent Art (exhibit), 146
Monumenta Judaica – 2000 Years of Jewish History and Culture on the Rhine (exhibit), 139–40
Moriyama, Raymond, 184, 186, 190, 192, 193, 195–7, 199n26
Murphy, Frank, 84n24
Museum of the 1984 Winter Olympic Games (Sarajevo), 128
Museum of the Art and History of Judaism (Paris), 161, 165, 172
Museum of Ethnography (Vienna), 149
Museum of Ethnology (Vienna), 149
Museum of Free Derry (Northern Ireland), 96
Museum of the History of Polish Jews, 6, 7, 8, 10, 157–78: display of Holocaust, 163–5; display and film in, 162–5, 167; and Polish anti-Semitism, 165, 169–70; and Polish-Jewish reconciliation, 163, 169–70; and restitution of Jewish property, 179; visitors' experiences, 163–7

Museum of Literary and Theatrical Arts (Sarajevo), 128
Museum of Natural History (Vienna), 149
Museum of the Old Orthodox Church (Sarajevo), 118, 135n32 and 33
Museum of the Republic of Serbia, 109, 130n2
Museum of Revolution (Sarajevo), 120–2, 128
Museum of the Warsaw Uprising (Warsaw), 177n30
museums: and democracy, 3, 8, 120; as educational spaces, 4; and film (*see* film); and globalization, 3; and healing, 142, 151; and integration, 9; Jewish 139–54, 157–78; and memory, 151–5; and narrative (*see* narrative); and nations, 4, 5, 6, 17, 157–78; and national identities, 3, 5, 183, 185; narrative historical, 160; pedagogical role, 146; and racial tolerance, 110–20, 146, 157–8; and reconciliation, 152, 163, 169–70; and redemption, 143; and regeneration, 9; and remembrance, 139–54; and restitution, 9, 150, 170; and social activism, 95–7, and technology, 6; use of new media, 194; visitors (*see* viewers); war museums, 183–99
Mussolini, Benito, 74

Nagy, Imre: reburial of, 57, 66, 71, 76
narrative: and exhibits, 4, 15, 16, 17, 20–1, 22; and museums, 4, 7, 160–1
National Gallery of Canada, 192, 194
nationalism, 5, 9; in Bosnia, 110, 116, 118–19, 123, 129, 131n; and exhibits, 26

National Library (Sarajevo), 121
National Library (Vienna), 149
National Museum (Bosnia), 6, 7, 9–10, 110–20. *See also* Sarajevo Haggadah
National War Memorial (Canada), 185, 187, 190, 191, 198n7
nationalism, 161–2, 169; in Bosnia (*see* Bosnia)
Naumann, Michael, 205, 206, 207, 208
Nazism. *See* Holocaust
Negri, Antonio, 40n7
Neuropolitics, in museums and exhibits, 8, 195
Newry (Northern Ireland), 99–100
Nora, Pierre, 4
Northern Ireland: Battle of the Boyne, 97; Bloody Sunday Trust, 96; Coiste na n-larchimi, 96; Community Relations Council, 92; Conflict Resolution and Peace-Building Learning Centre, 95; Falls Community Council (FCC), 95, 97; exhibition and healing, 100–3; Healing Through Remembering Project, 100, 102; Loyalists, 93; Northern Ireland Regional Curators Group, 92; Orange Culture Week, 98; Orange Order, 97–9; Republicans, 93; Troubles (displays of), 90–105
Nuremberg Laws, 68
Nussbaum, Felix, 142

Obala Art Center (Sarajevo), 121
Oberlander, Cornelia, 198n8
Obermeyer, Arthur, 151
Offe, Sabine, 141, 143

OHR (Office of the High Representative), 114, 116, 120, 127, 138n60
Oppenheim, Dennis. 120
Orbán, Viktor, 71–2, 78

Paolini, Giulio, *Mimesi* (sculpture), 31–3
Partners (The Teddy Bear Project) (exhibit), 7, 8, 9, 10, 15–41; visitors' experiences, 19, 20, 26, 29, 33
Passerini, Luisa, 5
Pawlak, Grażyna, 158–9, 167–8
Paziński, Piotr, 171
Peace Tower (Ottawa), 189, 190, 191, 197
peacekeeping: and Canadian identity, 189–90; in Bosnia, 118–19
Peacekeeping Monument (Ottawa), 198n8
Peres, Shimon, 169
Péter, Gábor, 70
photography, 48–9: as an exhibition medium, 16, 17; and film, 22–3, 26, 27, 30, 37–40; and memory, 36, 37, 100; in reportage, 83n21, 86n40
Physical and Psychological Appearance of the Jews (exhibit), 149
Pia, Secondo, 82–3n6
Pianist (film), 163, 165
Piano, Renzo, bridge in Sarajevo, 121, 123, 137n48
Pinay, Lloyd, 188
Pistoletto, Michelangelo, 120, 122
Poland: anti-Semitism in, 165, 169–71; ethnic pluralism in, 170; and globalization, 173–4, Holocaust in, 167–70; Jedwabne, 170; politics of forgetting, 171

politics of looking, 35
Poznanski, Kazimierz, 173

Radio Free Europe, 'items' collection, 51–2
Radunsky, Peter, 207
Rajk László, 62, 63, 76
Rákosi, Mátyás, 69–70
Rendez-Vous (art collection), 121
Richarz, Monika, 141
Riefenstahl, Leni, *Triumph of the Will*, 28
Roma (Hungarian), 71
Ronald S. Lauder Foundation, 158
Ronte, Dieter, 207
Rosensaft, Menachem, 171
Rosh, Lea, 206, 207
Rubin, Miri, 8

Sadovy, George: reports of Hungarian Revolution, 47–8
Safdie, Moishe, 192
St-Jean-en-Grève (France), 78–9
Saloon (installation). *See* Paul McCarthy
Sándor, Pál, *Dániel Szerencsés*, 80
Sarajevo Haggadah, 7, 9, 10, 110–20, 125–7, 129–32, 133n12–15, 138n60
Sarfatti, Margherita, 74
Sartre, Jean-Paul, 76
Schindler's List (film), 165, 172
Schleswig-Holstein Regional Museum/Gottdorf Castle (Germany), 142
Schroeder, Gerhard, 205, 206
Schroeder, Richard, 208
Serra, Richard, 200, 210, 202n
Shandler, Jeffrey, 174
Shoah. *See* Holocaust

Shoba, Nebojša Šerić, 123
Silverman, Kaja, 29, 36
simulacra, 38
Sironi, Mario, 75–6
Smith, Martin, 167
Solender, Stephen, 159–60, 169, 170, 171, 174, 176n7
Sontag, Susan, 83n21
Soviet Union, 53–4, 65, 67–72. *See also* Gulag
Spanish Civil War, photo reportage of, 47, 81–2n1
Spero, Nancy, *Remembrance* (installation), 145
Stalin, Joseph, 70
Stalinism, 62, 65. *See also* Gulag
Steinhardt, Jakob, 142
Struggles of Poland (television film), 167
Synagoga (exhibit), 139
Szabó, István, 80

Terragni, Giuseppe, 76
Tomb of the Unknown Soldier (Ottawa), 187
Tower Museum (Derry/Londonderry), 92
Treaty of Trianon, 67
Trudeau, Pierre Elliot, 189

Ulster Museum, 92
UN (United Nations), 114–15, 118, 127
UNESCO (United Nations Educational, Scientific and Cultural Organization), 6, 63, 122–6
UNHCR (United Nations High Commission for Refugees), 124–5
UNMIBH (United Nations Mission in Bosnia and Herzegovina), 114–16, 118, 120, 138n60

United States Holocaust Memorial Museum, 73, 75–6, 158, 160–1, 165, 167, 172–3, 176n3, 185

Varda, Agnès, *Ydessa, les ours et etc.,* 28, 41n10
Venice Biennale 2003, 122–3
Victims of the Counter-Revolution Monument (Budapest), 57
Vietnam Veterans Memorial (Washington, DC), 192
viewers: at Canadian War Museum, 195; experiences in museums and exhibits, 8; at House of Terror, 68–9, 73, 74, 75, 79; at Memorial to Murdered Jews of Europe, 201, 202–3, 204, 211; at Museum of the History of Polish Jews, 163–7; at *Partners (The Teddy Pear Project),* 19, 20, 26, 29, 33
Viola, Bill, 122
Volksbund, 48, 53
Voolen, Edward von, 172

Wall, Jeff, *Stumbling Block* (tableaux), 34, 36, 41n12
Warsaw Ghetto Memorial, 159, 165, 167, 175
Wassermann, Jakob, 146
WAVE Trauma Centre (Northern Ireland), 100
Weinberg, Jeshajahu (Shaike), 160–1
Weiner, Lawrence, *Vis intertiae* (installation), 38
West Belfast Living History Museum (Northern Ireland), 95
Whelan, Richard, 81–2n1
Whitney Museum of American Art, 64

Wilcken, Dagmar von, 209
William III, (king), 47
world memory, 7, 9, 17, 30, 34, 35–7, 39

Yad Vashem (Israel), 73, 172
Yamashita, Tomayuki, 84n24

Žižek, Slavoj, on culture 120

GERMAN AND EUROPEAN STUDIES

General Editor: Jennifer Jenkins

1 Emanuel Adler, Beverly Crawford, Federica Bicchi, and Rafaella Del Sarto, eds., *The Convergence of Civilizations: Constructing a Mediterranean Region*
2 James Retallack, *The German Right, 1860–1920: Political Limits of the Authoritarian Imagination*
3 Silvija Jestrovic, *Theatre of Estrangement: Theory, Practice, Ideology*
4 Susan Gross Solomon, ed., *Doing Medicine Together: Germany and Russia between the Wars*
5 Laurence McFalls, ed., *Max Weber's 'Objectivity' Revisited*
6 Robin Ostow, ed., *(Re)visualizing National History: Museums and National Identities in Europe in the New Millenium*